THE HISTORY OF
SOUTHERN AFRICA

THE HISTORY OF
SOUTHERN AFRICA

EDITED BY AMY MCKENNA, SENIOR EDITOR, GEOGRAPHY AND HISTORY

IN ASSOCIATION WITH

Published in 2011 by Britannica Educational Publishing
(a trademark of Encyclopædia Britannica, Inc.)
in association with Rosen Educational Services, LLC
29 East 21st Street, New York, NY 10010.

First Edition

Britannica Educational Publishing
Michael I. Levy: Executive Editor
J.E. Luebering: Senior Manager
Marilyn L. Barton: Senior Coordinator, Production Control
Steven Bosco: Director, Editorial Technologies
Lisa S. Braucher: Senior Producer and Data Editor
Yvette Charboneau: Senior Copy Editor
Kathy Nakamura: Manager, Media Acquisition
Amy McKenna: Senior Editor, Geography and History

Rosen Educational Services
Jeanne Nagle: Senior Editor
Nelson Sá: Art Director
Cindy Reiman: Photography Manager
Nicole Russo: Designer
Matthew Cauli: Cover Design
Introduction by Andrew Barbour

Library of Congress Cataloging-in-Publication Data

The history of southern Africa / edited by Amy McKenna.—1st ed.
    p. cm.—(The Britannica guide to Africa)
"In association with Britannica Educational Publishing, Rosen Educational Services."
Includes bibliographical references and index.
ISBN 978-1-61530-312-0 (library binding)
1. Africa, Southern--History. I. McKenna, Amy, 1969
DT1079.H57 2011
968—dc22

                                                            2010019433

Manufactured in the United States of America

On the cover: Xhosa boys prepare for a traditional manhood ceremony in South Africa. *Per-Anders Pettersson/Reportage/Getty Images*

On pages 1, 15, 49, 72, 82, 91, 101, 110, 120, 132, 180, 186, 198: A tree towers over the spot where, as legend has it, missionary and explorer David Livingstone's heart is buried. *Hulton Archive/Getty Images*

CONTENTS

Chapter 3: Southern Africa from 1899 Through Decolonization

40

50

57

62

69

87

124

134

147

156

169

176

INTRODUCTION

The Southern African region today is a vibrant mix of people and cultures with a rich history. Throughout this history rests the story of how peoples and cultures have collided during the struggle to control the area's great riches—gold, diamonds, ivory, land, and, distressingly, the very people themselves—and how these peoples and cultures have risen to the challenge of finding ways to prosper and coexist.

Archaeological findings have indicated that Southern Africa is the land from which humankind's ancestors evolved, between 3 million and 1 million years ago. Indeed, it is probable that the indigenous San, Pygmy, and Khoekhoe peoples of Southern Africa are linked genetically to that earlier, ancient population. Little, if anything, is known about interaction among these particular early groups, which emerged 17,000–22,000 years ago. Starting around 100 CE, though, a cultural collision occurred when Bantu peoples—the ancestors of many of the region's current population—migrated southward through Africa. While some of the indigenous groups existed peaceably with the new arrivals, others were displaced from the region's prime lands, often retreating to the desert margins.

The new arrivals were largely farmers, and their charges—cattle and other livestock—would later become an important element of more prosperous, settled societies. Long before Portuguese explorer Bartolomeu Dias rounded Cape Agulhas, at the southernmost portion of Africa, in 1488, the region was home to a series of impressive settlements that rose and fell between the 7th and 15th centuries. From the 11th century onward, however, the wealth of these settlements relied on more than just cattle and ivory, which had also become important. Trade in gold and copper enriched Mapungubwe, near the Zimbabwe border in present-day South Africa, and Ingombe Ilede, in present-day Zambia. The impressive stone ruins of Great Zimbabwe, located in southeastern Zimbabwe, are testament to the power and technological achievements of these more complex societies.

This new wealth was built on the development of trade routes, most notably along the Limpopo and Save river valleys, connecting the interior with the sophisticated Swahili culture that had spread south along the Indian Ocean coast. Between the 11th and 15th centuries, some three dozen Afro-Arab towns were founded along the coastline. For many African groups, it was probably their first contact with the outside world. It's ironic that the trade in gold and ivory that allowed these early settlements to flourish would, in no small part, play a role in the demise of the region's African societies during the colonial period. The establishment of trade routes with the coasts paved the way for the later,

Workers at the Kimberley diamond mines in South Africa. Diamonds were discovered at the site in 1867. Gray Marrets/Hulton Archive/Getty Images

large-scale exploitation of the region's resources by outside powers.

The Portuguese were the first Europeans to enter Southern Africa, as they searched for a sea route to the wealth of India. A Portuguese settlement was established at Luanda in present-day Angola in 1575, and the Portuguese wrested control of the port city of Sofala in Mozambique from the Arabs in the early 16th century.

Slavery had long been a feature among African societies, as it had in many other parts of the world. European and Arab traders engaged with African societies to secure slave labour. With growth in the 18th century of labour-intensive sugar, coffee, and cotton plantations in the New World, however, the demand for slaves skyrocketed. In the eastern part of the region, in present-day Mozambique, the old trade routes for ivory and gold were now tapped to supply another resource—humans.

The enormous demand for slaves had a destabilizing effect throughout the region, as many pursued the profits to be won by selling slaves to traders on the coasts. Slave raids, particularly against settled agrarian populations, soared. Warfare and banditry led to a surge in famine and disease, and a large percentage of the indigenous population of the region was enslaved or displaced.

To facilitate their slave raids and give them an advantage in war, some African groups purchased firearms from European and Arab traders. In so doing, they also obtained the mechanism for the exploitation of another of the region's great resources, ivory. Hunters had been killing elephants for their ivory for centuries. Yet when Britain finally banned the slave trade in 1807, the focus—at least in the western part of the region—switched more intensely to ivory. Firearms, coupled with the growing demand for ivory in Europe and elsewhere, now sealed the fate of most of the region's elephant herds. By 1880, the ivory trade almost collapsed due to the virtual extermination of elephants in Southern Africa.

The Portuguese, who had originally hoped to profit from gold in the interior, had gone on to profit from slavery instead. The arrival in Southern Africa of the Dutch, and later the British, was prompted by different goals. By the late 16th century, European ships regularly stopped at the Cape of Good Hope for fresh water and to trade for cattle with the Khoekhoe. In 1652, the Dutch East India Company established a permanent settlement there to grow provisions for ships en route to its possessions in the Far East.

As the Cape settlement grew, Dutch farmers pushed further into the hinterland, coming into conflict with the Khoekhoe and San. Starting in 1659, a series of guerrilla wars were waged between the Dutch colonists and the Khoisan, as the two indigenous peoples are collectively known. Only in 1803 were the Khoisan finally defeated. By then, the expansion of the colonists' territory had already brought them into conflict with the Xhosa, a Bantu group that was migrating southward toward the Cape, driven by overpopulation and a shortage of land.

While the colonists—by then referred to as Boers—and Xhosa skirmished in the west, unprecedented warfare broke out among the Nguni chiefdoms in the southeast. Control of the cattle and ivory trade no doubt played a part, but the conflict again appears to have originated in disputes over land, exacerbated perhaps by a series of devastating droughts between 1800 and 1818.

Out of this turmoil arose the Zulu, who, under the brilliant military leadership of Shaka, developed into the most powerful state in southeastern Africa. Shaka embarked on a series of wars that displaced numerous groups which, in turn, clashed with the peoples in their path.

A similar event occurred in the east, much of which was now known as the Cape Colony, as displaced Khoisan and escaped slaves, often armed with guns, pushed into areas occupied by the Tswana and Nama. The twin effects of these settler and Zulu wars ultimately sent whole populations on the move, changing the entire region as far north as Tanzania and Zambia.

The struggle for control of the region's lands intensified after the British annexed the Cape Colony in 1806 to protect the sea route to India during the Napoleonic Wars. Their introduction of more progressive labour laws and the abolition of slavery in the Cape in 1834 irritated the Boers at a time when they were also somewhat intrigued with the reports of easy victories over indigenous African populations further inland as well as the prospect of more land. In what is known as the Great Trek, Boers loaded up their ox wagons and headed into the interior to establish their own republics. Inevitably, this led to even further conflict with African groups, including the Zulu. At the Battle of Blood River in 1838, the Boers defeated the Zulu.

Through the first six decades of the 19th century, arable and grazing lands were the resources at the heart of many conflicts. An additional source of conflict was added in 1867 with the discovery of diamonds beyond the Cape Colony, in Griqualand West, opening up the next great struggle for the wealth to be had in Southern Africa. By 1871, nearly 50,000 people—black and white—had descended on the diamond diggings at Kimberley. Seduced by riches, the fledgling Boer republics and Tswana chiefs were among those who laid claim to the diamond zone, but Britain maneuvered to annex the area for itself, establishing a pattern for the expansion of its imperial territories in Southern Africa.

The diamond fields of Kimberley were important for another reason as well. There, mining magnates pioneered the kind of exploitative labour policies that would become endemic throughout the region. By 1888, thousands of claims that had originally been worked by individual diggers had been overtaken by the De Beers Mining Company, under the control of Cecil Rhodes. Labour in the De Beers-controlled mines was provided almost exclusively by migrant blacks who were housed in closed compounds and paid low wages.

This labour trend accelerated with the discovery in 1886 of yet another stunning resource—the world's richest goldfields—on the site of present-day Johannesburg. The mines there employed tens of thousands, the majority of whom were black migrants drawn from all over the region. The discovery of these rich mineral deposits accelerated the colonial land grab in Southern Africa. In 1884, the Germans annexed territory that is now in present-day Namibia. The rumors of ancient gold diggings beyond the Limpopo River lured the British north. By 1894, Rhodes, who also served as prime minister of the Cape Colony, had gained control of a vast territory that today comprises Malawi, Zambia, and Zimbabwe.

When hopes of finding a second large gold strike in the north dimmed, the British turned their attention back to the mother lode in Johannesburg, which was then part of the Boer-controlled South African Republic. The South African War (1899–1902), a bloody conflict between British troops and the Boer republics (the Free State, another Boer republic, fought along side of the South African Republic), left the goldfields in British hands and laid the foundation for the creation of present-day South Africa.

The wealth created by the mineral discoveries transformed the region quickly from a primarily agricultural society to one with an increasingly sophisticated manufacturing base, transportation networks, and a modern economy. Not surprisingly, the demand for labour soared. Back in the 18th and early 19th centuries, the demand for labour—slave labour—had come primarily from New World plantations. Now, the demand came from within. Means other than slavery were needed to create a large supply of cheap, controllable workers. The seizure of land by white settlers, coupled with high taxes, drove increasing numbers of blacks into the labour market. From the turn of the 20th century, pro-white legislative acts, which often deprived blacks and other non-whites of the right to vote or own land, further swelled the pool of cheap labourers.

Although it varied from colony to colony, the ideology of segregation was embraced to some degree by almost every government in Southern Africa. Nowhere was this truer than in South Africa where, in the mid-20th century, racially discriminatory practices that had been in place for decades were further broadened and solidified under a policy of apartheid, which segregated the races and sanctioned economic, residential, and political discrimination against non-whites.

African groups did not acquiesce quietly. Political opposition to the entrenchment of white power extended back to the end of the South African War in 1902, but it became far more energized during World War II, when economic expansion drew large numbers of blacks to settle permanently in the cities. In the wake of the war, the imperial powers also came under external pressure to give up their colonial possessions. The process of decolonization was relatively peaceful in British territories such as present-day Zambia, Lesotho, Malawi, Swaziland, and Botswana. In other areas, however, the transition to black-majority rule was a long and violent process.

The Portuguese colonies of Angola and Mozambique, and, to a lesser extent, South Africa-controlled Namibia (known then as South West Africa, administered by South Africa after the Germans lost the territory in World War I) were wracked by decades of war. After unilaterally declaring its independence from Britain in 1965, white minority-ruled Zimbabwe (then Rhodesia) also was afflicted by conflict, which ended only with the election of a black-majority government in 1980.

South Africa played a major role in slowing the transition to black-majority rule in all of these countries, often by direct military intervention or by support. By 1990, however, South Africa was ringed by countries with black-majority governments and isolated through international sanctions. Increasing unrest, labour strikes, and violence within the country finally led to the release of Nelson Mandela, a longtime leader of the African National Congress who had been jailed since the 1960s, and the unraveling of apartheid. In 1994, during the country's first free elections, Mandela was elected president of South Africa, drawing the curtain on white rule in the region—as well as a new era of independence for the countries of Southern Africa.

CHAPTER 1

EARLY HISTORY

Southern Africa comprises the countries of Angola, Botswana, Lesotho, Malawi, Mozambique, Namibia, South Africa, Swaziland, Zambia, and Zimbabwe. The history of Southern Africa cannot be written as a single narrative, as shifting geographic and political boundaries and changing historiographical perspectives render this impossible. Research into local history in the late 20th and early 21st century has presented fragmented historical knowledge, and older generalizations have given way to a complex polyphony of voices as new subfields of history—gender and sexuality, health, and the environment, to name but a few—have developed. Archaeological and historical inquiry has been extremely uneven in the countries of the Southern African subcontinent, with Namibia the least and South Africa the most intensely studied. Divided societies produce divided histories, and there is hardly an episode in the region's history that is not now open to debate. This is as true of prehistory as of the more recent past.

The uncertainties of evidence for the long preliterate past—where a bone or potsherd can undermine previous interpretations and where recent research has subverted even terminology—are matched by conflicting representations of the colonial and postcolonial periods. In Southern Africa, history is not a set of neutrally observed and agreed-upon facts. Present concerns colour interpretations of even the remote

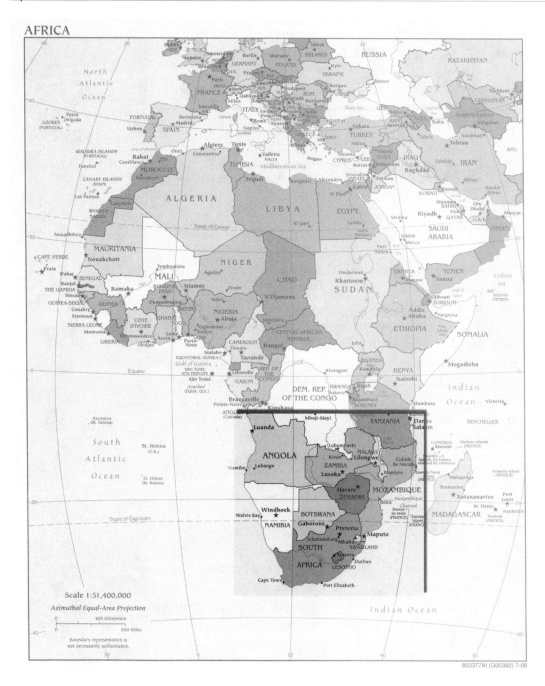

Map of Africa, emphasizing the countries of Southern Africa. Courtesy of the University of Texas Libraries, The University of Texas at Austin

past. For all the contestants in contemporary Southern Africa there has been a conscious struggle to control the past in order to legitimate the present and lay claim to the future. Who is telling what history for which Africa is a question that needs constantly to be addressed.

EARLY HUMANS AND STONE AGE SOCIETY

The controversies in Southern African history begin with the discovery of a fossilized hominin skull in a limestone cave at Taung near the Harts River north of Kimberley in 1924, followed in 1936 by discoveries in similar caves in the Transvaal (now Limpopo and Gauteng provinces) and Northern Cape province, in South Africa. Other significant hominin finds were made in the Sterkfontein Valley (in Gauteng province) beginning in the 1940s. For some time the significance of these finds and their relationship to the evolution of early humans were unappreciated, perhaps because the finds could not be dated, and stone tools—long regarded as the defining characteristic of early humans—had not been found with them.

Since that time, similar but datable discoveries in eastern Africa as well as discoveries in the Makapansgat Valley in South Africa have made it possible to place the South African remains in sequence and identify them as australopithecines, upright-walking creatures who are the earliest human ancestors. The australopithecines who roamed the highland savanna plains of Southern Africa date from about 3 million to 1 million years ago. There can be little doubt that for hundreds of thousands of years Southern Africa, like eastern Africa, was in the forefront of human development and technological innovation.

Controversies remain, however. The connections between australopithecines and earlier potentially hominin forms remain unclear, while a number of species of australopithecines have been identified. Their evolution into the species *Homo habilis* and then into the species *Homo erectus*—which displayed the larger brain, upright posture, teeth, and hands resembling those of modern humans and from whom *Homo sapiens* almost certainly evolved—is still fiercely debated. *Homo erectus* appears to have roamed the open savanna lands of eastern and Southern Africa, collecting fruits and berries—and perhaps roots—and either scavenging or hunting. Acheulean industry appeared during the Early Stone Age (c. 2.5 million to 150,000 years ago) and was characterized by the use of simple stone hand axes, choppers, and cleavers. First evident about 1.5 million years ago, it seems to have spread from eastern Africa throughout the continent and also to Europe and Asia during the Middle Pleistocene Epoch, reaching Southern Africa about 1 million years ago. Acheulean industry remained dominant for more than 1 million years.

During this time early humans also developed those social, cognitive, and linguistic traits that distinguish *Homo sapiens.* Some of the earliest fossils associated with *Homo sapiens,* dated from about 120,000 to 80,000 years ago, have been found in South Africa at the Klasies River Mouth Cave in Eastern Cape province, while at Border Cave on the South Africa–Swaziland border a date of about 90,000 years ago has been claimed for similar Middle Stone Age (150,000 to 30,000 years ago) skeletal remains.

With the emergence of *Homo sapiens,* experimentation and regional diversification displaced the undifferentiated Acheulean tool kit, and a far more efficient small blade (also called microlithic) technology evolved. Through the controlled use of fire, denser, more mobile populations could move for the first time into heavily wooded areas and caves. Wood, bark, and leather were used for tools and clothing, while vegetable foods were also probably more important than their archaeological survival suggests.

Some scholars believe that the addition of organized hunting to gathering and scavenging transformed human society. The large number of distinctive Late Stone Age (30,000 to 2,000 years ago) industries that emerged reflect increasing specialization as hunter-gatherers exploited different environments, often moving seasonally between them, and developed different subsistence strategies. As in many parts of the world, changes in technology seem to mark a shift to the consumption of smaller game, fish, invertebrates, and plants. Late Stone Age peoples used bows and arrows and a variety of snares and traps for hunting, as well as grindstones and digging sticks for gathering plant food. Using hooks, barbed spears, and wicker baskets, they also were able to catch fish and thus exploit rivers, lakeshores, and seacoasts more effectively.

Despite the ever-increasing number of radiocarbon dates available for the many Late Stone Age sites excavated in Southern Africa, the reasons for changed consumption patterns and variations in technology are poorly understood. Until the 1960s, population explosion and migration were the common explanations; subsequent explanations have stressed adaptation. Yet the reasons for adaptation are equally unclear and the model equally controversial. Environmental changes do not seem to have been directly responsible, while the evidence for social change is elusive. Nevertheless, the appearance

Engraving of a rhinoceros, an example of San rock painting and engraving in South Africa. Courtesy of A.R. Willcox; photograph.

of cave art, careful burials, and ostrich-eggshell beads for adornment suggests more sophisticated behaviour and new patterns of culture. These developments apparently are associated with the emergence between 20,000 and 15,000 BCE of the earliest of the historically recognizable populations of Southern Africa: the Pygmy, San, and Khoekhoe peoples, who were probably genetically related to the ancient population that evolved in the African subcontinent.

Although many scholars attempt to deduce the nature of Late Stone Age societies by examining contemporary hunter-gatherer societies, this method is fraught with difficulties. Evidence from Botswana and Namibia suggests that many contemporary hunter-gatherers recently have been dispossessed and that their present way of life, far from being the result of thousands of years of stagnation and isolation, has resulted from their integration into the modern world economy. This hardly provides an adequate model for reconstructions of earlier societies.

During historic times hunter-gatherers were organized in loosely knit bands, of which the family was the basic unit, although wider alliances with neighbouring bands were essential for survival. Each group had its own territory, in which special importance was attached to natural resources, and in many instances bands moved seasonally from small to large camping sites, following water, game, and vegetation. Labour was allocated by gender, with men responsible for hunting game, women for snaring small animals, collecting plant foods, and undertaking domestic chores. These patterns are also evident in the recent archaeological record, but it is unclear how far they can be safely projected back.

Contrary to the popular view that the hunter-gatherer way of life was impoverished and brutish, Late Stone Age people were highly skilled and had a good deal of leisure and a rich spiritual life, as their cave paintings and rock engravings show. While exact dating of cave paintings is problematic, paintings at the Apollo 11 Cave in southern Namibia appear to be some 26,000 to 28,000 years old. Whereas the art in the northern woodlands is stylized and schematic, that of the savanna and coastlands seems more naturalistic, showing scenes of hunting and fishing, of ritual and celebration. The latter vividly portrays the Late Stone Age cosmology and way of life. The motives of the artists remain obscure, but many paintings appear linked to the trance experiences of medicine men, in which the antelope (eland) was a key symbol. In later rock paintings there is also the first hint of the advent of new groups of herders and farmers.

THE KHOISAN

In the long run these new groups of herders and farmers transformed the hunter-gatherer way of life. Initially, however, distinctions between early pastoralists, farmers, and hunter-gatherers

SAN

The San are an indigenous people of Southern Africa, related to the Khoekhoe. They live chiefly in Botswana, Namibia, and southeastern Angola. Contrary to earlier descriptions, the San are not readily identifiable by physical features, language, or culture. In modern times, they are for the most part indistinguishable from the Khoekhoe or their Bantu-speaking neighbours.

Nevertheless, a San culture did once exist and, among some groups, still exists. It centred on the band, which might comprise several families (totaling between 25 and 60 persons). The elementary family within the band is composed of husband, wife, and their dependent children, but it is occasionally enlarged by polygynous marriage. Often all band members are related. Considerable interaction through trade, visiting, and particularly marriage may take place between bands. Kinship, both real and fictional, has wide ramifications, thus facilitating the frequent movement of people from band to band, so that the composition of any particular band may fluctuate considerably in time. Each band is an autonomous, somewhat leaderless unit within its own territory, and in most bands influence rather than authority is exercised in particular situations by skilled hunters or older men.

Many of the rural San live in lightweight, semicircular structures of branches laced with twigs and thatched with grass. Their equipment is portable, their possessions few and lightweight. Woods, reeds, and animals (and, formerly, stone) are the main raw materials from which their skin clothing, carrying bags, water containers, and hunting weapons are made. For hunting they use bows and poisoned arrows, snares, throwing sticks, and sometimes spears. They have probably always fed on game, wild vegetables, fruits, nuts, and insects. As game becomes less plentiful, they are forced to rely increasingly on gathering or, ultimately, into abandoning their old means of subsistence altogether.

The religions of two San groups, the !Kung and the |Gui, seem to be similar, in that both groups believe in two supernatural beings, one of which is the creator of the world and of living things whereas the other has lesser powers but is partly an agent of sickness and death. The !Kung and the |Gui also believe in spirits of the dead but do not practice ancestor worship.

were not overwhelming, and in many areas the various groups coexisted. The first evidence of pastoralism in the subcontinent occurs on a scattering of sites in the more arid west. There the bones of sheep and goats, accompanied by stone tools and pottery, date to some 2,000 years ago, about 200 years before iron-using farmers first arrived in the better-watered eastern half of the region. It is with the origins of these food-producing communities and their evolution into the contemporary societies of Southern Africa that much of the precolonial history of the subcontinent has been concerned.

When Europeans first rounded the Cape of Good Hope, they encountered herding people, whom they called Hottentots (a name now considered pejorative) but who called themselves Khoekhoe, meaning "men of men." At that time they inhabited the fertile southwestern Cape region as well as its more arid hinterland to the northwest, where rainfall did not permit crop cultivation, but they may once have grazed their stock on the more luxuriant central grasslands of Southern Africa. Linguistic evidence suggests that the languages of the later Khoekhoe (the so-called Khoisan languages) originated in one of the hunter-gatherer languages of northern Botswana. In the colonial period, destitute Khoekhoe often reverted to a hunter-gatherer existence. Herders and hunters were also frequently physically indistinguishable and used identical stone tools. Thus, the Dutch, and many subsequent social scientists, believed they belonged to a single population following different modes of subsistence, including hunting, foraging, beachcombing, and herding. For this reason the groups are often referred to as Khoisan, a compound word referring to Khoekhoe and San, as the Nama called hunter-gatherers without livestock (Bushmen, in the terminology of the colonists, is now considered pejorative).

The archaeological remains of nomadic pastoralists living in impermanent polities are frustratingly sparse, but in the upper Zambezi River valley, southwestern Zimbabwe, and Botswana, herding and pottery appear late in the 1st millennium BCE. Cattle and milking appear somewhat later than small stock and were perhaps acquired from iron-using farmers in western Zimbabwe or northeastern South Africa. The loosely organized herders expanded rapidly, driven by their need for fresh grazing areas. Along with pastoralism and pottery came other signs of change: domestic dogs, changes in stone tool kits, altered settlement patterns, larger ostrich-eggshell beads, and the appearance of marine shells in the interior, which suggests the existence of long-distance trade.

Most of Southern Africa's early agricultural communities shared a common culture, which spread across the region remarkably quickly from the 2nd century CE. By the second half of the 1st millennium CE, farming communities were living in relatively large, semipermanent villages. They cultivated sorghum, millet, and legumes and herded sheep, goats, and some cattle; made pottery and fashioned iron tools to turn the soil and cut their crops; and engaged in long-distance trade. Salt, iron implements, pottery, and possibly copper ornaments passed from hand to hand and were traded widely. Some communities settled near exceptionally good salt, metal, or clay deposits or became known for their specialist craftsmen.

THE KHOEKHOE TODAY

Most Khoekhoe are either Nama or Orlams, the latter term denoting remnants of the "Cape Hottentots" together with many of mixed ancestry. The main Nama groups are the Bondelswart, Rooinasie, Zwartbooi, and Topnaar; the main Orlams groups are the Witbooi, Amraal, Berseba, and Bethanie. The Khoekhoe are not physically distinguishable from the San.

War, disease, and absorption into the Cape Coloured communities have dissipated most of the original Khoe groups. Their traditional economy and social organization have thus changed drastically. Formerly their economy was based on herding, hunting, and gathering. Although some independent families still lead a nomadic pastoral life, the majority have settled and live by selling their labour; they have adopted the material equipment, dress, language, and general mode of living of their Europeanized rural environment. It is claimed that most Khoekhoe have become Christian. The former nomadic unit—the patriarchal group of related families—now finds expression as the ward of a village. The clans, to which persons were affiliated by descent and within which interclan affairs were administered by a council of clan heads, have given way to reserve groups. These are often administered as political units by chiefs and headmen, loyalty to whom defines group membership.

THE SPREAD OF BANTU LANGUAGES

Archaeologists are divided over whether all these cultural and economic attributes arrived with a single group of new immigrants speaking a new language or resulted from a more piecemeal development of different skills and the adoption of new techniques by indigenous hunter-gatherers, as has already been suggested in the case of herding among the Khoekhoe. Moreover, archaeologists disagree about the routes and modes of dispersal as well as its timing. It seems likely, however, that a movement of immigrants into Southern Africa occurred in two streams and was part of a wider expansion of populations speaking Bantu languages that ultimately derived from the Niger-Congo languages of western Africa some 2,000 to 3,000 years ago.

"Eastern-stream" Bantu speakers, associated with the earliest farming communities in the well-watered eastern half of Southern Africa, date from the 2nd to the 5th century CE. Similar pottery has been found stretching from northeastern Tanzania and coastal Kenya through southern Zimbabwe into eastern South Africa, Mozambique, and Swaziland. These early farmers settled on arable soils along coastal dunes, rivers, and valley basins. Where possible, they exploited marine resources, planted cereals, and worked iron. Cattle and long-distance trade were insignificant.

"Western-stream" Bantu speakers were initially more familiar with fishing, oil palms, and the cultivation of vegetables than with cereals or cattle. Even before the 1st millennium CE, pottery similar to that of the eastern stream was being made in the upper Zambezi valley, and pottery of a slightly more recent date has been found in parts of northern Angola. It was probably from these communities that the Bantu speakers spread into the more arid western half of the subcontinent, northwestern Zambia, southwestern Zimbabwe, along the eastern margins of the Kalahari into Botswana, and later into eastern South Africa and Mozambique. Like their counterparts in the east, western-stream Bantu speakers cultivated cereals, worked metal, and made pottery, but the evidence of livestock is far more clear-cut. At first they primarily raised sheep and goats, slightly later cattle. While some argue that the shift to livestock raising merely reflects the human impact on the environment as new lands were opened up for grazing animals, others associate the appearance of domestic stock with the emergence of a different and distinctive tradition of ceramics and a characteristic settlement pattern—known as the Central Cattle Pattern—that embodied both the new centrality of cattle and the different nature of hierarchy in these communities.

FOOD PRODUCTION

Although at first the impact of food production was probably less momentous than is often assumed, agriculture combined with pastoralism and metallurgy could support far larger settled communities than previously had been possible and enabled a more complex social and political organization to develop. Cattle raising led to increased social stratification between rich and poor and established new divisions of labour between men and women; the accumulation of cattle and the continuous site occupation inherent in cereal production enabled the storage of wealth and the deployment of more organized political power. Archaeologists argue about how easily groups made the transition from a way of life based on hunting and gathering to one centred on herding or agriculture, but an increasing number of excavations suggest that these boundaries were often permeable. The relationships established among hunters, herders, and agriculturalists over more than 2,000 years of socioeconomic change ranged from total resistance to total assimilation. For the indigenous people of Southern Africa the frontiers between different modes of subsistence presented new dangers and opportunities.

As the new culture spread, larger, more successful farming communities were established. In many areas the new way of life was adopted by the hunter-gatherers. Even in the apparently inhospitable and isolated Kalahari it is now clear that there was intense interaction and exchange between hunter-gatherers and food producers, leading to the development of hybrid

A farmer tends to his cattle in Soweto, South Africa. Raising cattle was a means of food production and an indication of status in early Southern African civilizations. Gallo Images/ Getty Images

amalgams of pastoralism, agriculture, and foraging. Contemporary Bantu-speaking peoples of Southern Africa are genetically very similar to the Late Stone Age people of Africa. Their close relationship also is evidenced by the presence of Khoisan "click" sounds (in Xhosa, Zulu, and Shona) and loanwords in southeastern Bantu and from the iron and stone tools, cattle and wild animal bones, pottery, and ostrich-eggshell beads on early farming sites such as Broederstroom in east-central South Africa and Hola-Hola in Mozambique.

THE RISE OF MORE COMPLEX STATES

From about the turn of the 1st millennium CE, in some areas of what are now central Zambia, southeastern Zimbabwe, Malawi, and eastern South Africa, changes in ceramic style were paralleled by a change in the location and nature of settlements. More sophisticated techniques of ironworking, more extensive gold and copper mining, and a great increase in stone building suggest the evolution of more complex state structures, the growth of social inequalities, and the emergence of new religious and spiritual ideas. These changes were, however, neither simultaneous nor evenly spread.

The nature of these transitions and the differences among the sites are still poorly understood, and, again, archaeologists disagree as to whether the changes can be explained by local developments or are best explained by the arrival of migrating populations. In part the controversy may reflect regional differences. In most of Zambia and Malawi a sharply distinguishable pottery style appears at this time, probably from southeastern Democratic Republic of the Congo, and forms the basis of the ceramics made by several different societies. Farther west, however, there are greater continuities with the earlier wares, while in southeastern Africa locally driven increases in population and cattle—which led to expansion into less favourable environments but which also brought new ideas and new methods of political control—may hold the key.

TOUTSWE

Whatever the explanation, many of the changes appear for the first time at Toutswe in eastern Botswana with the appearance about the 7th century CE of a new ceramic tradition, new technology, and new forms of social and economic organization. There, larger, well-defended hilltop capitals probably dominated a series of smaller sites with access to water over a wide region. Toutswe may provide evidence for a new population; on the other hand, the evidence of its large cattle herds provides insight into the way in which the natural buildup of herds in a favourable environment could stimulate social change and territorial expansion. Cattle underpinned both material and symbolic power in Southern Africa and served to

VELD

Veld, meaning field in Afrikaans, is the name given to various types of open country in Southern Africa that is used for pasturage and farmland. To most South African farmers today the "veld" refers to the land they work, much of which has long since ceased to be "natural."

Various types of veld may be discerned, depending upon local characteristics such as elevation, cultivation, and climate. Thus, there is a high veld, a middle veld, a low veld, a bush veld, a thorn veld, and a grass veld. The boundary between these different varieties of veld is frequently vague, and all of them are usually referred to with the general term veld by the local inhabitants. For convenience, its major regions—Highveld, Middleveld, and Lowveld—are distinguished on the basis of elevation.

cement social obligations through bride-wealth and loan arrangements. Cattle were also an ideal medium for exchange, and the increase in herding necessitated increased specialization and the extension of trading networks. Patrilineal and polygynous cattle-keeping farmers thus had immense advantages over communities that lacked these new forms of wealth and social organization. Similarities between Toutswe and the material culture of later sites in the Limpopo valley and Zimbabwe suggest that Toutswe also may have inspired new forms of social and economic organization for peoples further afield.

SWAHILI CULTURE

Greater stratification and more complex social organization were also probably accelerated by the growth of trading with the outside world and by competition for access to it. In the early centuries CE the northeastern African coast was well known to the traders of the Greco-Roman world. These contacts diminished with the rise of Islam, and the east coast became part of the Indian Ocean trading network. By the 8th century Arab traders had begun to visit more southerly harbours, and between the 11th and 15th centuries they founded some three dozen new towns. Although they never united politically, these towns developed a common Afro-Arabic, or Swahili, culture and a splendour that amazed the first European arrivals.

The Limpopo and Save rivers were early arteries of the trade from the southernmost Arab trading posts, with African intermediaries initially bringing ivory and perhaps animal skins, and later copper and gold, to the coast. In the 8th century the presence of Persian potsherds at Chibuene on the coast of Mozambique and snapped cane glass beads at various locations—Kruger National Park, Schroda on the Limpopo, Botswana, the

Zimbabwe plateau, and the Mngeni River near Durban—all attest to the influence of this long-distance trade in the region and its early integration into the Indian Ocean networks.

MAPUNGUBWE AND GREAT ZIMBABWE

At 9th- and 10th-century sites such as Schroda and Bambandyanalo in the Limpopo valley, the ivory and cattle trade seems to have been of major importance, but later sites such as Mapungubwe (a hilltop above Bambandyanalo), Manekweni (in southwestern Mozambique), and Great Zimbabwe, which date from the late 11th to the mid-15th century, owed their prosperity to the export of gold. Farther north the 14th-century site of Ingombe Ilede (near the Zambezi-Kafue confluence) probably also owed its prosperity in copper and gold—and its social stratification—to the rise of the east coast trade. Although they do not typify the later Iron Age as a whole, the conspicuous consumption at these sites and the bias in oral sources toward centralized states means they have attracted perhaps a disproportionate share of scholarly attention.

In Mapungubwe and Great Zimbabwe a wealthy and privileged elite built with stone and were buried with gold and copper ornaments, exotic beads, and fine imported pottery and cloth. Their homes, diet, and ostentatious burials are in stark contrast to those of the common folk, whose dwellings cluster at the foot of the sites where they probably laboured. Large quantities of stone were brought to build walls on these hilltop sites, which suggests considerable labour. All were centres of political authority, controlling trade and cattle movement over a wide area stretching from eastern Botswana in the west to Mozambique in the east. Cattle, gold, and copper came in trade or tribute from settlements hundreds of miles away. Skilled craftsmen made elegant pottery, sculpture, and fine bone tools for local use and for trade, while the presence of spindle whorls suggests local weaving.

In the past, fierce controversy raged concerning the identity of Mapungubwe's occupants, and, as in the case of Great Zimbabwe, early excavators refused to accept that it could have been built by Africans. Mapungubwe's skeletal and cultural remains are, however, identical to those found at other Iron Age settlements in the subcontinent, and there is little reason to doubt the African origin and medieval date of both sites.

TORWA, MUTAPA, AND ROZWI

In the second half of the 15th century Great Zimbabwe came to an abrupt end. Its successor in the southwest was Torwa, with its centre at Khami; in the north it was replaced by the Mutapa state. The new culture at Khami developed both the stone building techniques and the pottery styles found at Great Zimbabwe and seeded a number of smaller sites over a wide region of the southern and western plateau. The Torwa kingdom seems to have lasted until the end of the 17th century, when it was replaced by the Rozwi Changamire dynasty from the central plateau, which lasted well into the 19th century. The domination of the Mutapa state extended into Mozambique. Contrary to earlier historical opinion, there is little evidence to link the origins of Mutapa directly to Great Zimbabwe, and Mutapa did not reach the magnitude suggested in some accounts. It was, nevertheless, of considerable size by the beginning of the 16th century; the capital alone contained several thousand people. Like the rulers of Great Zimbabwe, the Torwa, Mutapa, and Rozwi dynasties maintained the coastal gold and ivory trade, although cereal agriculture and cattle remained the basis of the economy.

SMALL-SCALE SOCIETIES

In the first half of the 2nd millennium CE the majority of Southern Africa's peoples were probably relatively unaffected by the formation of these larger trading states. Most lived in small-scale societies, based on kinship, in which political authority was exercised by a chief who claimed seniority by virtue of his royal genealogy but who may have risen to power through his access to mineral resources, hunting, or ritual skills. By 1500 most of the farming communities had stabilized in roughly their present-day habitats, reaching their ecological frontier on the dry southern Highveld of South Africa and gradually clearing the coastal forests.

CHAPTER 2

EUROPEAN AND AFRICAN INTERACTION

The first Europeans to enter Southern Africa were the Portuguese, who from the 15th century edged their way around the African coast in the hope of outflanking Islam, finding a sea route to the riches of India, and discovering additional sources of food. They reached the Kongo kingdom in northwestern Angola in 1482–83. Early in 1488, Bartolomeu Dias rounded the southern tip of the continent, and just over a decade later, Vasco da Gama sailed along the east coast of Africa before striking out to India. Although the voyages were initially unpromising, they marked the beginning of the integration of the subcontinent into the new world economy and the dominance of Europeans over the indigenous inhabitants.

THE PORTUGUESE IN WEST-CENTRAL AND SOUTHWESTERN AFRICA

Portuguese influence in west-central Africa radiated over a far wider area and was much more dramatic and destructive than on the east coast. Initially the Portuguese crown and Jesuit missionaries forged peaceful links with the kingdom of the Kongo, converting its king to Christianity. Almost immediately, however, slave traders followed in the wake of priests and teachers, and west-central Africa became tied to the demands of the São Tomé sugar planters and the transatlantic slave trade.

Until 1560 the Kongo kings had an effective monopoly in west-central Africa over trade with metropolitan Portugal, which showed relatively little interest in its African possessions. By the 1520s, however, Afro-Portuguese traders and landowners from São Tomé were intervening in the affairs of the Ndongo kingdom to the south, supporting the ruler, or *ngola*, in his military campaigns and taking his war captives and surplus dependents as slaves. By

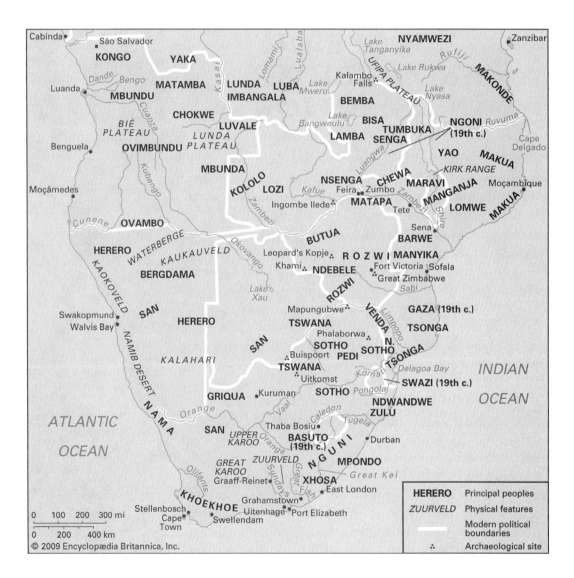

Principal peoples of Southern Africa, 17th to mid-19th century.

the mid-16th century Ndongo, with Portuguese assistance, had become a major kingdom extending over a wide area between the Dande, Lukala, and Kwanza rivers.

By the last third of the 16th century, the Portuguese attitude toward Africa had changed. Rumours of fabulous gold and silver to be found in the interior led in 1569 to the dispatch in the east of Francisco Barreto to discover the sources of gold in the Mutapa kingdom, as well as the appointment in 1575 of Paulo Dias de Novais to search for what turned out to be mythical silver mines in the west. Dias established himself as captain-general, or governor, in Luanda, with jurisdiction over an undefined area between the Dande and Kwanza rivers. A few years after his arrival a century of almost constant warfare was initiated. The wars soon resolved themselves into slave-raiding campaigns, as Europeans demanded labour rather than tropical products in exchange for their merchandise, and African societies rapidly exhausted local supplies of war captives and criminals.

Chiefs exchanged slaves for European firearms and luxury goods and secured further dependents with cheaply produced textiles and Brazilian alcohol. Impelled by the increased demand for slaves for the sugar plantations of São Tomé and later Brazil, and relying on African mercenaries and allies, the military governors of Luanda launched armed incursions against the people of the interior. States rose and fell as African rulers were ineluctably drawn into the slave trade and were as often destroyed by it.

THE IMBANGALA

New warlords emerged at the head of bands of starving refugees, who from the late 16th until the 18th century swarmed down from the hills, fought one another, and devastated the settled kingdoms. By the end of the 16th century well-organized military bands of marauders, known as the Imbangala, began to appear along the coast south of Luanda. In their eagerness to swell slave numbers, Portuguese governors allied with these war bands, and together they dealt the final blow to the Ndongo kingdom about 1622. By that time the Imbangala had retreated to the middle Kwango, where they founded the kingdom of Kasanje. Over the next two centuries this kingdom replaced Ndongo as the chief slave-trading entrepôt between the coast and the east, where the highly centralized and militarist Lunda kingdoms became increasingly important in supplying slaves by the 18th century.

THE CHOKWE

As the Portuguese were penetrating inland from Luanda at the beginning of the 17th century, they also moved southward. In 1617 they established a colony at Benguela, which, as in the case of the Kongo kingdom, was annexed as part of

Angola in the 19th century. Expansion inland from Benguela, however, like the initial expansion farther north, was spearheaded by Afro-Portuguese slave traders, who used southern ports to out-flank Portuguese control. As the slave frontier moved south, the process of constructing and then destroying slave-trading warrior kingdoms was repeated. Those who were not crushed by the process sought safety in woodlands and swamps or joined new heteroge-neous communities of refugees, like the Chokwe ("Those Who Fled") of the western savanna. These new com-munities often became slave raiders themselves.

THE OVIMBUNDU

Through the 18th and early 19th cen-turies the slave trade remained at the centre of Angola's economic existence, with Benguela replacing Luanda as the chief port. As a result, the Ovimbundu kingdoms on the Bié Plateau, which probably were formed by refugees from the Imbangala and Mbundu kingdoms in the late 16th and 17th centuries, dis-placed Kasanje as the main source of slaves. The expansion of plantations in the New World doubled the num-bers of slaves exported in the last third of the 18th century, when trade routes stretched as far as the Kunene River in the south and met up with the routes from Mozambique.

Although a brief Dutch occupation of Luanda in the mid-17th century did not seriously challenge the Portuguese hold over Angola, Dutch, British, French, and Brazilian manufactures increasingly undercut those of the Portuguese, and after 1763 the French became the chief traders on the southwest coast. Portuguese attempts to maintain their position led to Ovimbundu resistance and drastic Portuguese intervention in the Benguela hinterland in an attempt to install compli-ant rulers in the 1770s. Despite military victory, the Portuguese were unable to control the Ovimbundu effectively until more than a century later.

THE PORTUGUESE IN SOUTHEASTERN AFRICA

Initially the southeastern coast was of far less concern to the Portuguese than west-central Africa. Within a few years of their arrival, however, they had seized its wealthy but divided cities and had estab-lished themselves at Moçambique and Sofala, which soon became key ports of call for ships on the way to India.

The Portuguese conquests led to the economic and cultural decline of the east coast cities. Yet the newcom-ers soon discovered that they were unable to control the vast area they had conquered. They faced resistance from coastal communities throughout the 16th century, and the profits they expected from the gold trade failed to materialize. In an attempt to control the trade and to discover the precious min-erals for themselves, the Portuguese, following in the tracks of Muslim traders from the coast, expanded into the Zambezi valley about 1530.

THE ZAMBEZI VALLEY

In the Zambezi valley the Portuguese penetrated the Mutapa state, with its heartland in the northeast between the Zambezi and Mazoe rivers. Portuguese records shed some light on the complex world of African politics to the north and south of the Zambezi River, which provided an unbroken waterway 300 miles into the interior. By the 1530s the Portuguese dominated the trade exits from the coast and had established fortresses and trade fairs along the Zambezi and on the plateau, where Africans came to exchange ivory and gold for beads and cloth. After 1541 Portuguese residents at these outposts elected representatives who were delegated certain powers by the Mwene (ruler of) Mutapa. Individual Portuguese and Goans (from southwest Asia) also were able to get land grants and judicial rights from local rulers,

Slaves being marched to work under armed guard. During the 17th and 19th centuries in the Zambezi valley, Afro-Portuguese landholders and warlords were quite active in the slave trade. Time & Life Pictures/Getty Images

which enabled them to extract tribute from the local population. These early grants formed the basis of what became known as the *prazo* system of landholding. Between the 17th and 19th centuries *prazeros* became immensely powerful and interfered in local African politics, creating an Afro-Portuguese society in the lower Zambezi valley independent of either African or Portuguese jurisdiction. Assisted by slave-soldiers known as the Chikunda, Afro-Portuguese warlords engaged in the slave and ivory trade, unsettling a wide area of east-central Africa.

The effect of Portuguese traders along the Zambezi valley on the Mutapa state was minimal until the late 16th century. In the 1560s, however, their hold was probably strengthened with the appearance in Zambesia of people known as the Zimba, a term applied to any marauders. They seem to have been Maravi people, who had first migrated from Luba territory to the southern end of Lake Nyasa in the 14th century. There they broke up into a number of chiefdoms, usually under the paramountcy of the most powerful chief, who controlled the rain shrine at the heart of the local religion. The reasons for the emergence of the Zimba are far from clear, however. The Maravi attacked chiefs friendly to the Portuguese, as well as their settlements at Sena and Tete and on the coast. By 1601 the Mwene Mutapa was forced to call on the Portuguese for assistance, and this led to almost a century of increasingly disruptive Portuguese intervention in the affairs of Shona kingdoms to the south of the Zambezi.

OTHER SOUTHEASTERN AFRICAN STATES

Although attempts to drive the Portuguese from the Zambezi valley were unsuccessful until the late 17th century, when they were driven out by the armies of the Rozwi kingdom, this appearance of Portuguese power was deceptive: the Portuguese never had the resources to control the interior, and it was the Afro-Portuguese *prazeros* and the Rozwi Changamire dynasty who truly exploited the Mwene Mutapa's weakness.

In addition to gold, the Portuguese were interested in ivory and other mineral resources of the eastern African interior, particularly after 1700, when the gold appeared exhausted. A search for silver mines had led them first into Malawi in the 17th century, and from that point there is direct, though fragmentary, evidence of developments in the region. While the Portuguese records suggest that before 1590 there were no large states in the region, by the first decades of the 17th century a powerful state had emerged under Muzura, perhaps out of an earlier system of small Maravi states at the southern end of Lake Nyasa. Although initially Muzura was assisted by the Portuguese, his power was based on exacting tribute from the Portuguese and their allies south of the Zambezi.

In the early 1630s dissident Karanga and Manyika attempted once more to

MARAVI CONFEDERACY

The Maravi Confederacy, or Maravi empire, was a centralized system of government established in Southern Africa about 1480. The members of the confederacy were related ethnolinguistic groups who had migrated from the north into what is now central and southern Malawi. The confederacy was ruled by a karonga (king), whose authority was passed down through the leaders of each clan.

The main body of the confederacy was settled in an area southwest of Lake Nyasa (Lake Malawi); two groups moved south into the Shire River valley during the 15th or 16th century, and other groups moved into territories now in Zambia and Mozambique. The confederacy reached its peak during the 17th century, administering a large area that stretched north of the Zambezi River to the Dwangwa River, west to the Luangwa River, and east to the Mozambique coast. Its decline began when clan leaders, who traded with the Portuguese and Arabs in ivory, slaves, and iron, became increasingly independent of the central authority of the karonga. By 1720 the confederacy had broken into several autonomous factions. The Chewa and Nyanja peoples of modern Malawi are descendants of the original Maravi clans.

expel the Portuguese from Zambesia; Muzura joined the alliance and unsuccessfully attacked the coastal town of Quelimane. This defeat seems to have ended his challenge to the Portuguese. Thereafter he concentrated on controlling the territory in the western Shire Highlands to the north, trading ivory and, increasingly, slaves with the Portuguese to the south.

By mid-century Muzura was eclipsed by the Kalonga, whose capital lay on the southwestern shore of Lake Nyasa, while by the turn of the 18th century the rise of the well-armed Yao in the trade between Lake Nyasa and the coast, and of the Bisa as middlemen to the west, contributed to the disintegration of the Maravi confederacy into several more or less autonomous fragments. This process was further accelerated by the wars

and slave raids of the 19th century and the introduction of missionaries. By the early 18th century the Portuguese also had penetrated into present-day Zambia, establishing trading fairs at Zumbo and Feira on the Zambezi. Although there were no highly organized broker kingdoms in the area, *prazeros* traded gold and slaves to the coast.

THE DECLINING POWER OF THE PORTUGUESE

As in west-central Africa, from the beginning of the 17th century the Portuguese faced increasingly severe competition from Dutch and British ships in the Indian Ocean, while north of Cape Delgado the Arabs also took advantage of Portuguese weakness. In 1631 a series of revolts began on the east coast. By the beginning of the 18th century the Portuguese had been driven from the coast north of the Rovuma River. The Portuguese then turned their attention southward, where they had traded at Delagoa Bay with the local Tsonga inhabitants since the mid-16th century. They were unable to establish themselves at the bay permanently, however, and through the 18th century Dutch, English, and Austrian ships competed for the local ivory while North American whalers also traded there for food and cattle. Local chiefdoms vied for this market, and this competition contributed to the buildup of larger states in the hinterland of Delagoa Bay from the mid-18th century. Doubtless there was also trade in slaves, although the numbers seem to have remained relatively small before the 19th century.

THE DUTCH AT THE CAPE

Apart from the Portuguese enclaves in Angola and Mozambique, the only other area of European settlement in Southern Africa in the 17th and 18th centuries was the Dutch settlement at the Cape of Good Hope. In the late 16th century the Cape had become a regular port of call for the crews of European ships, who found local people (Khoekhoe) ready to barter cattle in exchange for iron, copper, beads, tobacco, and brandy. By the mid-17th century Khoekhoe intermediaries traded far into the interior. These trade relationships profoundly affected the nature of contact between the Khoekhoe and the Dutch.

FIRST KHOEKHOE-DUTCH CONTACT

In 1652 the Dutch East India Company dispatched Commander Jan van Riebeeck and 125 men to set up a provisioning station at the Cape. This outpost soon grew into a colony of settlement. In 1657 the company released a number of its servants as free burghers (citizens) in order to cultivate land and herd cattle on its behalf. Slaves arrived the next year via a Dutch ship, which had captured them from a Portuguese vessel bound from Angola to Brazil. Thereafter slaves continued to arrive at the Cape from Madagascar and parts of western and eastern Africa. Although the company prohibited the enslavement of the local inhabitants, in order to protect the cattle trade, the loosely organized Khoekhoe were soon undermined by the incessant Dutch demands for their cattle and encroachment on their grazing lands and waterholes. As one group became impoverished and reluctant to trade, another would take its place. The climate of the Cape was well suited to Europeans, and their birth rate was high; whereas in Angola and Mozambique the Portuguese were ravaged by disease, at the Cape it was the indigenes who were decimated by epidemics of smallpox, influenza, and measles brought by Europeans.

BOER EXPANSION

By the end of the 18th century, Cape settlers—called Boers (Dutch *boer*, "farmer")—were far more numerous than their Portuguese counterparts, largely because of natural increase. Men outnumbered women 3 to 2. Despite the varied European origins of the settlers, their shared vicissitudes and the company's insistence that all settlers speak Dutch and practice Calvinism led to a certain cultural uniformity and sense of group identity. The settlers began to call themselves "Afrikaners"—Africans. Nevertheless, class divisions in Cape Town and its environs were marked. A small group of affluent merchants and status-conscious company servants lived in Cape Town. In the neighbouring farming districts of the southwestern Cape, a wealthy gentry used slave labour to produce wine and wheat for passing ships. Independent small farmers eked out a living on the land, and a number of landless whites worked for others, generally as supervisors.

In the arid interior, economic necessity and ecology dictated a pastoral way of life for the Dutch cattle farmers, or trekboers. The poor soil and inadequate rainfall of the region necessitated vast, scattered farms, and the white population was thus thinly spread over an immense area. Although earlier literature stresses their mobility and subsistence economy, most frontier families occupied the same farms during their lifetime and remained dependent on the market for essentials such as arms and ammunition as well as for luxuries such as tea, coffee, tobacco, and sugar.

The greatest barrier to Dutch expansion was the range of mountains inland from Cape Town. Once these were crossed and Khoisan resistance overcome, trekboers expanded rapidly to the east and north, while the company made only sporadic attempts to follow them. The new districts of Stellenbosch (1679), Drakenstein (1687), Swellendam (1745), and Graaff-Reinet (1785) were large and unwieldy, and their centres were far from the expanding colonists. Governmental authority was weak, and on the frontier trekboers were left to crush Khoisan resistance and mount their own defense through the commando system. They became accustomed to handling emergencies on their own and to ruling over their slaves and Khoisan servants and clients as they saw fit, often with a ferocity born of fear. As the settlers expanded, their impact—through forced trade, plunder, and human and cattle disease—was increasingly destructive for the inland Khoisan, who retaliated by stealing settlers' cattle and burning homesteads.

SLAVERY AT THE CAPE

The number of slaves increased along with the settler population, especially in the arable districts. Experiments in the use of indentured European labour were unsuccessful, and by the mid-18th century about half the burghers at the Cape owned at least one slave, though few owned more than 10. Slaves spoke the creolized Dutch that in the 19th century became Afrikaans. Many adopted Islam, which alarmed the ruling class. Divided in origin and dispersed geographically, slaves did not establish a cohesive culture or mount effective rebellions. Individual acts of defiance were frequent, however, and in the early 19th century there were two small uprisings. Nevertheless, in Cape Town itself slave culture provided the basis for a working-class culture after emancipation.

Slavery at the Cape is often portrayed as benign, but mortality rates were high and birth rates low. Punishments for even minor misdemeanours were fierce, perhaps because adult male slaves greatly outnumbered their owners. Emancipation, baptism, and intermarriage rates were also low, although newcomers and poorer burghers married slave women and, more rarely, Khoekhoe women. Cohabitation with indigenous women was more common, especially in frontier districts where there were few white women. The children of these interracial unions, however, took on the unprivileged status of their mothers, so the practice did not affect the racially defined class structure of the society forming at the Cape. By the late 18th century in the Cape most blacks were servants and most Europeans were masters.

The existence of slavery affected the status and opportunities of the dispossessed Khoisan who entered the labour market in increasing numbers from the late 17th century. Although theoretically they were free, compulsion governed the relationship between master and servant, and the legal status of the Khoisan increasingly approximated that of slaves, especially when, during the wars of the late 18th century, the trekboers were allowed to employ captive women and children. As the Cape became increasingly involved in the world economy, the demand for food for European ships escalated, as did calls for increased controls over Khoisan labour. In 1775 a system of "apprenticing" Khoisan children until the age of 25 was established, and by the end of the century the Khoisan were subject to a pass system similar to that which curtailed slave mobility. As they lost their cattle and grazing areas, the Khoisan became virtual serfs on settler farms, although some groups managed to escape beyond colonial borders.

KHOISAN RESISTANCE TO THE DUTCH

Khoisan resistance to Dutch colonialism erupted into guerrilla war on three occasions in the 17th century; the first, in 1659, nearly destroyed the settlement. Cattle raids punctuated almost every decade of the 18th century. The raids and counterraids became increasingly violent as the Dutch expanded into the northeast where sheep could be grazed; by the last quarter of the 18th century the colony's northern frontier was under arms, and numerous settlers had been driven from their lands. Between 1799 and 1803 dispossessed Khoisan farm-workers in Graaff-Reinet, many with horses and guns, rose in revolt, challenging the entire colonial order. The Dutch feared that the Khoisan would attack the arable farms of the southwest, especially as they were joined by Xhosa allies. The intervention of government troops, divisions among Khoisan and Xhosa forces, and sheer bloodletting led to the defeat of the uprising, although it haunted the colonial imagination well into the 19th century. This was the last time the Khoisan fought under their traditional leaders to regain their lost lands.

XHOSA-DUTCH CONFLICT

Settler expansion to the Cape's eastern frontier was blocked by the 1770s when trekboers came up against numerous Xhosa farmers in the area of the Great Fish River. During the 18th century the Xhosa had been embroiled in two major civil wars over the chiefly succession, of which the more important was the dispute, between the paramount Gcaleka and his ambitious brother Rarabe, that split the Xhosa kingdom. After both struggles, the unsuccessful contestants fled west across the Great Kei River, where they bore the brunt of the Xhosa wars against

the Dutch and later the British. Various attempts to separate the colonists and the Xhosa were unavailing. In 1778 the Dutch decreed the Great Fish River to be the boundary between the Xhosa and the Dutch, but Xhosa lived in the contested area to the west known as the Zuurveld, while trekboers were embedded in Xhosa territory to the east.

The establishment of the district of Graaff-Reinet in 1785 hardly improved matters. The area of magisterial jurisdiction was vast and its inhabitants unruly. Before the century was over, minor cattle raids had escalated into two frontier wars, the prelude to a struggle that lasted almost 100 years; the trekboers only expanded again after moving north and outflanking the Xhosa. While the Dutch had superior firearms, the Xhosa had superior numbers, and both sides were internally divided. Thus, the first two frontier wars resulted in a stalemate, which ended only when the British acquired the colony permanently in the early 19th century.

By the end of the 18th century, then, when the British took over, the small Dutch East India Company outpost at the Cape had grown into a sprawling settlement in which some 22,000 whites dominated a labouring class of about 25,000 slaves and approximately as many Khoisan, as well as free blacks and "Prize Negroes"—slaves seized by the Royal Navy and reenslaved in the Cape—in Cape Town and a growing number of Xhosa in the eastern districts.

"LEGITIMATE" TRADE AND THE PERSISTENCE OF SLAVERY

By the time the Cape changed hands during the Napoleonic Wars, humanitarians were vigorously campaigning against slavery, and in 1807 they succeeded in persuading Britain to abolish the trade. British antislavery ships soon patrolled the western coast of Africa. Ivory became the most important export from west-central Africa, satisfying the growing demand in Europe. The western port of Benguela was the main outlet, and the Ovimbundu and Chokwe, renowned hunters, were the major suppliers. They penetrated deep into south-central Africa, decimating the elephant populations with their firearms. By 1850 they were in Luvale and Lozi country and were penetrating the southern Congo forests.

The more sparse, agricultural Ovambo peoples to the south also were drawn into the ivory trade. Initially trading in salt, copper, and iron from the Etosha Pan region to the north, and supplying hides and ivory to Portuguese traders, the Ovambo largely had been able to avoid the slave trade that ravaged their more populous neighbours. By the mid-19th century the advent of firearms led to a vast increase in the volume of the ivory trade, though the trade collapsed as the elephants were nearly exterminated by the 1880s. By then, traders from Angola, the Cape Colony, and Walvis Bay sought cattle as well as ivory. With the firearms acquired through the trade, Ovambo chiefs built up their power, raiding the pastoral Herero and Nama people in the vast, arid region to their south.

THE CONTINUATION OF THE SLAVE TRADE

British antislavery patrols drove the slave trade east, where ivory had been more significant. In the first decades of the 19th century, slave traders for the French sugar plantations on the islands of Réunion and Mauritius, who had previously drawn the majority of their slaves from the island of Madagascar, turned their attentions to the coast of Mozambique, while the demand from Cuba and Brazil also escalated. Thus, by the late 1820s Mozambique's slave exports were outstripping those of Angola, with demand from the French islands rivaling that of Brazil by the 1830s. The flow of slaves was augmented by turmoil in the interior of Southern Africa and by slaves captured by the Chikunda soldiers of the Zambezi warlords. By the 1840s rival Zambezi armies were competing to control the trade routes to south-central Africa.

The most important area of slave raiding appears to have been in Malawi and northeastern Zambia, where predatory overlords devastated a wide area. To the east of Lake Nyasa, the Yao—keen ivory traders from the 17th century—turned to slave raiding, obtaining firearms from the Arabs, subjugating the Chewa agriculturalists, and building up powerful polities under new commercial and military leaders. Displaced from northern Mozambique by the Ngoni in the 19th century, the Yao in turn pressured the Manganja peoples of the Shire Highlands. The Bemba also were able to increase their power through the slave and ivory trade, raiding the loosely organized Maravi peoples to the west of the lake from their stockaded villages on the infertile Zambian plateau. Although they never became large-scale slave traders, preferring instead to incorporate their captives, the Ngoni invaders added to the turmoil.

While the first European observers probably exaggerated the extent of the depopulation, the political geography of the region was transformed as people moved into stockaded villages and towns and began to raid one another for captive women to work the fields while the men engaged in warfare. Vast numbers of people, especially women, were torn from their social settings, and earlier divisions based on kin came to matter less than new relationships between patron and client, protector and protected.

British pressure on the sultan of Zanzibar to ban the slave trade was easily circumvented, and, though the abolition treaty forced on the Zanzibaris in 1873 was more effective, the reduced coastal demand for slaves led to even more ruthless methods in the interior of east-central Africa; slaves were no longer needed for export and thus were exploited locally. East coast Arabs began to play a much more active role in the interior. Initially operating through local chiefs, they came to exercise wide military and political jurisdiction over the northern routes from strategically placed commercial centres. Many of these became slave-based plantations.

EFFECTS OF THE SLAVE TRADE

It is not possible to compile an exact balance sheet of the devastation caused to Southern Africa by the slave trade, and historians differ in their estimation of the numbers involved and of the extent of the damage inflicted. In the 17th century some 10,000 to 12,000 slaves were exported annually from Luanda. Although this figure includes captives from both north and south of the bay, it does not include those smuggled out to escape official taxation. In the 18th century about a third of the slaves exported to the Americas probably came from Angola. The figure probably represents a relatively small proportion of the total population of a huge area in any one year, but it was a significant proportion of economically active adults. The figure also does not take account of the depopulation and social dislocation resulting from incessant warfare and banditry, resulting famine and disease, and the intensification of slavery within African society, where it was usually the young women who were taken as captive "wives" because of their utility as kinless and therefore unprotected agricultural labour.

The better-watered regions may have recouped their population losses within a couple of generations, supported by the introduction of new food crops such as manioc and corn (maize), which the Portuguese imported from South America. Nevertheless, the effects of the slave trade were, in social terms, incalculable. Accounts of Ndongo as rich and populous in the 16th century gave way to lamentations about its desolation in the 17th. The processes of border raids, wars of conquest, and civil strife, which affected the Ndongo and then the kingdoms of the Kwango River valley in the 17th century, were repeated to the south and east in the course of the 18th century as the slave frontier expanded. The ending of more overt violence as the slave frontier moved on left the weak—women, children, and the poor—vulnerable to innumerable personal acts of kidnapping and betrayal, a process exacerbated by the indebtedness of local traders to coastal merchants and the dependence of the traders on the transatlantic economy.

Neither Portugal's attempt to ban its nationals from slave trading in 1836 nor even the abolition of slavery in Brazil in the 1880s ended slavery in west-central Africa. Local merchants, chiefs, and elders turned to slaves to produce the tropical products demanded by Europeans and to serve as porters for the growing quantities of wax and ivory from the 1840s and '50s and rubber from the 1870s. By 1910 wild rubber accounted for more than three-quarters of Angola's exports by volume. Although the rubber trade was successful in the short term, excessive collection of wild rubber destroyed an irreplaceable natural resource, while new concentrations of population upset the ecological balance of a drought-prone environment.

THE "TIME OF TURMOIL"

Given the turbulence caused by slave raiding in east- and west-central Africa, it is tempting to blame this for the unprecedented warfare in Southern Africa in the second and third decades of the 19th century; the Mfecane, or Difaqane ("Crushing"), as this warfare is known, is currently much debated. As yet, however, there seems little evidence for extensive slave trading south of Quelimane until the 1820s, and the slave trade from Inhambane and Delagoa Bay remained paltry until 1823–44. The trade from these ports thus seems more a consequence than a cause of the wars.

Demand for cattle and ivory at Delagoa Bay seems rather more important in the emergence, by the late 18th century, of a number of larger states in the hinterland of Delagoa Bay. Trade gave chiefs new ways of attracting followers, while elephant hunting and cattle raiding honed military organization. In the early 19th century, however, the number of European ships calling at Delagoa Bay appears to have contracted, and this may have increased competition for the cattle and ivory trade. Together with a series of devastating droughts (in 1800–03, 1812, and 1816–18), this competition may better account for the debilitating wars in which the larger northern Nguni chiefdoms in Zululand were embroiled by the second decade of the century; indeed, oral sources attribute the first battles to conflicts over land. These battles occurred even before the rise of the Zulu king Shaka, whom an early historiography holds almost solely responsible for turmoil as far afield as the Cape Colony, Tanzania, and western Zambia.

SHAKA AND THE CREATION OF THE ZULU

Shaka, who until about 1817 was subject to the Mthethwa king, was thus the heir

Shaka, lithograph by W. Bagg, 1836. Courtesy of the trustees of the British Museum; photograph, J.R. Freeman & Co. Ltd.

to, rather than the originator of, the intensified warfare in Zululand. Nevertheless, his military brilliance led to the emergence of the Zulu as the most important power in southeastern Africa. Within a few years Shaka had consolidated the numerous chiefdoms between the Tugela and Pongola rivers into a centralized military state. However, divisions within the royal family culminated in his assassination in 1828.

Initially, Shaka's most formidable rivals were the Ndwandwe, under the leadership of Zwide, who had driven the Ngwane people led by Matiwane onto the Highveld and the Ngwane led by Sobhuza north across the Pongola river, beyond the Zulu orbit. There Sobhuza established the new conquest state of Swaziland (named for his successor, Mswati). In 1820 and again in 1823, Shaka defeated Zwide's armies, which broke into several groups. Zwide himself retired, but his generals fled northward. Clashing with one another and with the peoples in their path, the Ndwandwe (or Ngoni, as they became known) eventually established military states in northern Zimbabwe, Malawi, Zambia, and Tanzania, while the Ndwandwe general Soshangane established the extensive Gaza kingdom in south-central Mozambique. At its height, the Gaza kingdom stretched between the Zambezi and the Komati rivers; Soshangane engaged in slave trading with the Portuguese and reduced neighbouring Shona to tributary status.

Adding greatly to the social dislocation of east-central Africa, Ngoni

ZULU

The Zulu are a nation of Nguni-speaking people in KwaZulu-Natal province, South Africa. They are a branch of the southern Bantu and have close ethnic, linguistic, and cultural ties with the Swazi and Xhosa peoples. The Zulu are the single largest ethnic group in South Africa.

Traditionally grain farmers, they also kept large herds of cattle on the lightly wooded grasslands, replenishing their herds mainly by raiding their neighbours. European settlers wrested grazing and water resources from the Zulu in prolonged warfare during the 19th century, and, with much of their wealth lost, modern Zulu depend largely on wage labour on farms owned by individuals of European descent or work in the cities of South Africa.

Before they joined with the neighbouring Natal Nguni under their leader Shaka in the early 19th century to form a Zulu empire, the Zulu were only one of many Nguni clans; Shaka gave the clan name to the new nation. Such clans continue to be a basic unit of Zulu social organization; they comprise several patrilineal households, each with rights in its own fields and herds and under the domestic authority of its senior man. Paternal authority is so strong that the Zulu may be called patriarchal. Polygyny is practiced; a man's wives are ranked by strict seniority under the "great wife," the mother of his heir. The levirate, in which a widow goes to live with a deceased husband's brother and continues to bear children in the name of the dead husband, is also practiced.

The genealogically senior man of each clan is its chief, traditionally its leader in war and its judge in peace. Headmen (induna), usually close kin of the chief, continue to have charge of sections of the clan. This clan system was adopted nationwide under the Zulu king, to whom most clan chiefs are related in one way or another. When the Zulu nation was formed, many chiefs were married to women of royal clan or were royal kinsmen installed to replace dissident clan heads. The king relied on confidential advisers, and chiefs and subchiefs formed a council to advise him on administrative and judicial matters.

Boys in this highly organized military society were initiated at adolescence in groups called age sets. Each age set constituted a unit of the Zulu army and was stationed away from home at royal barracks under direct control of the king. Formed into regiments (impi), these men could marry only when the king gave permission to the age set as a whole.

Traditional Zulu religion was based on ancestor worship and on beliefs in a creator god, witches, and sorcerers. The king was responsible for all national magic and rainmaking; rites performed by the king on behalf of the entire nation (at planting season, in war, drought, or famine) centred on the ancestors of the royal line. Modern Zulu Christianity has been marked by the growth of independent or separatist churches under prophets, some of great wealth and influence.

The power and importance of the king, chiefs, and military system have declined substantially. Knowledge of and strong pride in traditional culture and history are, however, almost universal among contemporary Zulu.

movements were dictated by the need to avoid more powerful African polities and to find new food resources after local cattle and crops had been exhausted through their raids. Within their military states, the Ngoni aristocracy monopolized cattle, incorporated the women and children of conquered peoples, and exacted tribute from those whom they were unable to permanently subdue.

INCREASING VIOLENCE IN OTHER PARTS OF SOUTHERN AFRICA

As in eastern Africa, where violence intersected with the intensifying activities of slave raiders, so in Southern Africa the violence of this period is multifactorial and needs to be more closely analyzed. Warfare among the northern Ngoni preceded the expansion of the Zulu kingdom, and its rise does not sufficiently explain the violence in the hinterland of the Cape Colony. There the destructiveness of the settler presence was increasingly felt from the mid-18th century, as displaced groups of Khoisan and escaped slaves, carrying with them the commando system and the guns—and sometimes also the religion and the genes—of the white man, fled beyond the confines of the colony. In central and northwestern South Africa and southern Namibia these heterogenous groups of people, known variously as Basters, Griqua, Korana, Bergenaars, and Oorlams, competed for land and water with the Tswana and Nama communities and traded for or raided their ivory

and cattle in the late 18th and early 19th centuries. By the 1800s the extension of the firearms frontier was disrupting the Orange River valley and intensifying conflict between the Sotho-Tswana chiefdoms beyond.

The upheaval affected the southern chiefdoms and rebellious tributaries attacked by Shaka as far away as Pondoland. Many of the refugees fled either into the eastern Cape or west onto the Highveld, although their precise number is a matter of dispute. In both areas the arrival of the refugees added to upheavals of very different origin. The Mfengu, as the refugee population was known in the Cape, included in their ranks starving Xhosa victims of the 1834–35 frontier war, while the Mantatee or Fetcani (as the displaced population was known in the interior) were probably largely the product of labour raids by Griqua and Korana allies of frontier farmers.

Others shattered by the dual impact of the wars emanating from Zululand and the activities of labour raiders from the south scrambled to safety in the mountain fortresses of what is now Lesotho. There Moshoeshoe, the Koena leader, built a new kingdom at Thaba Bosiu, defeating and then incorporating his main rivals. Moshoeshoe quickly appreciated the utility of firearms and horses in the new warfare and of missionaries as diplomatic intermediaries. Shrewd diplomatic marriages extended his sway, and by the mid-19th century he had attracted some 80,000 followers, based on his ability to provide them with cattle and protection.

Other dislodged Highveld peoples joined the Griqua polities along the Orange River or continued raiding along the Vaal and into the western Transvaal region, where the disorders prepared the way for the coming of Mzilikazi. Originally one of Shaka's commanders, Mzilikazi fled from Zululand in 1823 with some 300 of his followers, known as the Ndebele (or Matabele). Over the next 15 years Mzilikazi created a 20,000-strong raiding kingdom in east-central South Africa by absorbing local Sotho-speaking peoples into his regiments. Nevertheless, he was constantly harried by Griqua raiders from the south, Zulu armies from the east, and the Pedi kingdom, which was establishing itself as the most formidable power in the northeastern Transvaal region. In 1837, harassed by his many enemies and defeated by expanding white farmers from the Cape Colony, Mzilikazi retreated across the Limpopo into southwestern Zimbabwe.

There Mzilikazi established himself relatively easily, for the Shona polities were ill-prepared for the new form of warfare and were already weakened by the earlier incursions of the Ngoni and by drought. As in northeastern South Africa, the local populace was absorbed into Ndebele age-set regiments. A castelike society evolved, with the original Ngoni on top, Sotho in the middle, and Shona at the bottom. The relationships that the Ndebele established with groups beyond their immediate settlement ranged from friendly alliances to the regular exaction of tribute and random raiding. Beyond the range of Mzilikazi's armies, however, many Shona chiefdoms remained independent. By the 1870s they were trading firearms to resist Ndebele incursions.

Yet another group dislodged by the warfare of this time, the composite Sotho group known as the Kololo, made its mark in west-central Africa. Defeated in warfare among the western Tswana, about 1840 Sebetwane led his followers across the Zambezi into northwestern Zambia. There they conquered the Lozi kingdom, which had been built up in the 18th century, and then dominated western Zambia. The Kololo triumph was short-lived, however. By 1864 the ravages of malaria, the accession of a weak and diseased king, and the revival of Lozi royal fortunes put an end to their hegemony. Nevertheless, a variant of Sotho is still the language of the region.

BRITISH DEVELOPMENT OF THE CAPE COLONY

Britain occupied the Cape Colony at the turn of the 19th century. During the Napoleonic Wars the Cape passed first to the British (1795–1803), then to the Batavian Republic (1803–06), and to the British again in 1806. The main impulse behind Britain's annexation was to protect its sea route to India. However, the British demands that the colony pay for its administration, produce raw materials for the metropole, and provide a market for Britain's manufactures and a home for its unemployed ineluctably drew Britain into defending the colonists, expanding their territory, and transforming the Cape's mercantile economy. The displacement of Dutch East India Company rule by an imperial state in the early stages of its industrial revolution greatly expanded local opportunities for trade and increased demands for labour, just as the slave trade was abolished in the British Empire.

In its constitutional development the Cape Colony followed the pattern set by Britain's other settler colonies in the 19th century. It was initially a crown colony governed by an autocratic governor, whose more extreme powers were modified by the presence in Cape Town of an articulate middle class and by the arrival in 1820 of some 5,000 British settlers. These groups demanded a free press, an independent legal system, the rooting out of corruption, and more representative institutions. After intense political struggle, Cape men were granted representative government in 1853, with a nonracial franchise that included a low property threshold, which, it was hoped, would defuse the discontent of both Afrikaners and the rebellious creolized Khoisan/Coloured population.

CHANGES IN THE STATUS OF AFRICANS

In 1872 the Cape gained full responsible government. The colour-blind franchise was retained but came under increasing attack. As a strategy for incorporating the more prosperous black peasants and artisans, it had been supported by white merchants, professionals, and officials. With the annexation of African territories and the creation of a mass black working class, however, it proved vulnerable, and in 1887 and 1892 the franchise qualifications were changed in order to restrict the number of black voters.

Initially, imperial protection expanded Cape wheat and wine production, while the British did little to alter existing social and property relations. By the mid-1820s, however, imperial attempts to create a "free market" in labour—including the abolition of preferential tariffs and reform in the system of land tenure—had an explosive effect on the class relations of a colony dependent on slaves and serfs. New regulations ensured standards of treatment and established equality before the law for "masters" and "servants." Ordinance 50 of 1828, which ensured Khoisan mobility on the labour market, caused an uproar; in 1834 slaves were finally emancipated. Despite their formal equality before the law, however, newly emancipated slaves received only modest protection, from the handful of mission stations, against exploitative and often brutal conditions. By 1841, largely through "masters and servants" legislation, settlers had reimposed much of their old authority.

Although the underclass received only limited benefits, the British land and labour policies—together with a restructuring of local government—threatened many Afrikaners. Between 1834 and 1838, in a movement known as the Great Trek, parties of Voortrekkers ("Pioneers"), with their families and dependents, departed the Cape Colony. Their exodus was to become the central saga of 20th-century Afrikaner nationalism. Beyond the confines of the colony, they established separate republics in Natal, the Orange Free State, and the Transvaal, outflanking the Xhosa along the southeast coast, where the British were confronted by a series of interlocking crises.

Continuing Settler-Xhosa Wars

The first of these crises had erupted in 1799 shortly after the British first occupied the Cape. This was the third war between settlers and Xhosa in the Zuurveld and coincided with a mass uprising of Khoisan in Graaff-Reinet. Although peace was restored in 1803, the Xhosa remained in the Zuurveld until British troops drove them east of the Great Fish River in 1811–12; subsequent near-constant skirmishing again exploded into war in 1818–19, 1834–35, and 1846. For most of the century the Cape was dependent on British troops for its defense and for the further conquest of African territory.

By mid-century the western Xhosa were formidable foes who used firearms and adopted guerrilla tactics. Thus, the eighth war (1850–53) was the most drawn-out and costly of all. As in 1799, a simultaneous uprising of Khoisan/Coloured people at the Kat River settlement in the eastern Cape north of Fort Beaufort (established as a buffer for the colony in 1828) weakened the colonists' position. In the end, it was not British arms or settler prowess that defeated the Xhosa but internal tensions resulting from the activities of white traders, missionaries, and settlers. These pressures were increased by the confiscation of Xhosa land and cattle, the apportionment after each war of captives as labour to settlers, the arrival of refugees from wars beyond their frontiers, and the expansion of commercial sheep farming, which was the most important sector of the Cape economy by the 1840s. The Cape's northern frontier was now the Orange River, while in the east the land between the Great Fish and Great Kei rivers was appropriated for white settlement.

In 1857 the internally divided Xhosa, exhausted by years of attrition, in the midst of severe drought and cattle disease, and undermined by the aggressive policies of the British governor Sir George Grey, turned to millenarian prophecies. They slaughtered their cattle and destroyed their crops in the belief that doing so would raise their ancestors from their graves and drive the whites into the sea. When the awaited salvation failed to materialize, some 30,000–40,000 Xhosa streamed across the frontier to seek work in the colony. An equal number died of starvation. Although Xhosa farther east fought the colonists again in 1877 and 1879, the slaughter of the cattle marked the end of Xhosa political and economic integrity. Thereafter the annexation of the remaining African territories proceeded peacefully, if piecemeal. The last of the independent kingdoms to pass into Cape hands was Pondoland, in 1895.

GROWTH OF MISSIONARY ACTIVITY

From the end of the 18th century, European missionaries were crucial in the transformation of African society at the Cape. With Christianity came Victorian notions of progress and civilization. Progress meant that Africans produced agricultural products for export and entered into the labour market. The first converts in the Cape were the Khoisan, in the east and north, and the Griqua, who by the 1820s had formed a series of independent if schismatic states in the Vaal-Orange confluence. By the late 1820s these states were seen by the missionaries as destined to have a vast "civilizing" influence in the interior.

The neighbouring Sotho-Tswana communities were also early sites of missionary activity. Two of the most famous 19th-century Scottish missionaries to Southern Africa, Robert Moffat and David Livingstone, worked among the Tswana. The most notable of the Tswana converts were the Ngwato, under the king Khama III (reigned 1875–1923), who established a virtual theocracy among his people and was perhaps the most acclaimed Christian convert of his day, while in the eastern Cape the Mfengu were in the forefront of mission activity and peasant enterprise. In the second half of the 19th

century, increasing numbers of Xhosa also turned to Christianity. In Zululand and on the Highveld the missionaries both preceded and paved the way for white settlers and were sometimes their fiercest critics.

Initially Christianity tended to advance most rapidly among the disaffected and dispossessed, and especially among women, with those who depended on the slave trade less enthusiastic. It was usually only after a major disaster undermined their belief systems that considerable numbers of men turned to the new religion. By inculcating individualism and encouraging the stratification that was to lead so many of their converts onto the colonial labour markets, the missionaries attacked much that was central to African society and developed an ideology to accompany colonial subordination.

The first European missionaries to south-central Africa, inspired by Livingstone, set up their Universities Mission in 1861. Although this mission ended in tragedy and failure, after Livingstone's death in 1873 other missionaries followed. In 1875 the Free Church of Scotland established the Livingstonia Mission in his memory, while the established Church of Scotland began work among the Yao at Blantyre the following year. From Lake Nyasa the Scottish missions spread inland to northeastern Zambia and were followed by a large number of representatives of other Christian denominations in the last decades of the century. By the last quarter of the 19th century, European missionaries and African evangelists of almost every denomination were working among the peoples of Southern Africa, eroding chiefly authority and inculcating the new values and practices of the colonial world but also bringing new modes of resistance and educating many Christian Africans who later became outspoken critics of colonialism.

THE EXPANSION OF WHITE SETTLEMENT

If the expansion of white settlement under the British led to a vast expropriation of African land and labour, it also led to a rapid expansion of unequal trading relations. Black-white exchange existed in the frontier zone from the early 18th century. British traders soon crossed colonial frontiers and were at Shaka's court by the early 1820s. They exchanged African cattle and crops for beads and brandy, and on occasion may have purchased slaves, although even settlers well beyond colonial boundaries now disguised this as "apprenticeship" and "indenture." The establishment of republics throughout the 19th century meant that black Africans continued to lose land and ultimately their independence to white-dominated governments.

THE REPUBLIC OF NATALIA AND THE BRITISH COLONY OF NATAL

The establishment of trekker republics in Natal and on the Highveld greatly expanded the frontiers of white settlement. The Voortrekkers, however, did not display any sense of national unity, and the parties soon fell out and set off in different directions. The trekkers enjoyed some spectacular successes as a result of their firearms, horses, and use of ox-wagons to form laagers (protected encampments), as well as their strategic alliances with African chiefdoms; they found it far more difficult to establish permanent hegemony over the region.

Victory over the Zulu at the Battle of Blood River on Dec. 16, 1838, and divisions in the Zulu kingdom enabled the establishment of the short-lived Republic of Natalia, bounded to the north by the still-powerful Zulu kingdom and to the south by the Mpondo. In 1843, however, the British, anxious to control the sea route to India, fearful of trekker negotiations with foreign powers, and concerned that trekker raids would spread to the eastern frontier, annexed Natal, leaving the Zulu kingdom north of the Tugela River independent until its disintegration in the civil wars that followed its defeat by the British army in 1879.

For most of the 19th century, British Natal was surrounded by powerful African states and was heavily outnumbered by Africans within the colony. Constitutional development in Natal was slower and more erratic than in the Cape; colonists received responsible government only in 1893. Unlike the Cape, Natal never had a viable nonracial franchise. At the century's end few Africans had the vote, despite the existence of considerable numbers

BATTLE OF BLOOD RIVER

On Dec. 16, 1838, the Zulu and the Voortrekker Boers battled along the Ncome River, a tributary of the Buffalo (Mzinyathi) River, in Southern Africa. The battle stemmed from the many clashes between the two groups that occurred during 1837–38, as Boers migrating from the Cape Colony with their families and livestock advanced into the region along the southern borders of the Zulu kingdom, then ruled by Dingane. On Dec. 16, 1838, a Boer force led by Andries Pretorius induced a Zulu attack on a Boer laager (protected encampment) of wagons at Ncome River. The Zulu were handily defeated, suffering heavy losses caused by the Boers' firearms and cannon, and Ncome River became known as Blood River after its water reddened with the blood of thousands of slain Zulu. The Boers then overran the Zulu kingdom and forced the Zulu population loyal to Dingane north of the Mfolozi River. The Boer victory at Blood River helped undermine Dingane's power: in 1840 he was deposed by his brother, Mpande, and was later killed. Conflict between the Zulu and the Voortrekkers ceased under Mpande.

Before the battle, the Voortrekkers had taken a vow that, if they succeeded in defeating the Zulu, they would build a church and observe the day as a religious holiday. For more than 150 years, Boers (later Afrikaners) annually commemorated the victory as the Day of the Covenant.

of mission-educated black Christians. Racial practices in Natal—including the reservation of lands for African communal occupation, recognition of African ethnic group authorities, codification of customary law, and control over urbanization through labour registration and influx control—were born out of the colony's weakness and provided precedents for 20th-century segregationist policies.

Absentee landowners bought up land claimed and vacated by the Voortrekkers and extracted rent from African producers, hoping increased white immigration would raise land prices. Like the weak colonial administration, the absentees were anxious to avoid the conflict that would have resulted from the expropriation of land occupied by Africans demanded by smaller settler-farmers.

When in 1860 sugar was exploited successfully for the first time, indentured labour had to be brought from India to do the arduous work, because Africans—many of whom still had their own land and cattle—refused to work for the low wages offered on the plantations. By the last decades of the 19th century, however, a land shortage and high taxes had forced large numbers of Africans to seek work in colonial labour markets.

VOORTREKKER REPUBLICS IN THE INTERIOR

With the British annexation of Natal, most of the Voortrekkers rejoined their compatriots on the Highveld, where separate communities had been established in Transorangia (the region across the Orange River) and the western and northeastern Transvaal. Apart from a brief period in the mid-19th century, the British left them alone, controlling external trade and security threats through the coastal colonies. On the Highveld the Voortrekkers entered a vibrant and complex African world. To ensconce themselves in the interior, they fought major wars and established a series of accommodations with those Africans whom they were unable to conquer.

Compared with the British colonies, the racially exclusive republics between the Vaal, Hartz, and Limpopo rivers were weak members of the world economy, dependent on cattle ranching and hunting. Bitterly divided politically and ecclesiastically, these republics were unified in 1860 as the South African Republic, annexed as the British colony of the Transvaal between 1877 and 1881, and reconquered as the Transvaal during the South African War (1899–1902). The trekkers staked a claim to black lands, provided a framework for speculation and the beginnings of commerce, and established formal legal title to territory, though these claims were as yet barely effective. The incapacity of the settlers to wrest the indigenous inhabitants from their land resulted in the development of several types of labour coercion and control: slavery, clientship, indenture, debt bondage, and various forms of rent and labour tenancy.

The struggle to transform formal claims into actual landownership and control continued well into the 20th century. Money was short, and government officials were paid in land, usually along with its African occupants. The settlers' accumulation of wealth was often the result of random looting and forcible, though sporadic, extraction of tribute, tempered by the limited physical capacity of the commando system. Surrounded by a horseshoe of powerful African chiefdoms, it was only in the last third of the 19th century, during a period of renewed imperial interest in the interior, that the balance of power shifted decisively in favour of white farmers.

THE ORANGE FREE STATE AND BASUTOLAND

Farther south, in Transorangia, a far greater proportion of the small settler community was tied to Cape and British markets through wool production. Of a population in 1875 of some 125,000, only the 26,000 whites had citizenship, but many European observers considered the Orange Free State, with its parliament and written constitution, a model republic. Despite the Dutch ancestry of the majority of the settlers, English was the language of commerce and education into the 20th century.

The existence of Moshoeshoe's Basuto kingdom on the settlers' eastern flank meant constant friction. With the restoration of peace on the Highveld in the 1840s, many Africans attempted to return to their lands, only to find them occupied.

Despite Moshoeshoe's attempts to keep the peace, cattle raiding by his dispossessed subjects, together with increasing demands for land and labour from settler sheep farmers, led to war in 1858 and again in 1865–69. On the first occasion, the Orange Free State was forced to sue for peace. On the second, Basutoland, internally divided and starved of arms by the British decision to sell weapons to Afrikaners but not Africans, was beaten. Some chiefs, especially in the north, offered their allegiance to the Afrikaners and, with their followers, became labour-tenants on their farms. Others moved into the Transkei. In 1868, in response to repeated appeals from the Sotho, the governor of the Cape annexed Basutoland, leaving the Orange Free State in possession of the fertile Caledon River valley. In 1869 the frontiers of Basutoland were delimited, and shortly thereafter it was handed over to the Cape. In 1881, however, when the Cape government tried to disarm the Sotho, a war that the colony could not control broke out, and in 1884 Basutoland reverted to British rule.

The Orange Free State also constantly encroached on the better-watered land of its western neighbours, the Griqua and southern Tswana states, which were also under frequent attack from the South African Republic. These attacks led to a growing alliance among the Tswana kingdoms and to protest from the missionaries and Cape traders, who feared the Afrikaners would block the main route to the interior. Nevertheless, the area came under colonial rule only after the discovery in 1867 of diamonds in Griqualand West.

MINERALS AND THE SCRAMBLE FOR SOUTHERN AFRICA

From the 1860s it was known that there was gold in the interior of Southern Africa. In 1867 diamonds were discovered at Kimberley in Griqualand West to the north of the Cape Colony, followed shortly thereafter by discoveries of outcrop (surface) gold in the Transvaal and deep seams of gold on the Witwatersrand in 1886. The conjuncture of speculation in mining futures and land, the imposition of colonial or company rule, and an industrial revolution based on mineral extraction meant that the last third of the 19th century was one of the most traumatic in the history of the region. The language of racial domination, though hardly new, was now buttressed by social Darwinism and was particularly well suited to an era of intensified land and labour exploitation.

The mineral discoveries led to dramatic economic development. Roads, railways, and harbours were built. New coal mines were exploited. Manufacturing, though in its infancy, responded to the new markets, while the creation of an internal market for food was crucial in the commercialization of agriculture and the spread of African cash crop production. Land prices soared, and the demand for labour became insatiable. A working class—consisting of both whites and blacks—was created out of the pre-industrial societies. Colonial conquest subjugated the remaining independent African societies and destroyed the bargaining power of black workers.

THE DIAMOND INDUSTRY

Although most scholarly attention has focused on the gold mines, it was the diamond industry that pioneered many of the characteristics of Southern Africa's labour control policies. People from all

Miners at the entrance to a De Beers mines in the late 1800s. African miners typically had to show work passes and were confined to compounds when they weren't working. FPG/Archive Photos/ Getty Images

over the world came to Griqualand West to seek their fortune. Between 1871 and 1875, more than 50,000 Africans from all over the subcontinent came each year, many of them lured by the prospect of purchasing firearms. Within a few years there was hardly an African chiefdom, from the Transkei to the Limpopo, that was not armed with guns. Combined with the progressive encroachment on African lands and the intensifying demand for their labour, the rearming of Africans was a major source of the instability of these years.

Initially, claims on the diamond fields were limited, technology was primitive, and small-scale black diggers could compete with whites. In the mid-1870s, however, chaotic production conditions, a flooded world diamond market, and labour shortages made the transition to larger units of production necessary. Joint-stock companies were created, bringing international capital and a transformation of mining technology. By 1888 the thousands of claims of the previous decade had been monopolized by the De Beers Mining Company. For black and white workers the establishment of the De Beers monopoly was of immense significance. African migrant workers were now more rigorously controlled by pass laws, which limited their mobility, and by confinement to compounds for the duration of their work contracts. Many white miners lost their jobs or became overseers, and wages for all workers were sharply reduced.

THE DISCOVERY OF GOLD

With the discovery of the Witwatersrand, attention switched from Kimberley to the South African Republic, which was quickly transformed from a ramshackle and bankrupt agrarian outpost to the most important state in the subcontinent. The coastal colonies competed to control the lucrative Witwatersrand trade, and immigration mounted. In 1870 the total white population of Southern Africa was probably less than 250,000. By 1891 it had increased to more than 600,000, and by 1904 it was more than 1 million. When local capital proved inadequate, funds flowed in from Britain, Germany, and France. From the late 1880s gold outstripped diamonds as the region's most important export, and by 1898 the Witwatersrand produced about one-fifth of world gold output.

In 1889 the Chamber of Mines, an organization of mine owners, was formed to drive down the costs of production. This became even more important once deep-level mines were opened in the mid-1890s, because development costs were high, the ore low-grade, and the price of gold controlled. Skilled, unionized white workers from the mining frontiers of the world were able to protect their high wages, while the chamber formed two major recruiting organizations, the Witwatersrand Native Labour Association (Wenela) and the Native Recruiting Corporation, to extend, monopolize, and control the

CECIL RHODES

The story of how Cecil Rhodes came to South Africa to repair his frail health and stayed to become a millionaire on the diamond fields before he was 30 is legendary. In 1880 Rhodes entered the Cape parliament, and in the 1880s he played a key role in securing the British annexation of the Tswana kingdoms that straddled the road to the interior. One of the leading mine owners in Kimberley, by 1888 he had bought out his rivals and created the De Beers consortium. In 1890, when he became the Cape's prime minister, he was the most powerful man in Southern Africa.

Rhodes hoped to find in south-central Africa a "second Rand" to outflank the South African Republic. In 1888 his agents secured exclusive mining rights from Lobengula, the Ndebele king, for Rhodes's British South Africa Company (BSAC), which was granted a royal charter by the British government to exploit and extend administrative control over a vast area of south-central and Southern Africa. Across the Zambezi, where the British were anxious to preempt European rivals, Rhodes engaged the newly appointed British consul for Malawi and Mozambique, Harry (later Sir Harry) Johnston, to establish his company's claims.

THE RHODES COLOSSUS

Cecil Rhodes. Hulton Archive/Getty Images

A flurry of treaty making in 1888–89 left the BSAC with land and mineral concessions throughout present-day Malawi and Zambia. Despite the dubious legality of the treaties, the chiefs agreed to accept British jurisdiction over non-Africans in their domains and over external relations. In the European chancellories, where the frontiers of Africa were being decided, the treaties played an important role in negotiations. In 1890–91 British, Portuguese, and German conventions established the frontiers of many of the modern states of Southern Africa.

For Britain the BSAC's great advantage was its promise to make British occupation effective against contending European powers and to bring capitalist development at minimum cost. In 1890 Rhodes sent a "Pioneer Column," consisting of 200 white settlers and 150 blacks, backed by 500 police, into Mashonaland; the real goal was the Ndebele kingdom, which was conquered in a deliberately provoked war in 1893. Although Matabeleland's conquest brought an anticipated boom in BSAC shares, by the end of 1894 it was clear that there was no "second Rand" in south-central Africa and that the future lay with the new deep-level mines coming into operation farther south.

black labour supply throughout the subcontinent.

Throughout the region it was usually young men who were the first migrants, often sent by homestead heads, who tried to control their movement and their wages, or by chiefs who received a recruitment fee or a portion of the labourer's wages in tribute. For many young men a period of labour migration could bring independent access to bridewealth. Although the process had its roots in the migration of Africans to colonial labour markets earlier in the century, migrant labour expanded after the mineral discoveries and had profound ramifications for the control of senior men over juniors and colonial administrators over taxpayers. Chiefs thus became increasingly anxious over their lack of control over young men and women and struck alliances with colonial administrators and recruiting agents to secure the return of migrants.

THE ANNEXATION OF SOUTHERN AFRICA

The first move in the scramble for Southern Africa came with renewed assertions of British supremacy in the interior. After much dispute, Britain annexed Griqualand West as a crown colony in 1871, transferring it to the Cape Colony in 1881. The multiple crises following the diamond discoveries led during the 1870s to failed imperial schemes to confederate the Southern African territories, but imperial wars between 1878 and 1884 effectively ended the independence of the major African kingdoms. Of these conquests the best-known was the war in 1879 against the Zulu, which included a spectacular defeat of the British army at Isandhlwana. Nevertheless, wars against the southern Tswana and Griqua, the Pedi of the eastern Transvaal, the western Xhosa, and the southern Sotho were the essential precondition for the creation of a unified South Africa.

The mineral discoveries whetted German imperial ambitions, and in 1884 Germany annexed the vast, sparsely populated territory of South West Africa (now Namibia). The annexation challenged British hegemony in the region, raised fears of a German-Transvaal alliance, and accelerated the scramble for Southern Africa. The possibilities of mineral wealth in the interior also revived Portugal's dream of uniting its African colonies. Portugal received short shrift from the other powers, however. At the Berlin West Africa Conference of 1884–85, Portugal secured the Cabinda exclave and a portion of the left bank of the Congo River on the Atlantic coast—considerably less than it claimed—and in 1886 the Kunene-Okavango region went to Germany. Portugal gained even less in Mozambique, which remained a narrow coastal corridor.

With the discovery of gold, the remaining independent African polities south of the Limpopo were conquered and annexed, and both within and beyond colonial frontiers concessionaires were spurred by prospects of further discoveries and the availability of speculative capital. The Limpopo constituted no barrier, and between 1889 and 1895 all the African territories south of the Congo territory were annexed. In south-central Africa the British competed with the South African Republic, Portugal, Germany, and Belgium, while in east-central Africa, to the west and south of Lake Nyasa, the thrust from the south encountered the less powerful but still significant antislavery missionary and trading frontier from the east.

For many of the peoples of the subcontinent, the first phase of colonialism may have been overshadowed by the series of disasters that struck rural society in the mid-1890s, including locusts, drought, smallpox and other diseases, and a disastrous rinderpest epidemic that decimated African cattle holdings in 1896–97. Whereas before the colonial period such natural disasters would have killed large numbers in the short term but probably would have had little long-term consequence, the disasters of the 1890s drew considerable numbers of Africans into dependence on colonial labour markets for the first time and thus permanently changed the structure of African society.

From the 1860s it was known that there were "ancient gold workings" beyond the Limpopo, and by the mid-1880s Lobengula, the Ndebele king, was surrounded by concession hunters. In 1887–88 the high commissioner at the Cape, fearful of Transvaal expansion northward, declared the region a British sphere of interest.

As their hopes of discovering gold waned, settlers and the British South Africa Company (BSAC) began expropriating African land, labour, and cattle. Settlers who participated in the war were granted lavish farms and mineral claims, both of which soon passed to speculative syndicates. A land commission perfunctorily set aside two reserves for the Ndebele on poor soils. In 1896 the Ndebele rose in revolt and were joined by a number of eastern Shona polities. Only the arrival of imperial troops and the collaboration of other Shona groups saved the company state. The uprising led the British to intervene directly in BSAC affairs by appointing a resident commissioner in Bulawayo responsible to the imperial high commissioner in Cape Town.

These events left few resources for occupation north of the Zambezi until the late 1890s. Opposition from missionaries and the African Lakes Company ensured that the region around Lake Nyasa and the Shire River valley was separated from the BSAC sphere; it was declared the British Central African Protectorate in 1891, with Johnston as commissioner. Even before Johnston's arrival the British had been embroiled in open warfare with Arab slave traders, and during the early years of the protectorate Johnston engaged in a spate of wars against the Swahili and Yao slave and ivory traders, who feared the loss of their livelihood. Given the fragmentation and social divisions of the region, he found little difficulty in implementing a policy of divide and rule. Johnston's antislavery wars had the advantage of releasing labour for European employers. Wary of creating a landless proletariat, Johnston, like Rhodes, nevertheless believed that the protectorate's future development should be based on the marriage of white enterprise and black labour, assisted by Asian middlemen.

West of the protectorate, Africans were drawn more gradually under colonial rule, despite pleas from the Lozi king Lewanika that the British provide technical and financial assistance in exchange for mineral concessions, as promised in an 1890 treaty. Lewanika's scramble for protection in the 1890s was dictated by the same circumstances that initially had led him to invite whites into his kingdom in the mid-1880s. The 20 years following the restoration of the Lozi monarchy after the Kololo interregnum had been filled with civil war and succession disputes. By inviting the missionaries, and subsequently the BSAC, to Bulozi, Lewanika, like the Ngwato king Khama III to his south, hoped to bolster his internal position and gain the skills to enable him to deal with the intruders.

In 1897 the BSAC sent an administrator to Bulozi. Contrary to Lewanika's expectations, this spelled the end of Lozi independence. Despite Lewanika's "protected" status, over the next decade the powers of the king and the aristocracy were whittled away. British insistence on the abolition of serfdom and slavery in 1906 undermined the cultivation of the floodplain on which Lozi agriculture depended, and Lewanika's hopes to control the modernization of his state were not fulfilled. Bulozi became a protectorate within a protectorate, tied to the Southern African political economy.

In northeastern Zambia, too, the process of imposing colonial rule came later, but in the end it was swifter and less violent than it had been to the south or east. The natural disasters of the 1890s diminished the ability of the more powerful groups to resist, while weaker peoples at first welcomed the end of Bemba, Ngoni, and Swahili exactions. A lack of resources spared the region major confrontations with colonialism (by contrast, among the Ngoni led by Mpeseni, where gold was believed to exist, the onslaught was as dramatic as in Zimbabwe and the expropriation as brutal). Nevertheless, attempts to impose closer settlement, interfere with local agricultural techniques, and extract forced labour combined with natural disasters to produce extremely high morbidity and mortality rates in the early years of company rule.

PORTUGAL IN SOUTHERN AFRICA

For much of the 19th century, Portuguese colonists in Angola and Mozambique were fewer in number and weaker in authority than those in the interior of South Africa. At the beginning of the century, fewer than 1,000 settlers in each colony huddled on a number of estates around inland forts, along the Bengo and Dande rivers in Angola, and along the lower Zambezi in Mozambique. Most of them had intermarried with local peoples and were independent of Portugal. The metropolitan Portuguese were unable to control either the coastal trade or the activities of the merchants and warlords in the hinterland, who often acted in their name. In the absence of regular taxation or an effective system of customs and tariffs, the economies of the territories were poor and their administrations weak and corrupt. Despite a mythology that held that the Portuguese, unlike the northern Europeans, did not differentiate according to race, from early times it is clear that whites had superior status and prestige—if not always greater power—in Angola and Mozambique. Although both territories gained somewhat from the Napoleonic Wars, it was not until the end of the 19th century that Portugal regained any of its colonizing energy.

From the mid-19th century, Portuguese capital began to enter the colony. The Portuguese made land grants in the Luanda hinterland, and planters experimented with raising coffee, cotton, cacao, and sugarcane, using the slaves who could no longer be exported. In the absence of an adequate administration or communications network, the plantations in Angola were never highly successful, although coffee cultivation spread among African peasant farmers in the region. The appropriation of African land for plantations was resisted, and Portuguese attempts to expand their colonial nucleus led to a series of wars with African peoples, followed by famine and epidemics. The instability of the last decades of the 19th century paved the way for the colonial period that followed.

Portuguese attempts to develop Mozambique met with even less success, given the lack of investment and prevailing disorder, as escaped slaves, soldiers, and porters formed bandit bands in broken country and attacked Portuguese settlements and African villages. In many areas domestic slavery underpinned the migration of young men to the labour markets of the south by the 1850s. Liberal governments in Portugal from mid-century were anxious to outlaw the feudal aspects of the *prazo* system but were unsuccessful, despite four military campaigns and a declaration in 1880 that the *prazos* were crown property.

Until the 1890s the Portuguese had little authority beyond their coastal enclaves. The only bright spot in their fortunes in southeastern Africa was the growing prosperity of Delagoa Bay, as trade with the Transvaal increased. In 1875 Portuguese rights to Delagoa Bay were recognized internationally. With the discovery of gold in the South African Republic, the bay acquired a new importance as its closest outlet, and in 1888 Lourenço Marques became the capital of Mozambique.

Although Portugal failed in its major territorial ambitions in the late 19th century, it nonetheless acquired about 800,000 square miles (2 million square km) of African territory, of which it controlled about one-tenth. In both Portuguese territories "pacification" became a sine qua non of economic development, and there were military campaigns or police actions in almost every year between 1875 and 1924, a measure of Portugal's weakness as a colonial power. The greatest resistance came from those people with the longest experience of Portuguese rule and with the necessary firearms. In Angola the major campaigns were against the Kongo, Mbundu, and Ovambo peoples; in Mozambique, against peoples of the Zambezi valley, the Islamized Makua and Yao, and the Gaza kingdom, which was finally defeated in 1895.

The majority of Portuguese troops in both territories were black, a situation that turned every campaign into a potential civil war. Fragmentation of political authority, resistance of traditional elites threatened by colonial rule, and the precipitate introduction of taxes and forced labour policies also made resistance in the Portuguese colonies the most prolonged in early 20th-century Africa.

Colonial markets were of particular importance to Portugal, and tariff barriers were erected to protect its manufactures. Starved of capital and racked by financial crises, Portugal planned to develop the colonies by attracting immigration and foreign capital and by fostering plantation agriculture. In Mozambique, however, local employers could not compete with the Witwatersrand. Since the 1850s, Mozambican migrants had traveled to the farms and sugar plantations of South Africa, while by the 1870s sterling had begun to replace cattle and hoes

as bridewealth. By 1897 more than half the mine workers on the Rand came from Mozambique, while thousands worked on South African farms.

GERMANS IN SOUTH WEST AFRICA

The Germans were the last imperial power to arrive in Africa. Their annexation and control of South West Africa was eased by the intense cleavages that had opened up between the local Nama and the Herero chiefdoms, a result of their increasing involvement in the world economy during the 19th century.

Throughout the 19th century, displaced communities of Khoekhoe and Oorlams from the Cape had made their way into South West Africa, competing for the sparse water and grazing land. At first they settled peacefully on land granted them by the local populace, some of them establishing mission communities. The advent in the 1830s of the Oorlam chief Jonker Afrikaner and his well-armed followers significantly altered the regional balance of power. Responding to an appeal from the Nama, who were being driven from their grazing lands by Herero expansion, Afrikaner settled at Windhoek. By gaining control over the all-important trade routes from Walvis Bay and the Cape Colony, he ensured, until his death in 1861, Nama dominance over the Herero. Wars between the Nama and Herero were exacerbated from the mid-19th century by the increasing cattle and ivory trade and the availability of firearms; apart from a breathing space between 1870 and 1880, the Nama-Herero wars continued from 1863 to 1892.

Initially Germany hoped to exploit the territory through a concession company, but it could not raise sufficient capital. The government was increasingly forced to intervene in local affairs, especially when settlers appropriated Herero cattle and grazing lands. The most formidable opponent of the Germans was Hendrik Witbooi, a Nama chief who tried unsuccessfully to unite the Herero and Nama against the Germans. After a lengthy guerrilla war, he was defeated in 1894.

The rinderpest epidemic, the alienation of the better-watered highlands, unfair trading practices, and increasing indebtedness led to an uprising by the Nama and Herero peoples in 1904–07. They were crushed in a genocidal campaign: the Herero population fell from about 70,000 to about 16,000, with many dying in the desert while attempting to escape. The Nama were reduced by two-fifths. The handful of settlers had to turn for labour to the Cape Colony and Ovamboland, which was formally brought under colonial rule only when the South Africans took over South West Africa during World War I.

CHAPTER 3

SOUTHERN AFRICA FROM 1899 THROUGH DECOLONIZATION

I f the Nama-Herero wars were among the most savage in colonial Africa, an equally bitter, costly colonial war was fought by Britain against the two Boer (Afrikaner) republics—the South African Republic and the Orange Free State—at the end of the 19th century.

THE SOUTH AFRICAN WAR

The reasons for the South African War (1899–1902) remain controversial. Some historians portray it in personal terms, the result of clashes between the president of the South African Republic (also known as the Transvaal), Paul Kruger, and the representatives of British imperialism, Rhodes and the high commissioner, Sir Alfred Milner. Others argue that the British feared that the regional dominance of the South African Republic would open the way for German intervention in the subcontinent and endanger the sea route to India. Still others believe that the struggle was for supremacy over the richest gold mines in the world and the need to establish a state in the Transvaal that would fulfill the demands of the deep-level mine owners.

Even before the war, the South African Republic's inability to create and coerce a labour force was irksome to the deep-level mine owners, with their huge demand for labour

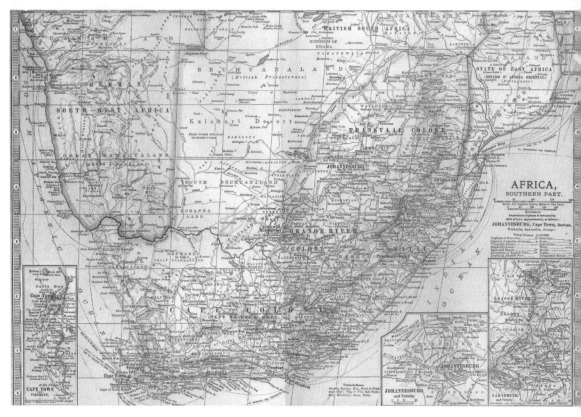

Map of Southern Africa, from the 10th edition of Encyclopædia Britannica, *published in 1902.*

and tight working costs. The liquor, railway, and dynamite policies of the South African Republic also angered the mine owners. Taking advantage of the fomented clamour of British immigrants over their lack of voting rights and secretly backed by the British colonial secretary Joseph Chamberlain, Rhodes plotted the armed overthrow of the republic by his lieutenant Leander Starr Jameson.

The Jameson Raid in December 1895 was a complete fiasco. There was no internal uprising, and the raiders were soon arrested. Rhodes was forced to resign from the premiership of the Cape Colony, and

the alliance he had carefully constructed between English and Afrikaners in the Cape was destroyed. Previously loyal to the empire, Cape Afrikaners now backed Kruger against the British, as did their fellows in the Orange Free State. Nascent pan-South African Afrikaner nationalism received a push. Milner's determination to assert British supremacy exacerbated matters, and in 1899 a rearmed South African Republic issued an ultimatum to the British that amounted to a declaration of war.

Over the next three and a half years, nearly 500,000 British troops were deployed against an Afrikaner force of

60,000 to 65,000, at great cost to the British taxpayers. Some 6,000 British soldiers died in action and another 16,000 of infectious diseases. The Afrikaners lost some 14,000 in action and 26,000 in concentration camps. The camps powerfully inflamed 20th-century Afrikaner nationalism. Although the total number of African dead is unrecorded, according to low official estimates, more than 100,000 were forced into camps and at least 13,000 died there. In the end, Britain's greater resources wore the Afrikaners down; their leaders were forced to sue for peace, and a treaty was signed on May 31, 1902.

Even before the war ended, Milner had begun to "reconstruct" the vanquished Afrikaner republics (the British annexed the South African Republic and the Orange Free State as the Crown Colony of the Transvaal and the Orange River Colony, respectively). The most serious grievances of the mine magnates were removed, and an efficient bureaucracy was established. The smooth functioning of the mining industry was crucial both politically and economically. An acute shortage of unskilled African labour was resolved by the importation of 60,000 Chinese, despite the bitter opposition of white workers, and ambitious schemes were hatched to reduce the cost of both black and white labour.

Africans were effectively disarmed and systematically taxed for the first time, and the pass laws were made more efficient. These changes also benefited white farmers, who were assisted in a variety of ways by the state. By 1906–07 the British were sufficiently confident of the new order they had established to grant self-governing institutions to male whites in the conquered territories. Under the South Africa Act passed by the British Parliament in 1909, the four South African colonies of Transvaal, Natal, Orange River (which would revert back to its previous name, Orange Free State), and the Cape were unified as provinces of the Union of South Africa in 1910. Although much British propaganda before and during the South African War had been concerned with the political rights of British subjects regardless of colour, outside the Cape province blacks remained excluded from citizenship.

THE NATURE OF COLONIAL RULE

By the beginning of the 20th century the subcontinent was under European rule, and its disparate societies were increasingly meshed into a single political economy. The annexation of African territories meant the establishment of new states, and colonial rule was given perceptible effect by policemen and soldiers, administrators, tax collectors, traders, prospectors, and labour recruiters. Railroads connected the coast with the interior, opening up new markets and releasing new sources of labour. New boundaries were drawn that lasted beyond the colonial period, and the Zambezi became the frontier between the settler south and the "tropical dependencies" of East and Central Africa, although Nyasaland (now Malawi) and Northern Rhodesia (now Zambia) occupied a middle ground.

THE CHANGING LABOUR MARKET

The exploitation of minerals, the capitalization of settler agriculture, and the establishment of manufacturing industries drew Africans into the world economy as workers and peasants, transforming class structures and political alignments and shifting the division of labour between men and women. Previously male occupations, such as hunting and warfare, declined. Indigenous production of

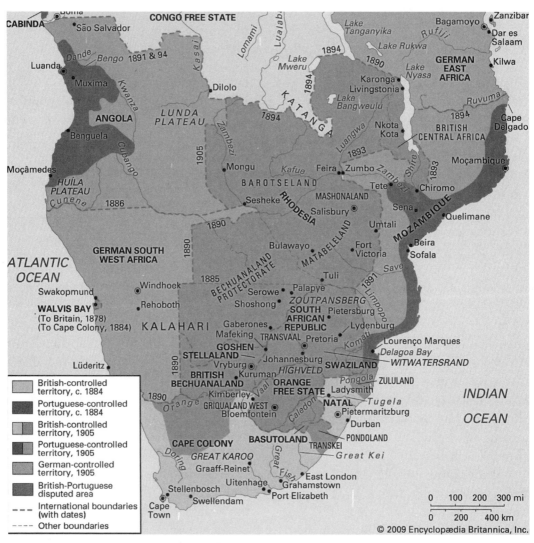

European penetration into Southern Africa in the late 19th and early 20th centuries.

nonagricultural commodities from cotton to iron suffered from the competition of cheap, mass-produced imports. The costs of colonialism were unequally distributed. In the areas of white colonization, the BSAC and the colonial powers supported the settlers. Elsewhere African ruling elites were able to strike compromises with their new overlords. On the reserves and protectorates of Southern Africa, chiefs and hereditary headmen still controlled their followings, although their authority was eroded as they became appointees of the colonial authorities. Again the process varied from area to area. Whereas colonial authorities initially attempted to destroy the overarching powers of the African kings and paramounts, who had led the military resistance to colonialism and symbolized the cohesion of their people, the role of intermediate chiefs in providing a cheap administrative infrastructure was soon recognized.

CHANGES FOR AFRIKANERS

Many Afrikaners also experienced a period of rapid change. In 1886 the South African Republic was still a preindustrial state controlled by a livestock-owning elite; by 1910 it was dominated by mining capital and formed the hub of the industrializing subcontinent. The injection of international capital, inflated land prices, the South African War, and imperial social engineering transformed Afrikaner society as painfully and perhaps more completely than African

society. For Afrikaners, too, there were winners and losers.

GROWTH OF RACISM

Some blacks and whites, particularly those who had been educated or had prior experience, were able to take advantage of economic opportunities developing in new towns and markets. Yet, for the growing numbers of mission-educated Africans and Coloured and for Indian communities in Southern Africa, the period was probably one of regression rather than advance. European racist ideology replaced an older tradition in the Cape of social dominance through economic control. Strident settler demands for urban segregation classified even wealthy Indian merchants as "uncivilized natives." Indian immigration into all the South African colonies was restricted, and in Natal a number of anti-Indian discriminatory measures followed the grant of responsible government in 1893. In the Cape, institutions became increasingly segregated. While the establishment of new colonial states contributed to the creation of new forms of national consciousness, black hopes of inclusion in the wider society were dashed by the South Africa Act of 1909 and by the establishment of settler-only representative institutions elsewhere. White racism, though still embryonic outside South Africa, fueled African nationalism throughout the region.

Racially discriminatory policies were prompted by settlers' fears of competition from blacks and the growth of black class consciousness; they were given an intellectual underpinning by anthropologists and administrators fearful of rapid social change. The Portuguese espoused policies of African assimilation, yet obstacles to progress for the Afro-Portuguese and acculturated African elite were more rigidly enforced in the 20th century than they had been in the 19th. Before 1945 the ideology of segregation was espoused by virtually all the governments of the region and by most whites regardless of political persuasion. Segregation had different meanings for different groups, but throughout Southern Africa it unified contradictory white interests under a single political slogan, buttressed white power and protected white workers and farmers, and attempted to defuse black militancy at a time of urbanization and social change. For blacks segregation meant exclusion from citizenship; incorporation into a restricted and racially segmented labour market based on the use of migrant labour; government control of movement, urban residence, and trade union organization; the consolidation of the authority of the chiefs; and a recognition or invention of black ethnic identity in the African reserves.

Basutoland, Bechuanaland, and Swaziland

South Africa was at the centre of Britain's Southern Africa policies. Nevertheless, until the 1930s the Union was poor, divided, and dominated by international capital. White settlers were Britain's closest allies. Although it overpowered its immediate neighbours, South Africa's expansionist ambitions in the region were largely blocked.

In 1910 the Union wished to incorporate Basutoland (now Lesotho), Bechuanaland (now Botswana), and Swaziland—three landlocked territories that, through a variety of historical accidents, had remained outside South African control. African and humanitarian opposition and Britain's desire for a foothold in the region prevented this incorporation, and the territories remained British protectorates. Until the mid-20th century, however, both Britain and South Africa assumed that the territories would ultimately become part of South Africa.

Although this did not happen, Basutoland, Bechuanaland, and Swaziland were locked into South Africa's economy. All three territories, which had been grain and cattle exporters at the turn of the century, became increasingly dependent on the South African labour market, especially after South Africa implemented protectionist measures for white farmers. Administrators were often South African, and the form of indirect rule they practiced strengthened the authority of conservative chiefs, leaving little room for political progress. This dual administration, as well as the dependent economies of the territories, were severely castigated by the Pim Commission of 1934–35, but, despite

POLICE ZONE

The German and later South African colonial administrations were able to establish effective European-style police control in the southern two-thirds of South West Africa (now Namibia) beginning in the early 20th century. The name of the area and its original boundary were adopted in 1919 by the South Africans from a 1911 German map of the territory on which the area was marked Polizei-Zone.

Spanning the north-central sector of what became the mandated territory of South West Africa, the Police Zone's boundary (often called the Red Line because it was printed on maps in red ink) extended from the Atlantic Ocean to Botswana in a generalized northward-arcing semicircle. The boundary separated indigenous African groups to the north, including the numerically significant Ambo (Ovambo) as well as other Bantu-speaking peoples, from white settlement areas to the south. Not all indigenous groups of South West Africa, however, lived north of the Police Zone. The numerically less significant Herero, together with groups of Khoekhoe and other groups of mixed origin, lived mostly within the Police Zone.

The Police Zone boundary was long inviolate. Whites were prohibited from entering the north, and the indigenous groups of the north were generally prohibited from entering the Police Zone except when hired as a "labour unit" contracted for a prescribed period. Many successive demarcation changes of the boundary between the 1920s and 1960s usually reflected the increasing white control of better farming areas. The name Police Zone was used less after the South African Odendaal Commission defined the geographic, economic, and political aspects of apartheid—the policy that sanctioned racial segregation and political and economic discrimination against nonwhites—in South West Africa. The commission's directive in 1964 led to the establishment of 10 reserves (homelands) in the 1970s for South West Africa's African peoples and groups of mixed origin; the eastern, southern, or western boundaries of the 6 reserves for the indigenous African groups to the north of the Police Zone followed the Police Zone boundary with slight alterations.

The 1977 South African agreement to create an interim government in Namibia until independence led to the Rural Areas Proclamation (1977), which revoked the regulations previously used to control the movement of black Africans and permitted all ethnic groups to take employment and residence wherever they chose. By the time of Namibia's independence in 1990, the effects of a Police Zone had ceased.

modest reforms, the territories remained poor and neglected.

OVAMBOLAND

The Union was more successful in acquiring the vast colony of South West Africa, which it conquered from the Germans during World War I. Despite a League of Nations mandate that South West Africa be administered as a "sacred trust" for its indigenous inhabitants, South Africa's concern was to foster mining, which dominated the economy, and to subsidize poor Afrikaner settlement in what was known as the "Police Zone." In 1917 Ovamboland, in the north, was annexed; better-watered and therefore more densely populated, Ovamboland had long been able to resist dispossession. During the interwar years South Africa was able to defy the many resolutions passed by the League of Nations urging African social and educational advancement, and the country continued to defy them even when the South African mandate was withdrawn by the United Nations in 1946.

SOUTHERN RHODESIA

South Africa also had designs on Southern Rhodesia (now Zimbabwe). In 1922, however, when the BSAC relinquished control of Southern Rhodesia, the predominantly British settlers opted for self-government under British rule, and the territory became a self-governing colony the following year. While British subjects of all races were enfranchised, high property qualifications excluded from voting the vast majority of Africans, who formed 95 percent of the population, and an essentially white parliament controlled all the colony's affairs. An imperial veto over discriminatory legislation was rarely exercised. Between the 1920s and '50s the governing party generally remained closely allied to the small group of mining companies that controlled the economy, while the opposition usually represented white farming and working-class interests.

NYASALAND AND NORTHERN RHODESIA

In Nyasaland and Northern Rhodesia, self-government for the handful of whites was clearly impossible, although in both colonies settlers were given some representation on the Legislative Councils that were established in Nyasaland in 1907 and in Northern Rhodesia in 1924. With the discovery of copper, the white population in Northern Rhodesia increased, but whites never achieved a political dominance comparable to that of their compatriots farther south.

Although copper mining was interrupted by the worldwide depression of the 1930s, by the eve of World War II Northern Rhodesia was a major producer, with nearly nine-tenths of its export earnings coming from copper. In 1939 there were about 13,000 whites in the territory. In Nyasaland the BSAC hoped settlers would develop the territory, but white immigration was restricted by Nyasaland's sluggish economic prospects. In both territories racially discriminatory policies protected the interests of white settlers over those of blacks in every sphere. Nevertheless, the small numbers of whites and British proclamations of the paramountcy of African interests, however limited in practice, differentiated these territories from those farther south.

SETTLERS IN MOZAMBIQUE AND ANGOLA

In Mozambique and Angola, too, settler numbers remained small, despite Portugal's schemes to encourage colonial immigration. Before World War I, colonists consisted mainly of illiterate and unskilled peasants. Power remained in the hands of the governor-general, the highest colonial representative of the Portuguese government. In Angola the collapse of rubber prices in 1913 added to settler problems, and many went bankrupt; in northern Mozambique, campaigns against the Germans during World War I led to famine, forced labour, and high mortality from combat and disease. After the war, however, the colonies attracted new settlers as their economies recovered on the strength of increasing world prices for tropical products. In Angola, diamond production in the northwest was an additional stimulus for settlement.

The regime of dictator António Salazar effectively quashed the political and economic ambitions of those living in Portuguese-controlled Southern Africa early in the 20th century. Evans/Hulton Archive/Getty Images

The republican period in Portugal (1910–26) was accompanied by a flurry of activity among settler political groups, some of them in alliance with the Afro-Portuguese and members of the Creole elite angered by bureaucratic inefficiency and corruption. With the inauguration of Portugal's authoritarian "New State" in the early 1930s under António Salazar, however, immigration schemes were dropped and strict vigilance was exercised over all political and economic activity in the colonies. Consultative institutions disappeared, and grand imperial rhetoric accompanied a return to protectionism, fostering Portugal's needs for cheap raw materials and a closed market.

Class and Ethnic Tensions Among White Settlers

In the new dispensation, whites, with state assistance, controlled private property and the means of production, while Africans were seen solely as labour. In South Africa after 1912 and the British colony of Southern Rhodesia after 1923, settlers controlled the police and armed forces; elsewhere Africans manned the police and armies of the colonial state, although imperial troops remained the ultimate authority.

Settlers everywhere were united in their determination to assert white supremacy but were divided by class and ethnicity. Particularly in South Africa, South West Africa, and Southern Rhodesia, political struggles among whites were often bitter. In South West Africa, German and Afrikaner settlers lived in uneasy tension, which increased in the 1930s when pro-Nazi demonstrations advocating a German takeover of the colony were common. In the Rhodesias, too, there was antagonism between British settlers and Afrikaners who made their way to the territory in the early years of the 20th century, as well as conflicts between the BSAC and white workers and farmers.

These political struggles were most intense in South Africa, which had the most developed economy, the largest and most diverse population (African, Indian, Coloured, and white), and the most acute class and ethnic differences. In the early 20th century "racial conflict" referred to the conflict between settlers of British origin and Afrikaners. Class warfare between white workers and the mine magnates on the Rand was fierce until the 1920s. The years after the creation of the Union were turbulent, with a civil war between Afrikaners when South Africa joined the British side in World War I. A series of mine strikes culminated in 1922 when recently proletarianized Afrikaners, still dreaming of restoring their republic, and members of the newly formed Communist Party of South Africa joined ranks. A five-day battle between white workers and troops on the Witwatersrand ended with 230 dead and the defeat of the workers after martial law was declared; the ringleaders were later hanged.

The South Africa Act of 1909 enfranchised white adult males, but, except for a diminishing proportion of black male property holders in the Cape, neither blacks nor women were enfranchised. Although white women received the vote in 1930, in 1936 Cape African men were removed from the common voters roll, and in 1956 the Coloured voters of the Cape were similarly disenfranchised. White men effectively were given control over the majority of blacks, and they retained this control until the first democratic, nonracial election in South Africa in April 1994.

LAND, LABOUR, AND TAXATION

Everywhere in early 20th-century Southern Africa the priority of administrations was for labour and revenue, and an extensive tax system was developed to address both needs. Where land shortages did not suffice to push Africans into the labour market, taxation frequently did. In many areas the colonial state was weak, and colonial administrators feared rousing widespread resistance; efforts to collect taxes were often followed by flogging, hut burning, and the confiscation of crops or cattle. Violence was often most intense where administrations were weakest. In areas that had been under colonial rule for more extended periods, legislation forced Africans who had not already been dispossessed of their land into the labour market.

As long as Africans had access to land, however, they had some bargaining power. Money for taxes could be earned by increasing crop production or by selling cattle. In many areas women did most

of the farming, and young men worked periodically on white farms and in mines to earn money for cattle, fertilizer, seed, and plows. In the long run, however, Africans became locked into the money economy, and land shortage and indebtedness brought ever-increasing numbers into the labour market.

WHITE AGRICULTURE AND AFRICAN RESERVES

At the beginning of the 20th century the vast majority of Africans in the subcontinent still lived by farming, though in many areas they had become rent- or labour-paying tenants and sharecroppers on land claimed by settlers, syndicates, and speculators. During the 20th century these various forms of tenancy were transformed into wage labour, as white farms became increasingly capitalized.

Throughout the subcontinent, lands were reserved for sole African occupation by administrations fearful that total dispossession would lead to widespread African resistance. In South Africa, mining capitalists also came to see the utility of the reserves in subsidizing cheap labour: the limited agricultural production of the reserves supported the families of migrants, who could then be paid as single workers. On the other hand, white farmers wanted to take over the African reserves for their own use, eliminate competition from African producers, and reduce the employment status of Africans from tenancy to labour service. The Native Lands Act of 1913 and supplementary legislation in 1936 harmonized these conflicting interests, setting aside about one-eighth of South African land for the some 4,000,000 Africans, while reserving the rest for about 1,250,000 whites.

In Swaziland the 3,000 whites who had gained land as temporary concessions from the king in the late 19th century retained virtually two-thirds of the total in land settlements in 1908 and 1915. In response the Swazi royal family gained much popular support by establishing a national fund to repurchase the alienated lands, and by 1968 it had acquired almost half of the total. Basutoland, which had been deprived of its most fertile lands in the 19th century, was a de facto reserve, although, as in Bechuanaland, land remaining in African hands was inalienable.

In Southern Rhodesia, too, where the BSAC developed commercial farming to attract immigrants and raise revenue, even the limited African reserves that had been set aside at imperial insistence were a subject of constant contention. The crucial legislation was the Land Apportionment Act of 1930, which barred African landownership outside the reserves, except in a special freehold purchase area set aside for "progressive farmers." The best land was allocated to whites; less than one-third went to Africans, while about one-fifth remained unassigned. From 1937 Africans not required as labour on white-owned lands were removed to the reserves, which became increasingly congested.

These land acts were part of a battery of legislation aimed at fostering settler agriculture. Throughout the region white capitalist agriculture was possible only with extensive state support, which was not granted to Africans. African farmers attracted state support only when cattle disease threatened to spread from black areas to white or when soil conservation became a matter of concern. The worldwide depression of the 1930s, which severely affected white farmers, intensified discrimination against African peasant production, and by the 1940s many rural areas were almost entirely dependent on migrant remittances.

Initially, similar policies were pursued north of the Zambezi. In Northern Rhodesia the colonial office attempted to increase settler numbers by opening nearly 12 million acres of the colony's best lands for white farming, while reserves were drawn up for African occupation. Although the reserves were large, like the reserves to the south, they were far from the railway line, contained poor soils, and were soon overcrowded and eroded. It was only after World War II that white landownership was limited in Northern Rhodesia and attempts were made to address African rural poverty.

In the Shire Highlands a handful of settlers owned nearly 34 million acres, while about one-eighth of all land belonged to the African Lakes Company until 1930, when it reverted to customary use. The plantations remained poor and inefficient until the 1920s and '30s, when tobacco and tea replaced coffee and cotton. Low pay, forced-labour practices, and squalid working conditions meant the plantations depended on labour tenants, sharecroppers, and migrants from Mozambique and the more marginal north.

South of the Shire Highlands, however, the administration began to encourage Africans to produce cash crops from about 1910. Despite this evidence of African enterprise, however, racial bias and Nyasaland's poverty tended to handicap peasant agriculture. By the 1930s increased numbers of migrants sought work in South Africa and Rhodesia, especially after the 1913 ban on recruiting "tropical" Africans for the South African mines was lifted.

Despite the status of South West Africa, Africans did not regain the land lost to the Germans; by 1946 the whites (who formed less than one-tenth of the population) controlled more than three-fifths of the land in the Police Zone. Located on arid lands capable of supporting only sparse human and animal populations, the African reserves served as labour reservoirs, subject to police raids and pass laws. As settler farms on the better lands in the centre and south of the territory blocked older patterns of transhumance, independent pastoral production became difficult. While a few African families were able to retain their hold on rural resources, the majority were forced to seek work in town. Farther north, where the Ovambo retained control over their more fertile lands, restrictions on their access to markets meant that by the

1930s they, too, were increasingly seeking work in the colonial economy.

THE INVENTION OF TRIBALISM

In the areas reserved for sole African occupation, governments made use of African political structures, creating "tribes" where none had existed and governing through compliant indigenous chiefs and headmen. Imperial authorities at first sought to curb and undermine the powers of chiefs, whom they saw as the embodiment of their people and as potential leaders of resistance; this was as true in the 19th-century Cape as it was in the Rhodesias and South West Africa in the early 20th century. Once the powers of the chiefs had been limited, however, fears of "detribalization" and the potential radicalization of African workers confronted administrations. In response, colonial governments throughout the region moved to bolster chiefs, granting them increased authority over their subjects while seeking to maintain their subordination to the colonial state and establishing local advisory councils as a substitute for popular enfranchisement and representation in central government. This creation of "tribal" institutions frequently created new identities and political interests.

Industrial development and increasing Westernization often made indirect rule through chiefs inappropriate to changing African needs, however. The extension of the market economy intensified divisions, especially as chiefs became identified with unpopular colonial policies and no longer had sufficient land to dispense to their followers. The state recognition of chiefs, the imposition of "tribal boundaries," and land shortages meant that dissatisfied commoners could no longer check arbitrary rule by attaching themselves to alternative polities, as they had in precolonial times. Although urban migration provided some outlet, restrictions on African movement into the colonial towns, together with the often squalid living conditions and low wages, meant that moving to the towns was not an easy option.

LABOUR AND THE MINING INDUSTRY

At the beginning of the 20th century by far the strongest demand for labour came from the gold mines of South Africa. With the creation of the Union of South Africa there was for the first time a state strong enough to ensure the effective implementation of the laws and labour policies that had developed in Kimberley and on the Witwatersrand to control the workforce. The development of South Africa as the most powerful

A gold miner toils in a cramped tunnel in 1940s Johannesburg. Working and living conditions for miners were difficult throughout Southern Africa, particularly for black workers. Popperfoto/ Getty Images

and industrialized country in modern Africa was built upon the labour of a poorly paid, mistreated, and disenfranchised workforce drawn from the entire subcontinent.

The early years of the century also saw intensified recruiting of African labour from Northern Rhodesia, Mozambique, and Nyasaland for the hundreds of small mines working scattered gold deposits in Southern Rhodesia. Because mining profits were so low in Southern Rhodesia, wages, food, housing, and health conditions were cut back ruthlessly, and disease and mortality rates were exceptionally high. Where possible, black workers bypassed the Rhodesian mines and made their way to the Witwatersrand.

Across the Zambezi the absence of mineral wealth meant that Africans in Nyasaland and Northern Rhodesia migrated to the mines in Katanga (now in the Democratic Republic of the Congo), Southern Rhodesia, and South Africa in search of money for food and taxation; the opening up of the copper mines shifted some migrant routes to the Copperbelt. In the interwar years Northern Rhodesia and northern Nyasaland were no more than massive labour reservoirs.

In Angola and Mozambique, too, the economy was sustained by labour migration as the recruitment of labour for South African, Rhodesian, and German enterprises provided revenue for tax and trade. The Portuguese government attempted to control the flow of labour from Mozambique to the gold mines through a series of conventions with the South African government. Tax fees on migrants were a major source of state income, while deferred pay ensured the migrant's return, tax payment, and purchase of Portuguese manufactures. Mozambique also received a fixed proportion of the Transvaal's railway traffic. In a similar system in Angola, contract labour was sent to São Tomé; when this system was terminated after allegations of slavery arose in 1908, the São Tomé planters also turned to Mozambique for labour.

Most Mozambican migrant labour came from the region south of the Save River. Farther north the Portuguese had granted wide mining, agricultural, and commercial concessions to chartered companies in the 1890s. Based on the old *prazos* system, the chartered companies controlled more than half of the colony's lands. Under Salazar the concessions were allowed to expire, but this brought little respite. Southern Mozambique was entrenched as a labour reserve for the Rand; elsewhere in the colony, as in Angola, Africans had to produce fixed quotas of cotton and rice. Confiscations and assaults were legion, despite a plethora of protective legislation. By 1945 more than four-fifths of Portugal's raw cotton came from Mozambique and Angola.

THE IMPACT OF MIGRANT LABOUR

It is difficult to determine the precise impact of migrant labour in Southern Africa in the 20th century. In south-central Africa, for example, the major agricultural communities probably did not send migrants, and the majority of migrants usually came from areas already decimated by slaving and raiding. In other regions, earnings from migrant labour were often used, at least initially, to increase agricultural production, and many migrants maintained their links with the rural areas and retired there in old age. However, many Africans became dependent on the money economy and became locked into the migrant labour system; rural impoverishment resulted from the increasing congestion and soil erosion on the reserves. The division of labour in the countryside began to change, and the burden of agriculture fell increasingly on women and children, although this trend, too, was uneven and may not have existed in some areas until well into the 20th century.

The cheapening of black labour through migrancy rendered skilled white workers vulnerable to attempts by mine owners to reduce costs by substituting cheaper semiskilled black labour for expensive overseas workers. Whites demanded a "colour bar" to protect their access to certain jobs. Initially formulated to reconcile white workers to Milner's decision to import Chinese labour, the colour bar was formally established in South Africa under the Mines and Works Act of 1911 and its amendment in 1926. At the same time, industrial conciliation legislation introduced after a 1922 strike excluded blacks from the wage-bargaining machinery. These examples were followed in the Rhodesias as well,

although in the Copperbelt white workers were weaker and the liberal impulse of government stronger, so that by the 1950s a skilled black workforce began to emerge there.

URBANIZATION AND MANUFACTURING

Mining shaped Southern Africa's experience of industrialization, although during the 19th century towns in the Cape and Natal engaged in small-scale manufacturing. This accelerated in response to the demands of the mining industry, but not until World War I did manufacturing make a significant contribution to the economy. By the end of the war the future of the mining industry seemed in doubt, while dispossessed rural Afrikaners began to enter the cities in search of work. The state thus encouraged the development of the manufacturing industry.

Although the plight of poor Afrikaners was frequently attributed to their refusal to do manual labour, they were at a double disadvantage in the towns. Unlike Africans—who had some access to the land—Afrikaners were totally dependent on their urban wages and lacked the skills of English-speaking workers. It was in response to this that the "civilized labour" policy, which favoured employers using white labour, was devised in the 1920s. The policy probably was more effective in spurring capital-intensive manufacturing and the employment of poorly paid Afrikaner women than in eliminating white poverty: by 1930 one in five Afrikaners was classified as "poor white." They formed an important constituency for the anti-imperialism of Afrikaner nationalism, which developed in the interwar years.

To meet the needs of Afrikaners in the cities, South Africa from 1924 promoted manufacturing through a number of techniques: the levying of tariffs, the use of the gold tax to subsidize infrastructure development, the provision of inexpensive food to manufacturing workers, and the imposition of stringent controls to ensure low wages for black labourers. However, the insulation of South Africa's fledgling industries from international competition during the worldwide depression and World War II may have been the most important factor in its economic expansion. Although Southern Rhodesia attempted some of the same strategies, its economy remained overshadowed by South Africa even after the establishment of the British Central African Federation in 1953, comprising Northern Rhodesia, Southern Rhodesia, and Nyasaland. The development of manufacturing in South Africa and Southern Rhodesia led to a sharp increase in the number of urban Africans in both territories. Until the war years their welfare needs were largely ignored.

THE AFRICAN RESPONSE

African peoples, who were so painfully drawn into the capitalist economy of Southern Africa and were subjected to ever-increasing administrative, economic, and political control, did not acquiesce in their subordination without resistance. Most engaged in daily struggles to survive and devised individual strategies to resist exploitation. Yet they did not all experience their subjection in the same way, and to some extent this weakened resistance. The 20th century witnessed the rise of new classes, with the emergence of an African petite bourgeoisie and working class in the towns and a considerable degree of stratification in the countryside. Migrant labour both undermined and strengthened the authority of the chiefs, especially in areas where the colonial state was anxious to retain traditional structures for purposes of social control. Alongside the growth of nationalist movements among the educated elite and the organization of trade unions among workers, there was a continuation of royal family politics, a restructuring of ethnic identification, and a resort to millenarian solutions.

ROYAL FAMILY POLITICS

In regions where large centralized states had existed at the time of the colonial takeover, royal politics continued to be of significance. In Barotseland, Swaziland, and Basutoland, where paramount chiefs were recognized by the British, the traditional aristocracy combined with the educated elite to protect their position and demand the redress of grievances. In both Matabeleland and Zululand, where the royal families had been militarily defeated, royalists combined to demand state recognition of the monarchy, while in Nyasaland in the 1930s there was an attempt to create a Tonga paramountcy and to restore the Ngoni king. The struggle for the recognition of the monarchy had anticolonial overtones. In general, the monarchies were most successful in the climate of indirect rule of the 1930s and in areas where settlers were weak.

POLITICAL ORGANIZATIONS AND TRADE UNIONS

Nonviolent African opposition to white rule—through the adoption of Western-style political organizations and the formation of trade unions—was longest and most intense south of the Limpopo, where the existence of substantial Coloured and Indian minorities gave an extra dimension to anticolonialism. In South Africa, between 1906 and 1913, Mahatma Gandhi formed the South African Indian Congress and led the first large-scale nonviolent resistance campaign against anti-Indian legislation. He gained limited success, although restrictions on Indian movement and immigration to South Africa remained in force. After his departure in 1914, however, the militancy of the Indian Congress was lost until after World War II, when younger, more radical groups won power from the middle class that had dominated the organization. Nevertheless, Gandhi's example influenced later African nationalists.

The Coloureds of the Cape and Transvaal also mobilized politically in the first nationwide black political organization, the African Political Organization (APO; later African People's Organization), founded in 1902, which sought to unite Africans in opposition to the South Africa Act of 1909. The formation of a separate Coloured Affairs Department to some extent diverted Coloured political energies from joint black action. Coloureds were prominent, however, in the All-African Convention, a body formed in 1935 that represented numerous African organizations. In 1943 the All-African Convention, along with several Coloured organizations, founded the Non-European Unity Movement, which rejected cooperation with the government and sought full democratic rights for all South Africans.

In 1912 educated Africans united various welfare associations, which had developed in the late 19th and early 20th centuries, into the South African Native National Congress (later the African National Congress [ANC]). They aimed to represent African grievances, overcome African ethnic divisions, and gain acceptance from whites through self-help, education, and the accumulation of property. Demands for industrial education, individual land tenure, and representation in Parliament were accompanied by attacks on the pass laws, the colour bar, and the Native Lands Act of 1913; until the 1940s the ANC's methods remained strictly constitutional and appealed mainly to the educated elite.

The ANC had its counterparts farther to the north, partly because many early nationalists had either studied or worked in South Africa. Native associations and welfare associations evolved among the educated elite from the second decade of the 20th century and gave birth to congresses in Southern Rhodesia in 1934, Nyasaland in 1944, and Northern Rhodesia in 1948, all forerunners of more radical anticolonial movements. Despite regional differences, the class composition and methods of struggle of these organizations were broadly similar until the 1950s, with the South African organizations leading the way.

Although Africans in South Africa were moving into industry by the end of World War I, their trade unions were hampered by pass laws, lack of recognition, and police harassment; strikes were illegal and often were put down with violence. Nevertheless, the period 1918–22 saw a great deal of working-class militancy, and in 1920 Clements Kadalie, a Nyasaland migrant, founded the Industrial and Commercial Workers' Union (ICU). Initially consisting of dockworkers in Cape Town, the ICU spread rapidly as a mass movement in the towns and in the countryside, where those who had been evicted responded with millenarian zeal to its message. At its height the ICU claimed 100,000 members and had branches as far afield as Southern Rhodesia and South West Africa, but by 1929 it had largely disintegrated. By that time the Communist Party of South Africa was organizing black workers. Black unions appeared elsewhere in the region after World War II.

From the early 1920s the South African government, seeking to preempt black radicalism, attempted to provide channels for the expression of African grievances through a variety of local consultative councils. In the Rhodesias and Nyasaland and, slightly later, in the smaller colonial territories, advisory councils, "tribal representatives," and rural "native authorities" played a similar role.

In Angola and Mozambique Africans had even fewer political rights, except for a brief republican period (1910–26) when political organizations, trade unions, and the press flourished. For a while it appeared that Africans and settlers in Angola would strive for similar reformist goals, but the Africans broke away to form organizations publicizing black grievances and demanding limited welfare and educational benefits. Crushed even before the advent of Salazar, these groups were revived as social and educational organizations, and it was only during the 1950s that they became overtly political.

CHRISTIANITY AND AFRICAN POPULAR RELIGION

Even at their height political organizations and trade unions never reached more than a fraction of the African population, especially in rural areas. In many areas witchcraft-eradication movements became a sensitive barometer of social distress: in 1933–34, for example, amid worldwide depression, drought, and locusts, a cult offering adherents a medicine called *mchape* that would deliver them from witchcraft swept central Nyasaland and eastern Northern Rhodesia. Antiwitchcraft cults and prophet movements drew on traditional religious and cultural beliefs, offering hope to a sorely pressed and poverty-stricken populace.

By the beginning of the 20th century, however, parts of South Africa had already experienced almost a century of Christian endeavour. The scope of mission work, already entrenched in the Shire Highlands and south of the Limpopo, was vastly extended as new societies appeared on the scene. The Roman Catholic church revived its presence in Angola and Mozambique and spread rapidly in the rest of the subcontinent, after its virtual disappearance by the late 19th century when Baptist and other Protestant missions began working there. The consolidation of colonialism and the new challenges facing African society gave mission activity renewed vitality, and throughout the region black education and health remained largely the responsibility of Christian missions until after World War II.

At the same time, by the late 19th century many missionaries had come to oppose African religious leadership and practiced their own colour bar. Thus, many Africans turned instead to the independent churches that emerged in South Africa in the late 19th century and spread rapidly throughout the subcontinent in the 20th century. Independent churches originated in the countryside but spread rapidly on the Rand, with the formation in 1892 of the Ethiopian church, which was linked to the African Methodist Episcopal church in the United States. Its "back to Africa" ideology was an essential part of what became known as Ethiopianism, a Christian movement that stressed African political solidarity and religious autonomy.

African independent churches were often characterized by a millenarian vision that disturbed missionaries, settlers, and administrators. In some areas whites sought to suppress them. Although the break with a mission church betokened a desire for independence from whites, there were many motives for separatism. In Nyasaland and Northern Rhodesia, adherents of the millennial Watch Tower sect violently confronted state authority, but among the rural Shona and Kongo in Angola the millenarian churches were not confrontational. Everywhere, however, the independent churches subverted the norms of colonial society but lacked the capacity to transform it.

THE IMPACT OF WORLD WAR II

Unlike World War I, World War II did not involve campaigns on Southern African soil, although large numbers of black and white soldiers fought elsewhere in Africa. Yet in many ways this war had a greater impact. In South Africa manufacturing overtook mining and agriculture in its contribution to the economy, and large numbers of Africans settled permanently in the major cities. In Southern Rhodesia, too, the war boosted the economy, and by its end tobacco farming and secondary industry had emerged as key economic sectors.

Economic expansion during the war led to increased organization among African workers, whose wages lagged far behind the rising cost of living. In South Africa these years saw a wave of African worker militancy, partly inspired by the Communist Party, and a reorganization of the African National Congress by a new, younger urban constituency. The brutal suppression of a 1946 strike by African mine workers further radicalized many African nationalists and brought about a closer alliance between the ANC and the Communist Party. This alliance became

Strikes that arose throughout post-World War II Southern Africa helped usher in a new age of political protest in the region. Decolonization and independence followed over the next few decades. AFP/Getty Images

even more important after the banning of the party in 1950.

In south-central Africa, too, the end of the war brought an eruption of strikes, particularly a strike by railway workers in 1945, which led to the founding of a large number of African trade unions in Southern Rhodesia. In 1947 the British government dispatched a trade union-ist to organize African mine workers in the Copperbelt, while the first union in Nyasaland followed in 1949. With gen-eral strikes in Bulawayo and Salisbury in 1948, a new form of political action had emerged.

World War II was important in shak-ing up the politics of the region in other ways as well. Thousands of Africans had joined the army, and some came back home with widened horizons, while their experiences of demobilization and discriminatory compensation fueled nationalist feeling. The 1941 Atlantic Charter, which proclaimed the right of all peoples to self-determination, also stimulated political activists in Southern Africa. In the 1940s the African National Congress began to demand full democratic rights in South Africa for the first time, and its influence, like that of the trade unions, began to be felt throughout the region, spread partly by returning migrant labourers, who formed similar organizations in neigh-bouring territories.

For those territories under the authority of the British colonial office, the Colonial Development and Welfare Acts of 1940 and 1945 signaled Britain's commitment to the development of empire at a time of internal weakness. Thus, after the war Britain attempted to expand agricultural production through agricultural research stations, extension programs, promotion of technology, and conservation measures. These efforts largely benefited white estate owners rather than African peasants, however, and the attempted restructuring of peasant production prompted consider-able rural unrest, providing anticolonial movements throughout the region with a large, disaffected constituency.

INDEPENDENCE AND DECOLONIZATION IN SOUTHERN AFRICA

After the war the imperial powers were under strong international pressure to decolonize. In Southern Africa, how-ever, the transfer of power to an African majority was greatly complicated by the presence of entrenched white set-tlers. After an initial phase from 1945 to about 1958, in which white power seemed to be consolidated, decoloni-zation proceeded in three stages: first, the relatively peaceful achievement by 1968 of independence by those territo-ries under direct British rule (the High Commission territories became Lesotho, Botswana, and Swaziland, and Northern Rhodesia and Nyasaland became Zambia and Malawi); second, the far bloodier struggle for independence in the Portuguese colonies and in Southern Rhodesia (from 1965 Rhodesia, which achieved independence as Zimbabwe in 1980); and, third, the denouement in South West Africa (which in 1990 achieved independence as Namibia) and in South Africa, where the black majority took power after nonracial, democratic elections in 1994. While at the end of the colonial period imperial interests still controlled the economies of the region, by the end of the 20th century South Africa had become the dominant economic power. The beginning of the 21st century ushered in attempts to finally create unity among all the countries in Southern Africa. Despite the spread of multiparty democracy, however, violence, inequality, and poverty persisted throughout the region.

CHAPTER 4

ANGOLA

A ngola is located on the central-southwest coast of Africa. The former Portuguese colony gained independence in 1975. Luanda is the capital.

EARLY ANGOLA

Most of the modern population of Angola developed from the agricultural cultures that appeared there from about 1000 to 500 BCE, which by the first centuries CE were also working iron. These people probably spoke the ancestral versions of Angola's present languages. Complex societies also may have been established at that time, and by 1500 several large kingdoms occupied the territory of Angola. Of these, Kongo, situated in the northern part of the country, south of the Congo River, was the largest and most centralized. Ndongo, with its centre in the highlands between the Cuanza (Kwanza) and the Lukala rivers, was an important rival. Other states, such as the kingdom of Benguela on the Bié Plateau, are less well known. Smaller states, including Bailundu, Ciyaka, and Kwanhama, were scattered between the larger kingdoms, sometimes remaining independent, sometimes falling under control of the larger kingdoms. The Chokwe, although they did not have a centralized government, established an important cultural centre in the northeastern part of the country.

THE KONGO KINGDOM AND THE COMING OF THE PORTUGUESE

The Kongo kingdom, the most powerful state to develop in the region, emerged in the 14th century as the Kongo people moved southward from the Congo River region into northern Angola. There they established Mbanza Kongo as their capital. Portuguese navigators reached Kongo, in the northwest, in 1483 and entered into diplomatic relations with the kingdom after that. Moreover, Kongo's king converted to Christianity, and his son Mvemba a Nzinga took the Christian name of Afonso I, establishing the religion permanently in the country, along with literacy in Portuguese and European customs. Disputes over control of trade, particularly regarding slaves from Kongo and its neighbours, led the Portuguese to look for new allies, especially the Ndongo kingdom. After undertaking several missions there, the Portuguese established a colony at Luanda in 1575. Subsequent wars with Ndongo, particularly after 1617, brought the Portuguese significantly more territory, despite the resistance of Queen Njinga Mbande of Ndongo and Matamba. Portuguese expansion was largely over by 1670, and further conflict involved attempts to redirect or tax trade.

Slaves were Angola's major export, and Portugal was actively involved in their acquisition, more so from the late 17th century. People were also enslaved through inter-African conflicts, such as the civil wars in Kongo after 1665, and conflicts that occurred during the rise of the great Lunda empire after 1750, in the Dembos region between Kongo and Matamba, and on the Bié Plateau. Population losses were considerable, and the demography was badly distorted; censuses from the late 18th century show that there were twice as many adult females as males.

The expansion of the slave trade was but one of several factors that played a role in the rise and fall of the region's kingdoms. Beset by civil wars, Kongo entered into a steep decline in the 17th century. The Loango kingdom flourished north of the Congo estuary until it was decentralized by the late 18th century. The Ndongo kingdom in the Malanje highlands reached its height in the late 16th century but was destroyed when the Portuguese pushed inland in the 17th century and was replaced by the Kasanje kingdom in the Cuango (Kwango) River valley.

COLONIAL TRANSITION (1820S–1910)

In the 18th and 19th centuries, the port of Cabinda was a major entrepôt, where slaves were an important commodity. The export of slaves was banned in Angola in 1836, but the trade did not end until the Brazilian market was closed in the early 1850s. Slavery itself was legally abolished in the Portuguese empire in 1875, but it continued in thinly disguised

LUNDA EMPIRE

The historic Bantu-speaking African state known as the Lunda empire was founded in the 16th century in the region of the upper Kasai River (now in northeastern Angola and western Democratic Republic of the Congo). Although the Lunda people had lived in the area from early times, their empire was founded by invaders coming west from Luba. Between 1600 and 1750, bands of Lunda adventurers established numerous satellites. The Lunda empire consisted of a centralized core, a ring of provinces closely tied to the capital, an outer ring of provinces that paid tribute but were otherwise autonomous, and a fringe of independent kingdoms that shared a common Lunda culture. The imperial boundaries were thus only loosely defined.

Lunda traded with both the Arabs on the Indian Ocean and, from about 1650, the Portuguese on the Atlantic. The leading exports were ivory and slaves; imports included cloth and guns. The empire reached the height of its power by the 1850s. Thereafter its might was eroded by the incursions of the neighbouring Chokwe. Portuguese troops arrived from Angola in the west in 1884 and Belgians from the Congo Free State in the northeast in 1898. Lunda was partitioned between them. Guerrilla warfare against the Congo Free State continued until 1909, when the Lunda leaders were captured and executed.

forms until 1911 and in many cases into the 1960s. Slaves were exported to the coffee and cocoa plantations of São Tomé from the 1860s and were used in Angola to produce coffee, cotton, sugar, and fish. But from the 1850s, exports came to be dominated by products hunted or collected by Africans, first ivory and wax and later wild rubber. These changes came about as the industrial revolution reorganized the world economy, and items such as cloth and metal goods were now available for import and at less expense than in the past. Africans responded to this by ceasing local production of these goods and instead paying for the imported versions with commodity exports of peanuts and wild products such as honey, animal skins, ivory, and eventually rubber.

The slave trade had primarily been a state business and did not greatly affect the local communities from an economic standpoint. In contrast, this new trade involved the whole population: hundreds of thousands of people were employed in the transport and production of these commodities, and their increasing wealth, involvement in the international economy, and interest in commercial policies led to many problems for both indigenous and colonial governments. The Ovimbundu turned from slave raiding to long-distance trade, and their caravans penetrated as far east as the East African coast. The Chokwe were expert hunters of elephants and collectors of wax and rubber, and they used their accumulated firearms to overthrow the Lunda empire in the 1880s. The Kasanje kingdom collapsed when illicit slave trading undermined the king's central slave market and newly enriched commoners demanded a stronger voice in government.

Angolans closer to the coast were more affected by the slow expansion of Portuguese colonialism and by the loss of land to settlers. Cotton and sugar were grown from the 1840s on oasis plantations along the coastal strip, and immigrants from the Algarve built up the fishing industry. Spontaneously occurring stands of coffee led the Portuguese to carve out plantations in the Malanje highlands beginning in the 1830s, and work on the railway from Luanda to Malanje commenced in 1885. Construction began in 1902 on the Benguela Railway, which was intended to serve the Katanga mines in the Belgian Congo (now the Democratic Republic of the Congo). Portuguese small farmers were settled in the Huíla highlands from the 1880s to counterbalance an influx of Boer trekkers from South Africa, and the southern railway was begun in 1905. In the Maiombe forest of

In the 1900s, while Angola was under colonial rule, cacao plantations, such as this one in neighbouring Congo, were owned by Portuguese settlers and worked by native Angolans. Roger Viollet/ Getty Images

the far north, plantations of cacao and oil palms were laid out in the 1900s.

Angola's borders, including those for Cabinda (an exclave located in the country of the Democratic Republic of the Congo), had been finally determined by negotiations in Europe in 1891, but the Portuguese focused exclusively on administering areas with plantations and railways and introduced systematic taxation of Africans only in 1906. Many positions in the colonial administration were held by Angolan Creoles, who were initially accepted as full Portuguese citizens. The spread of British and American Protestant missions from the 1870s was countered by government-subsidized French Roman Catholic missions.

FROM COLONIAL CONQUEST TO INDEPENDENCE (1910–75)

The proclamation of the Republic of Portugal in Lisbon in late 1910, followed in 1926 by the creation of the authoritarian New State (Estado Novo), marked the advent of modern Portuguese colonialism. The authorities stamped out slavery and undertook the systematic conquest of Angola. By 1920 all but the remote southeast of the colony was firmly under Portuguese control. Kingdoms were abolished, and the Portuguese worked directly through chiefs, headmen, and African policemen. Conversions to Christianity increased, and by 1940 there were about a million Christians in Angola, some three-fourths of them Roman Catholics. Angolan "natives"

were taxed and subjected to forced labour and forced cultivation, with a stringent set of tests imposed on the few nonwhite "assimilated persons" who applied to be exempted from these impositions. Increasingly, Portuguese immigrants replaced Creoles in the administration. This trend continued, forcing Creoles into positions with lower pay and prestige and ultimately leading to the growth of Creole-led nationalism.

Angola's economy was modernized and bound to that of Portugal by a system of protective tariffs. A network of dirt roads was built, and the Benguela Railway was completed to the boundary of the Belgian Congo in 1928. Lorries (trucks) and fixed stores replaced trading caravans. Coffee, sugar, palm products, and sisal came mainly from the estate sector, and corn (maize) and cattle from smallholders. The cultivation of cotton for Portuguese textile mills was imposed by force. Alluvial diamond mining dominated the northeast from 1912, the fishing industry expanded, and import-substitution industries were started.

After the independence of the Belgian Congo in 1960, a major revolt rocked northern Angola in 1961, followed by a long guerrilla war. Land alienation and forced labour sparked rebellion in the coffee zone, while in the Cuango valley the peasants rose against forced cotton cultivation. An attack on the prison in Luanda was led by frustrated Creoles. To contain the revolt, the Portuguese deployed large numbers of troops, set up strategic hamlets (forced settlements of rural Angolans), and, by encouraging Portuguese peasants to immigrate to Angola, raised the European population to about 330,000 by 1974.

At the same time, they tried to improve relations with Africans by abolishing forced cultivation, forced labour, and the stringent tests to gain assimilated status. They also improved education, health, and social welfare services and protected peasants from land alienation. The economy entered into a period of sustained boom, marked by rapid industrialization and the growth of oil production, and the standard of living rose for both urban workers and rural producers.

The armed struggle continued, but the anticolonial guerrillas were seriously weakened by dissension. The Popular Movement for the Liberation of Angola (Movimento Popular de Libertação de Angola; MPLA) was founded in 1956 with the help of the clandestine Portuguese Communist Party, and from 1962 it was led by Agostinho Neto. It was popular in Luanda and among some rural Mbundu, drawing foreign support from the Soviet Union. Initially based in the Republic of the Congo, the MPLA moved to Zambia in 1965. The National Front for the Liberation of Angola (Frente Nacional de Libertação de Angola; FNLA), founded in 1957 under another name and led by Holden Roberto, drew its support from the Kongo and some rural Mbundu. Based in Congo (now the Democratic Republic of the Congo; called Zaire from 1971 to 1997), the FNLA obtained aid from the United States and

China. In 1966 Jonas Savimbi set up a third movement, the National Union for the Total Independence of Angola (União Nacional para a Independência Total de Angola; UNITA), with a predominantly Ovimbundu leadership and with some support from the Chokwe and Ovambo (Ambo). UNITA enjoyed little official foreign backing (although China provided some aid) and lacked a secure foreign base because Zambia leaned toward the MPLA.

The divisions among and within these three movements, which at times degenerated into armed conflict, allowed the Portuguese to gain the upper hand by the early 1970s. When a military coup in Portugal overthrew that country's dictatorship in April 1974, all three guerrilla movements had been almost entirely expelled from Angolan soil.

INDEPENDENCE AND CIVIL WAR

The three liberation movements proved unable to constitute a united front after the Portuguese coup. The FNLA's internal support had dwindled to a few Kongo groups, but it had strong links with the regime in Zaire and was well armed; it thus made a bid to seize Luanda by force. The MPLA, with growing backing from the Portuguese Communist Party, Cuba, and the Soviet Union, defeated this onslaught and then turned on UNITA, chasing its representatives out of Luanda. UNITA was militarily the weakest movement, but it had the greatest potential electoral

Agostinho Neto

(b. Sept. 17, 1922, Icolo e Bengo, Angola—d. Sept. 10, 1979, Moscow, Russia, U.S.S.R.)

Agostinho Neto was a poet, physician, and first president of the People's Republic of Angola. Neto first became known in 1948, when he published a volume of poems in Luanda and joined a national cultural movement that was aimed at "rediscovering" indigenous Angolan culture (similar to the Negritude movement of the French-speaking African countries). His first of many arrests for political activities came shortly thereafter in Lisbon, where he had gone to study medicine.

Neto returned home as a doctor in 1959 but was arrested in the presence of his patients in June 1960 because of his militant opposition to the colonial authorities. When his patients protested his arrest, the police opened fire, killing some and injuring 200. Neto spent the next two years in detention in Cape Verde and in Portugal, where he produced a new volume of verse. In 1962 he managed to escape to Morocco, where he joined the Angolan liberation movement in exile. At the end of 1962 he was elected president of the Movimento Popular de Libertação de Angola (MPLA).

When in 1975 Angola became independent, it was divided among its three warring independence movements. The MPLA forces, however, with Cuban help, held the central part of the country, including the capital, and Neto, a Marxist, was proclaimed president.

Neto was widely recognized as a gifted poet. His work was published in a number of Portuguese and Angolan reviews and was included in Mário de Andrade's Antologia da Poesia Negra de Expressão Portuguesa *(1958).*

support, given the predominance of the Ovimbundu within the population, and it thus held out most strongly for elections. But the Portuguese army was tired of war and refused to impose peace and supervise elections. The Portuguese therefore withdrew from Angola in November 1975 without formally handing power to any movement, and nearly all the European settlers fled the country.

The MPLA, in control of the capital city, declared itself the government of independent Angola and managed to win recognition from many African countries. UNITA and the FNLA set up a rival government in Huambo and called on South African forces to eject the MPLA from Luanda. Cuba poured in troops to defend the MPLA, pushed the internationally isolated South Africans out of Angola, and gained control of all the provincial capitals. The Cuban expeditionary force, which eventually numbered some 40,000 to 50,000 soldiers, remained in Angola to pacify the country and ward off South African attacks. In 1977 the MPLA crushed an attempted coup by one of its leaders and, after a thorough purge, turned itself officially into a Marxist-Leninist party, adding Partido

Trabalhista (Party of Labour) to their name (MPLA-PT). The transformation of the economy along communist lines was pursued, with disastrous results. The major exception was the oil industry, which, managed by foreign companies, grew rapidly enough to enable Angola to stave off economic and military collapse. President Neto died in 1979 and was succeeded by the former minister of planning, José Eduardo dos Santos.

The FNLA withered away in exile, but UNITA reorganized itself with foreign backing as an effective guerrilla force. South Africa became a strong supporter in hopes that UNITA could counter the guerrilla campaigns of the South West Africa People's Organization into Namibia, actions supported by the MPLA-PT. In 1985 UNITA began receiving military aid from the United States, and its campaigns became more effective. When the MPLA-PT launched several large campaigns against UNITA in 1987, using armour and aircraft, South African forces returned to the region, and a military stalemate resulted as fighting engulfed the country. But late in 1988 the South Africans promised to grant independence to Namibia and to cease supporting UNITA, while the Cubans agreed to withdraw their expeditionary force from Angola by mid-1991. The MPLA-PT's initial response to the South African withdrawal was to try to capture the airfield at Mavinga, from which it would be able to launch an attack against UNITA's headquarters.

The failure of this costly campaign and the increasingly effective UNITA attacks on oil installations forced the MPLA-PT to adopt a more conciliatory posture. In June 1989 a historic meeting between Santos and Savimbi during negotiations brokered by Zaire produced a cease-fire, although it did not last; but with communist regimes collapsing in eastern Europe, the MPLA-PT lost its support and began negotiating more seriously. In mid-1990 the MPLA-PT abandoned the one-party state and produced a new constitution that included elections and participation by all, including UNITA. They also abandoned their strict Marxist-Leninist stance and dropped the words Partido Trabalhista (PT) from their name. Elections were held in 1992 under United Nations supervision; Dos Santos was elected president, and the MPLA gained a majority in the parliament, but UNITA made a strong showing, especially on the Bié Plateau. Charging election fraud, UNITA renewed the civil war, while its delegates in Luanda were massacred in a popular uprising that many believe had government backing.

The exclave of Cabinda became another focus of attention for postindependence government. Although this region is situated geographically within the country of the Democratic Republic of the Congo, Portugal gained control of it at the end of the 19th century. Cabinda was specifically made a part of Angola in 1975, but the Angolan government had to contend with independence movements there. The region is particularly valuable because a significant amount of Angola's oil is found there.

At the end of 1992, UNITA controlled approximately two-thirds of the country, including valuable diamond mines that were used to pay for the continuing costs of the war. Fighting raged throughout 1993 as the government gradually regained territory and won greater support abroad; both South Africa and the United States recognized the government of Angola in 1993, as did the United Kingdom by ending an arms embargo that had existed since 1975. Meanwhile, international pressure mounted on the two sides to reach a peaceful solution. Sanctions against UNITA were imposed by the UN in September 1993 after it disregarded a cease-fire it had accepted earlier, but it appeared that UNITA could continue the war for some time with its vast stockpile of weapons. Eventually, an agreement called the Lusaka Accord was signed by the government and UNITA on Nov. 20, 1994. The agreement allowed UNITA to be reintegrated into the government, provided fighting ceased on that date.

Although minor fighting between the two groups continued, dos Santos and Savimbi met several times over the next three years to resolve issues relating to the final form of the combined government. In August 1996 Savimbi finally agreed to accept the title of "leader of the opposition," but he declined to attend a ceremony in April 1997 at which UNITA delegates formally joined the government. Relations between the two groups were further complicated that year by the civil war in the Democratic Republic of the Congo. UNITA supported the

(Left to right, foreground): Angolan President José Eduardo dos Santos, Zambian President Fredrick Chiluba and UNITA leader Jonas Savimbi, during the signing of 1994's Lusaka Accord. Gary Bernard/AFP/Getty Images

crumbling Zairean regime because the group had been able to transport its diamonds through the country, while the Angolan government supported the victorious rebels led by Laurent Kabila.

ANGOLA IN THE 21ST CENTURY

By the beginning of the 21st century, hostilities between the government and UNITA had resumed, and the UNITA delegates had been expelled from the government. With the killing of Savimbi by government forces in February 2002, talks began again between the UNITA leadership and the government, finally culminating in a peace agreement in April. Although the country breathed a collective sigh of relief with the end of 27 years of civil war, the Angolan government was faced with the daunting challenge of rebuilding the country's physical and social welfare infrastructure, much of which was completely destroyed. In the early 21st century, there were repeated outbreaks of illness, such as cholera, due to poor sanitary conditions; there was also an epidemic of hemorrhagic fever caused by the deadly Marburg virus in 2005. It was estimated that the civil war had displaced more than four million people, and hundreds of thousands of Angolan refugees still needed to be resettled in the country. The resumption of agricultural production was also a challenge, further complicated by the thousands of land mines that were strewn haphazardly throughout the country during the conflict. The Angolan government also had to address the long-standing issue of separatist groups in oil-rich Cabinda and their demands for independence, which intensified in 2004. When the government and the main separatist group reached a peace agreement in 2006, Angolans looked to the future, hopeful that peace had finally come. Nonetheless, sporadic bouts of violence continued in the exclave in the years that followed.

Highly anticipated multiparty parliamentary elections—the first since 1992—were held on Sept. 5–6, 2008. Although there were some reports of fraud and intimidation, the elections were deemed valid by international observers, and the MPLA won about four-fifths of the vote. The long-awaited presidential election, however, was postponed. A new constitution promulgated in 2010 eliminated the direct election of the president and instead provided for the presidential post to be filled by the leader of the party with the largest share of the vote in parliamentary elections. Dos Santos was to remain president until the next round of elections, scheduled for 2012.

CHAPTER 5

BOTSWANA

The landlocked country of Botswana is located in the centre of Southern Africa. The former British protectorate gained independence in 1966. Gaborone is the capital.

EARLY PASTORAL AND FARMING PEOPLES

The history of Botswana is in general the history of the Kalahari area, intermediate between the more populated savanna of the north and east and the less populated steppe of the south and west. The historical record of the region begins with its early pastoral and farming inhabitants.

KHOISAN-SPEAKING HUNTERS AND HERDERS

People speaking Khoisan (Khoe and San) languages have lived in Botswana for many thousands of years. Depression Shelter in the Tsodilo Hills has evidence of continuous Khoisan occupation from about 17,000 BCE to about 1650 CE. During the final centuries of the last millennium before the Common Era, some of the Khoi (Tshu-khwe) people of northern Botswana converted to pastoralism, herding their cattle and sheep on the rich pastures revealed by the retreating lakes and wetlands.

BANTU-SPEAKING FARMERS

Meanwhile, the farming of grain crops and the speaking of Bantu languages were carried gradually southward from the Equator. By about 20 BCE such farmers were making and using iron tools on the upper Zambezi. The earliest dated Iron Age site in Botswana is an iron-smelting furnace in the Tswapong Hills near Palapye, dated about 190 CE and probably associated with Iron Age farmers from the Limpopo valley. The remains of small beehive-shaped houses made of grass matting, occupied by early Iron Age farmers around Molepolole, have been dated to about 420 CE.

There is also evidence of early farming settlement west of the Okavango delta, in the Tsodilo Hills alongside Khoisan hunter and pastoralist sites, dated to about 550 CE. Archaeologists

Animal images speckle a cliff face in Tsodilo Hills, a historically significant site in Botswana. Daryl Balfour/Gallo Images/ Getty Images

therefore have difficulty interpreting the hundreds of rock paintings in the Tsodilo Hills (designated a UNESCO World Heritage site in 2001) that were once assumed to be painted by San hunters remote from all pastoralist and farmer contact.

IRON AGE STATES AND CHIEFDOMS

As time progressed, the region saw the rise and fall of several new states and chiefdoms. The initial means for survival of these societies was primarily farming and pastoralism, which was later augmented or replaced by hunting and trading.

EASTERN STATES AND CHIEFDOMS

From about 1095 CE southeastern Botswana saw the rise of a new culture, characterized by a site on Moritsane hill near Gabane. The Moritsane culture is historically associated with the Khalagari (Kgalagadi) chiefdoms, the westernmost dialect group of Sotho (or Sotho-Tswana) speakers.

The area within 50 or 60 miles (80 or 100 km) of Serowe saw a thriving farming culture, dominated by rulers living on Toutswe hill, between about the 7th and 13th centuries. The prosperity of the state was based on cattle herding, with large corrals in the capital town and in scores of smaller hilltop villages. (Ancient cattle corrals are identified by the peculiar grass growing on them.) The Toutswe people also hunted westward into the Kalahari and traded eastward along the Limpopo River.

The Toutswe state appears to have been conquered by its neighbour, the Mapungubwe state, centred on a hill at the Limpopo-Shashi confluence, in the 13th century. But the triumph of Mapungubwe was short-lived, as it was superseded by the new state of Great Zimbabwe, north of the Limpopo River. Great Zimbabwe's successor from about 1450 was the Butua state, based at Khami (Kame) near Bulawayo in western Zimbabwe. Butua controlled trade in salt and hunting dogs from the eastern Makgadikgadi Pans, around which it built stone-walled command posts.

Western Chiefdoms

From about 850 CE farmers from the upper Zambezi, ancestors of the Mbukushu and Yei peoples, reached as far south and west as the Tsodilo Hills (Nqoma). The oral traditions of Herero and Mbanderu pastoralists, west of the Okavango, relate how they were split apart from their Mbandu parent stock by 17th-century Tswana cattle-raiding from the south.

Rise of Tswanadom

During the 13th and 14th centuries a number of powerful dynasties began to emerge among the Tswana in the western Transvaal region. Rolong chiefdoms spread westward over lands controlled by Khalagari peoples. Khalagari chiefdoms either accepted Rolong rulers or moved westward across the Kalahari.

The main Tswana dynasties of the Hurutshe, Kwena, and Kgatla were derived from the Phofu dynasty, which broke up in its home in the western Transvaal region in the 16th century. The archaeology of the Transvaal region shows that, after about 1700, stone-walled villages and some large towns developed on hills. These states were probably competing for cattle wealth and subject populations, for control of hunting and mineral tribute, and for control of trade with the east coast.

GROWTH OF TSWANA STATES

Kwena and Hurutshe migrants founded the Ngwaketse chiefdom among the Khalagari-Rolong in southeastern Botswana by 1795. After 1750 this chiefdom grew into a powerful military state controlling Kalahari hunting and cattle raiding and copper production west of Kanye. Meanwhile, other Kwena had settled around Molepolole, and a group of those Kwena thenceforth called Ngwato settled farther north at Shoshong. By about 1795 a group of Ngwato, called the Tawana, had even founded a state as far northwest as Lake Ngami.

Times of War

From about 1750, trading and raiding for ivory, cattle, and slaves spread inland

TSWANA

The Tswana are a westerly division of the Sotho, a Bantu-speaking people of South Africa and Botswana. They are also called Batswana or Botswana (formerly spelled Bechuana). The Tswana comprise several groupings, the most important of which, numerically speaking, are the Hurutshe, Kgatla, Kwena, Rolong, Tlhaping, and Tlokwa. They numbered about four million at the turn of the 21st century.

The Tswana live in a grassland environment where they practice animal husbandry and subsistence agriculture based on corn (maize) and sorghum. There is a seasonal and periodic migration of large numbers of men who work in the mining and industrial centres of South Africa.

Tswana material culture reflects the widespread intrusion of European goods and standards. Housing forms range from the traditional circular single-roomed dwelling with conical thatched roof to multiroomed rectangular houses with roofs of corrugated iron. Transport varies from ox-drawn sledges to motor vehicles. European dress prevails.

Every Tswana is affiliated to a patrilineal descent group, each group associated with a distinctive symbol that serves as a polite mode of address and sometimes as a surname. In self-administering political units, especially those in Botswana, the basic social unit is the ward, a readily identifiable, self-contained social and administrative entity comprising a number of lineally related families together with their dependents and servants. Its leader is usually the head of the senior family.

Although identification with a particular ward is strong, there also are age groups (age sets, or regiments) that cut across ward loyalties. New regiments are formed periodically and are important as organized labour units for public works.

Ethnic group membership includes alien elements, and Tswana members are often in a minority, so that a Tswana group accordingly lacks cultural and even linguistic uniformity. The chief rules with the assistance of advisers and officials, but at the same time all matters of public policy usually require the approval of a general council open to all adult male members.

from the coasts of Mozambique, the Cape Colony, and Angola. By 1800 raiders from the Cape had begun to attack the Ngwaketse. By 1824 the Ngwaketse were being attacked by the Kololo, a military nation on the move that had been expelled northwestward by raiders from the east. The great Ngwaketse warrior king Makaba II was killed, but the Kololo were pushed farther north by a counterattack in 1826.

The Kololo moved through Shoshong to the Boteti River, expelling the Tawana northward. About 1835 the Kololo settled on the Chobe River, extending their power to the upper Zambezi, until their final defeat there by their Lozi subjects in 1864. The Kololo were followed by the Ndebele, a military nation led by Mzilikazi, who settled in the Butua area of western Zimbabwe in 1838–40, after the local Rozvi state was conquered.

PROSPEROUS TRADING STATES

The Tswana states of the Ngwaketse, Kwena, Ngwato, and Tawana were reconstituted in the 1840s after the wars ended. The states competed with each other to benefit from the increasing trade in ivory and ostrich feathers being carried by wagons down new roads to the Cape Colony in the south. Those roads also brought Christian missionaries to Botswana and Boer trekkers who settled in the Transvaal to the east.

The most remarkable Tswana king of this period was Sechele (ruled 1829–92) of the Kwena around Molepolole. He allied himself with British traders and missionaries and was baptized by David Livingstone. He also fought the Boers, who tried to seize people who fled from the Transvaal to join Sechele's state. But by the later 1870s the Kwena had lost control of trade to the Ngwato under Khama III (ruled 1872–73; 1875–1923), whose power extended to the frontiers of the Tawana in the northwest, the Lozi in the north, and Ndebele in the northeast.

BRITISH PROTECTORATE

White miners and prospectors flooded Botswana in 1867–69 to start deep gold mining at Tati near Francistown. But the gold rush was short-lived, and the diamond mines at Kimberley south of Botswana became Southern Africa's first great industrial area from 1871. Migrant labourers from Botswana and countries farther north streamed to Kimberley and later to the gold mines of the Transvaal.

The "scramble for Africa" in the 1880s resulted in the German colonization of South West Africa. The new German colony threatened to join across the Kalahari with the independent Boer republic of the Transvaal. The British in the Cape Colony responded by using their missionary and trade connections with the Tswana states to keep the roads through Botswana open for British expansion to Zimbabwe and the Zambezi. In 1885 the British proclaimed a protectorate over their Tswana allies and the Kalahari as far north as the Ngwato. The protectorate was extended to the Tawana and the Chobe River in 1890.

British colonial expansion was privatized in the form of the British South Africa Company, which in 1890 used the road through the Bechuanaland Protectorate to colonize the area soon to be called Rhodesia (Zimbabwe). But the protectorate itself remained under the British crown, and white settlement remained restricted to a few border areas, after an attempt to hand it over to the company was foiled by a delegation of three Tswana kings to London in 1895. The kings, however, had to concede to the

SIR SERETSE KHAMA

(b. July 1, 1921, Serowe, Bechuanaland [now Botswana]—d. July 13, 1980, Gaborone, Bots.)

Seretse Khama served as the first president of Botswana (1966–80), after the former Bechuanaland protectorate gained independence from Great Britain.

The grandson of Khama III the Good, who had allied his kingdom in Bechuanaland with British colonizers in the late 19th century, Seretse Khama succeeded his father to the chieftainship of the Ngwato (Mangwato, or Bamangwato) people at age four. He was educated in South Africa and studied law at the University of Oxford. His marriage to Ruth Williams, a British woman, in 1948 caused considerable controversy in both Britain and Bechuanaland and was among the reasons the British government forced his exile from Bechuanaland until he agreed to renounce the chieftainship in 1956.

Following his return to Bechuanaland as a private citizen, he founded the Democratic Party in 1962, and in 1965 he became prime minister. He helped negotiate the terms of Botswana's independence, and he was knighted in 1966.

As president of Botswana, Khama promoted his ideal of a multiracial democracy. He achieved free universal education in Botswana and sought to diversify and strengthen the country's economy. He was reelected to successive terms and served as president of Botswana until his death. His son, Ian Khama, became president of Botswana in 2008.

Seretse Khama. Brian Seed/Time & Life Pictures/Getty Images

company the right to build a railway to Rhodesia through their lands.

The British government continued to regard the protectorate as a temporary expedient, until it could be handed over to Rhodesia or, after 1910, to the new Union of South Africa. Hence, the administrative capital remained at Mafeking (Mafikeng)—actually outside the protectorate's borders in South Africa—from 1895 until 1964. Investment and administrative development within the territory were kept to a minimum. It declined into a mere appendage of South Africa, for which it provided migrant labour and the rail transit route to Rhodesia. Short-lived attempts to reform administration and to initiate mining and agricultural development in the 1930s were hotly disputed by leading Tswana chiefs, on the grounds that they would only enhance colonial control and white settlement. The territory remained divided into eight largely self-administering "tribal" reserves and five white settler farm blocks, with the remainder classified as crown (i.e., state) lands.

The extent of the Bechuanaland Protectorate's subordination to the interests of South Africa was revealed in 1950. In a case that caused political controversy in Britain and the empire, the British government barred Seretse Khama from the chieftainship of the Ngwato and exiled him from Botswana for six years. This, as secret documents have since confirmed, was in order to satisfy the South African government, which objected to Seretse Khama's marriage to a white Englishwoman at a time when racial segregation was being reinforced in South Africa under apartheid.

ADVANCE TO INDEPENDENCE

From the late 1950s it became clear that Bechuanaland could no longer be handed over to South Africa and must be developed toward political and economic self-sufficiency. The supporters of Seretse Khama began to organize political movements from 1952, and there was a nationalist spirit even among older "tribal" leaders. Ngwato "tribal" negotiations for the start of copper mining led to an agreement in 1959. A legislative council was eventually set up in 1961 after limited national elections. The Bechuanaland People's Party was founded in 1960, and the Bechuanaland Democratic Party (BDP; later known as the Botswana Democratic Party)—led by Seretse Khama—was founded in 1962.

After long resistance to constitutional advance before economic development could pay for it, the British began to push political change in 1964. A new administrative capital was rapidly built at Gaborone. Bechuanaland became self-governing in 1965, under an elected BDP government with Seretse Khama as prime minister. In 1966 the country became the Republic of Botswana, with Seretse Khama as its first president.

For its first five years of political independence, Botswana remained financially dependent on Britain to cover the full cost of administration and development. The planning and execution of economic development took off in 1967–71 after the discovery of diamonds at Orapa. The essential precondition for this was renegotiation of the customs union with South Africa, so that state revenue would benefit from rising capital imports and mineral exports rather than remain at a fixed percentage of total customs union income. This renegotiation was achieved in 1969.

BOTSWANA SINCE INDEPENDENCE

From 1969 Botswana began to play a more significant role in international politics, putting itself forward as a nonracial, liberal democratic alternative to South African apartheid. In 1974 Botswana was—together with Zambia and Tanzania and later Mozambique and Angola—one of the "Frontline States" seeking to bring majority rule to Zimbabwe, Namibia, and South Africa. The organization of the Frontline States led in 1980 to the formation of the Southern African Development Coordination Conference (SADCC; since 1992 known as the Southern African Development Community [SADC]). The idea behind the SADCC, largely structured by Khama, was to build a better future for the region by coordinating disparate economies and promoting development in each of the member countries.

Benefiting from a rapidly expanding economy in the 1970s and '80s, Botswana was able to extend basic infrastructure for mining development and basic social services for its population. More diamond mines were opened, on relatively favourable terms of income to the state. The BDP was consistently reelected with a large majority, though the Botswana National Front (BNF; founded 1965) became a significant threat after 1969, when "tribal" conservatives joined the socialists in BNF ranks attacking the "bourgeois" policies of government.

Khama died in 1980 and was succeeded by Quett Masire, a BDP party member who had been his deputy since 1965. Masire was faced with such internal issues as a high rate of unemployment and the increasing gap between urban rich and rural poor, as well as with international concerns. Between 1984 and 1990, Botswana suffered from upheavals in South Africa when South African troops raided the Frontline States. Two raids on Gaborone by the South African army in 1985 and 1986 killed 15 civilians. But a new era in Southern African relations dawned after Namibia gained independence in 1990, and the internal political changes in South Africa resulted in full diplomatic relations being established with Botswana in 1994.

The economic expansion of previous decades slowed and even reversed in the early 1990s but bounced back within a few years. However, there were still other issues facing the country. Looting and rioting, unusual behaviour in Botswana, killed one person in 1995. Although the apparent cause of the violence was outrage over the release of three people charged in the murder of a

Ian Khama, the son of independent Botswana's first president, was elected to the country's highest political office for a full term in 2009. Getty Images

young girl, critics of the BDP-led government asserted that frustration with social conditions and the high rate of unemployment were the underlying reasons that fueled the unrest. Of greater concern was the AIDS epidemic that had exploded in the country during the 1990s, leaving Botswana with one of the highest rates of infection in the world. The government responded aggressively by increasing HIV/AIDS awareness and by coordinating efforts to curtail the epidemic. In the early 21st century Botswana became the first African country to provide free HIV antiretroviral medication to all citizens.

Masire retired in 1998 and was succeeded by the BDP's Festus Mogae, a former cabinet minister and vice

president. Following BDP victories in the 1999 and 2004 elections, Mogae was elected by the National Assembly in 1999 to serve a full term as president and was reelected in 2004. Meanwhile, in 1998 more than 2,400 refugees from Namibia's Caprivi Strip began fleeing into Botswana; some were Caprivian secession leaders that Namibia demanded be extradited. Botswana's decision to instead grant them refugee status led to tension between the two countries. Mogae's administration also had to address worldwide criticism over the relocation of the Basarwa (San), which had been an issue under Masire's administration as well. The reasons for relocating the Basarwa to settlements outside the Central Kalahari Game Reserve (the Basarwa ancestral land) and the methods used to carry out the relocation continued to be a source of domestic and international consternation. Although the Basarwa were eventually awarded the right to return to their land in a December 2006 ruling from the Botswana High Court, disagreements remained between the Basarwa and the government about such issues as hunting and water rights.

Mogae retired in April 2008 and was succeeded by vice president Ian Khama, a BDP party member and the son of Botswana's first president, Seretse Khama. In elections held on Oct. 16, 2009, the BDP won a decisive victory, extending its majority in the National Assembly and securing for Khama a full term as president; he was inaugurated on October 20.

CHAPTER 6

LESOTHO

The Southern African country of Lesotho is completely encircled by the Republic of South Africa. A former British protectorate, Lesotho gained independence in 1966. Maseru is the capital.

EARLY HISTORY

The territory now known as Lesotho was occupied as early as the Neolithic Period (New Stone Age) by Khoisan-speaking hunter-gatherers. From about the 16th century, African farmers—the ancestors of the present population—moved across the grasslands of Southern Africa and settled in the fertile valleys of the Caledon River, where they came to dominate the hunters of the region. These stock-keeping agriculturalists belonged to the large Sotho group and were divided into numerous clans that formed the nucleus of chiefdoms, whose members occupied villages.

THE SOTHO KINGDOM (1824–69)

The violent upheavals of the early 19th century among the chiefdoms of Southern Africa intensified in Lesotho in the 1820s. During this turbulent period, known as the Difaqane (also spelled Lifaqane; Sotho: "crushing"; also known by its Zulu name, Mfecane), the members of many chiefdoms were annihilated,

Moshoeshoe I was instrumental in the creation of the kingdom of Sotho, which later became the country of Lesotho. Fotosearch/Archive Photos/Getty Images

dispersed, or incorporated into stronger, reorganized, and larger chiefdoms positioned in strategically advantageous areas.

The leaders who headed the new chiefdoms had the ability to offer greater protection; one of these was Moshoeshoe I of the Moketeli, a minor lineage of the Kwena (Bakwena). In 1824 he occupied Thaba Bosiu ("Mountain at Night"), the defensive centre from which he incorporated many other individuals, lineages, and chiefdoms into what became the kingdom of the Sotho (subsequently also called Basutoland). Moshoeshoe was a man of remarkable political and diplomatic skill. By cooperating with other chiefdoms and extending the influence of his own lineage, he was able to create a Sotho identity and unity, both of which were used to repel the external forces that threatened their autonomy and independence. Moshoeshoe also acknowledged the importance of acquiring the skills of farmers, settlers, hunters, and adventurers, who increasingly moved across his borders from the south. He therefore welcomed the missionaries from the Paris Evangelical Missionary Society as a source of information about the rest of the world when they arrived at Thaba Bosiu in 1833. He placed them in strategically important parts of the kingdom, where they gave the Sotho their first experience with Christianity, literacy, and commodity production for long-distance trading.

Large numbers of Boer trekkers from the Cape Colony began to settle on the western margins of the kingdom in 1834 and to challenge the right of the Sotho to their land. The next 30 years were characterized by conflict and outbursts of warfare between the Sotho and the Boers. Ultimately, the Sotho lost most of their territory west of the Caledon River to the Boers. The British, to whom Moshoeshoe appealed for intervention, were unable to resolve the dispute over where the boundary should be drawn.

MOSHOESHOE

(b. c. 1786, near the upper Caledon River, northern Basutoland [now in Lesotho]—d. March 11, 1870, Thaba Bosiu, Basutoland)

Moshoeshoe (also spelled Mshweshwe, Moshweshwe, or Moshesh) was the founder and first paramount chief of the Sotho (Basuto, Basotho) nation. One of the most successful Southern African leaders of the 19th century, Moshoeshoe combined aggressive military counteraction and adroit diplomacy against colonial invasions. He created a large African state in the face of attacks by the Boers and the British, raiders from the south east coastal lowlands of Africa, and local African rivals.

Moshoeshoe, or Lepoqo (as was his original name), was the son of Mokhachane, the chief of the Mokoteli. As a young man, Moshoeshoe—then known by his post circumcision name of Letlama ("The Binder")—won a reputation for leadership by conducting daring cattle raids. In early adulthood he took the name Moshoeshoe, an imitation of the sounds made by a knife in shaving that symbolized his deft skills at rustling cattle. His acquaintance with the chief Mohlomi, who was revered as a wise man, strengthened his capacity for generous treatment of allies and enemies alike.

In the late 1810s and early '20s, European land invasions, labour needs, and trade heightened Southern African disturbances and led to migration in the region. Moshoeshoe led his people south to the nearly impregnable stronghold of Thaba Bosiu ("Mountain at Night") in the western Maloti Mountains, where his following expanded to other African peoples attracted by the protection he was able to provide. He eventually united the various small groups to form the Sotho nation, called Basutoland by English-speaking persons. He strengthened his new nation by raiding local Tembu and Xhosa groups for cattle and adopting the use of horses and firearms. In the cold Highveld he was able to defeat mounted Griqua and Korana raiders with his own mounted cavalry and expanded his control into the Caledon valley.

In 1833 he welcomed missionaries of the Paris Evangelical Missionary Society (though he never became a Christian himself), and he used them to cultivate good diplomatic relationships with British politicians in Cape Town. Moshoeshoe's greatest threat (and opportunity) came with the Boer invasions—the Great Trek—after the mid-1830s. The rival Boer and Sotho groups fought for control of the fertile farming lands of the Caledon valley.

In 1848, when the British annexed the Orange River Sovereignty (previously the Boer's territory) to the east of Moshoeshoe's stronghold, he found himself exposed to direct Anglo-Boer invasion. Moshoeshoe's Sotho forces twice defeated overconfident and undersupported British armies, first in 1851 at Viervoet and again in late 1852 at the battle of Berea near Thaba Bosiu. Moshoeshoe continued to fight against encroachment on Sotho lands, and in the following year he defeated and absorbed the Tlokwa, local African rivals.

Wanting to avoid the time and expense required to defeat the Sotho, the British gave the Boers of the Orange River Sovereignty (renamed the Orange Free State) independence at the Bloemfontein Convention of 1854. During the next 10 years, Moshoeshoe was able to inflict further defeats on the Boers, who were disorganized in their efforts to unite and repel the Sotho. At the Treaty of Aliwal North in 1858, the Sotho regained control of land on both sides of the Caledon River, a perhaps unparalleled assertion of black expansionism against contending whites in Southern Africa.

After the Boers of the Orange Free State united behind Pres. J.H. Brand in 1864, however, the long land war turned against Moshoeshoe. He was forced to give up most of his earlier gains at the Treaty of Thaba Bosiu in 1866, and during 1867 he faced complete defeat. This was prevented when the British high commissioner of the Cape Colony, Sir Philip Wodehouse, annexed Moshoeshoe's now truncated territory as Basutoland in 1868. Though Moshoeshoe's power waned in the last years of his life, the Sotho continue to venerate his name, and he is considered to be the father of his country.

Devastating wars in the late 1860s prompted Moshoeshoe to again appeal to the British for assistance, as he feared the dispersal and possible extinction of his people. Sir Philip Wodehouse, governor and high commissioner of the Cape Colony, concerned with the region's stability and British interests in Southern Africa, annexed the kingdom to the British crown in 1868.

Basutoland remained a British protectorate until Moshoeshoe's death in 1870 (he was buried on Thaba Bosiu). The next year the colony was annexed to the Cape Colony without the consent of Basutoland. The former independent African mountain kingdom lost much of its most productive land to the Boers and its political autonomy to the British. Nonetheless, the Sotho still retained some of their land and their social and cultural independence.

BASUTOLAND

Attempts by the Cape Colony administration to disarm the Sotho led to the Gun War (1880–81). The Cape Colony relinquished Basutoland to British rule in 1884, when it became one of three British High Commission Territories in Southern Africa; Swaziland and Bechuanaland (now Botswana) were the other two.

At the end of the 19th century, mineral discoveries were made whose enormous potential laid the foundation for the creation of the Union of South Africa (1910). In order to acquire cheap labour and to end competition from independent African agricultural producers, landowners and miners encouraged the adoption of policies that deprived the indigenous population of its social and political rights and most of its land. Sotho farmers took advantage of the markets for foodstuffs in the growing South African mining centres, however. They utilized new farming techniques to produce substantial surpluses of grain, which they sold on the South African markets. Sotho workers also traveled to the mines to sell their labour for cash and firearms.

Lesotho's history in the 20th century was dominated by an increasing dependence on labour migration to South Africa, which was made necessary by taxation, population growth behind a closed border, the depletion of the soil, and the need for resources to supplement agricultural production. Sotho workers became an important element of the South African mining industry, and Basutoland became the classic example of the Southern African labour reserve, its people dependent on work in South Africa for their survival.

The British set up a system of dual rule and left considerable power in the hands of the paramount chiefs—Letsie (1870–91), Lerotholi (1891–1905), Letsie II (1905–13), Griffith (1913–39), Seeiso (1939–40), and the regent 'Mantsebo (1940–60)—all of whom were descendants of Moshoeshoe. Under these leaders, authority was delegated through ranked regional chiefs drawn from the royal lineage and the

THE GUN WAR

In the Gun War of 1880–81, the Sotho (also Basuto or Basotho) people of Basutoland (present-day Lesotho) threw off the rule by the Cape Colony. It is one of the few examples in Southern African history of black Africans' winning a conflict with colonial powers in the 19th century.

In 1871 Basutoland was annexed—without its consent—to the Cape Colony. As in other areas where the Cape Colony ruled over black Africans, the Sotho people were forced off their land to work on white-owned farms or mines. The Cape Colony's government intended to destroy the powers of the Sotho chiefs and revise their traditional laws, and attractive land in Basutoland was earmarked for white occupation. The former independent African mountain kingdom quickly lost much of its most productive land and its political autonomy. In 1879 the chiefs of southern Basutoland attacked Cape Colony magistrates and took a stand on the issues of self-rule and sovereignty. In retaliation, troops from the Cape Colony were sent into Basutoland.

In 1880 the Cape authorities doubled the already controversial hut tax on the Sotho and tried to enforce the 1879 Disarmament Act, ordering the Sotho to disarm and hand in their guns. These demands split the Sotho into rebels and collaborators, and this led to civil war between the Sotho chiefs, who were already in conflict over the paramountcy. In September 1880 a Cape Colony army attacked Sotho rebels led by Lerotholi and other chiefs. In October the rebels were able to inflict a sound defeat on Cape troops at Qalabani: while fighting from defensive positions in rugged mountainous country and using horses, the Sotho rebels ambushed a column of Cape soldiers, killing or wounding 39 of them. Unwilling or unable to commit the large number of troops that would have been necessary to destroy the rebel armies, the Cape Colony made peace with the Sotho in April 1881.

After the war the Sotho were permitted to retain their arms, though they were to pay an annual tax on each gun. By 1882, however, the Sotho were refusing to register their firearms and thus evaded the tax. That year a Cape army under Gen. Charles Gordon was sent in, but it retired without achieving anything. The Cape Colony, faced with prospects of endless war, gave over responsibility for Basutoland directly to the British government in 1884. Basutoland became a British High Commission Territory, and the powers of the Sotho chiefs were left relatively intact. This change in status is why Basutoland was not included in the surrounding Union of South Africa when it was formed in 1910. Instead, the Sotho nation remained under British oversight until 1966, when it became the independent country of Lesotho.

most important chiefdoms. A system of customary law was adopted, with the land held in trust by the paramount chief for the people, while crucial aspects of local government were also left to the chiefs. The colonial government was headed by a resident commissioner and advised by the Basutoland National Council, which was led by the paramount chief and dominated by his nominated members.

The British administration was concerned primarily with balancing Basutoland's budget, which it facilitated by ensuring that a substantial proportion of the population worked for wages in South Africa. The local chiefs could do little to halt the increasing social and economic deprivation within Basutoland. Education was left to the missionary societies, and there was little development of economic infrastructure or social services. Between 1929 and 1933 the Great Depression coincided with a massive drought, driving so many people into South Africa that the population in Basutoland hardly increased for a decade.

Opposition to the colonial system grew, but no organizations were able to topple the colonial administration and its traditionalist allies. The Sotho were unified, however, in their opposition to Basutoland's incorporation into South Africa and their fear that the British might cede the territory to South Africa without consulting them.

In the early 1930s the British attempted to reduce the number of chiefs, but after World War II (during which more than 20,000 Sotho served for the British in North Africa, Europe, and the Middle East) the development of nationalist parties pressing for independence outweighed the need for reform. Three major political parties emerged at this time: the Basutoland Congress Party (BCP; at independence the Basotho Congress Party) in 1952, under Ntsu Mokhehle; the more conservative Basutoland National Party (BNP;

at independence the Basotho National Party) in 1958, under Chief Leabua Jonathan, which was supported by the South African government and was associated with chiefly power and the Roman Catholic Church; and the Marema-Tlou Freedom Party (1963), which was identified with the defense of the powers of the country's principal chiefs.

The Basutoland Council, in existence since 1903, obtained the right to control the internal affairs of the territory in 1955. The region became self-governing in 1965, and general elections held in that year for a new legislative assembly were dominated by the BNP.

THE KINGDOM OF LESOTHO

On Oct. 4, 1966, when Basutoland received its independence from Britain, it was renamed the Kingdom of Lesotho and headed by paramount chief Moshoeshoe II (named for the nation's founder) as king and Chief Jonathan as prime minister. Executive power was given to the prime minister in 1967.

THE FIRST TWO DECADES

In the first postindependence general elections (January 1970), the opposition BCP gained a majority of seats. The results were never released, however, and Chief Jonathan suspended the constitution, arrested leading members of the opposition, and temporarily exiled the king. Resistance to these moves was met with considerable violence, but, after a short delay, Britain accepted the actions of Chief Jonathan.

The BNP used legislation and violence—and the distribution of state patronage—to silence and control its opponents. In 1974 the BCP attempted to overthrow the regime, but this coup was put down, and Mokhehle, the BCP's leader, went into exile.

During the 1970s Lesotho received an increasing amount of foreign aid in support of its struggle against the discriminatory apartheid policy of South Africa. The funding helped to increase the pace of modernization and urban development, spur economic improvements in infrastructure, education, and communications, and create a privileged bureaucracy. It failed, however, to alleviate the long-standing problems of poverty and dependence. Thus, although mine wages and payments from the Southern African Customs Union increased in the 1970s, Lesotho was unable to use these revenues productively and remained dependent on South Africa.

Chief Jonathan criticized South Africa's apartheid policy on numerous occasions through the late 1970s. The government's hostility toward the South African regime became more serious when the country began accepting refugees from South Africa. As part of its strategy to destabilize its African neighbours, South Africa gave support to the armed wing of the BCP, the Lesotho Liberation Army. In December 1982 the South African Defence Force attacked houses in Maseru that it alleged were guerilla bases for the African National Congress. More than 40 people were killed, many of whom were Lesotho citizens. Relations between the governments deteriorated as South Africa demanded the expulsion of South African refugees in Lesotho.

Differences also began to appear among leading figures within the Lesotho government. One faction advocated a policy more amenable to South African demands. In January 1986 the South African authorities placed severe restrictions on the movement of goods and people across the border, effectively closing it. In response, the pro-South African faction in Lesotho, led by Maj. Gen. Justin Lekhanya, deposed Chief Jonathan and established military rule, making the king head of state.

When the Military Council banned open political activity and deported a number of South African refugees, South Africa responded by lifting the blockade. In October 1986 Lesotho and South Africa signed the Lesotho Highlands Water Treaty, and the following year a South African trade mission was established in Lesotho. However, Lesotho's economic impasse continued as a recession in South Africa deepened and the South African gold mining industry reduced its production.

POLITICAL CRISIS

Conflict arose in February 1990 within the Military Council, headed by Maj.

Gen. Lekhanya, but King Moshoeshoe II refused to approve several dismissals from the council. He was dethroned and went into exile, and his eldest son, Mohato, was sworn in as King Letsie III. Maj. Gen. Lekhanya was forced to resign in April 1991 after a successful coup led by Col. Elias Tutsoane Ramaema, who lifted the ban on political activity and promised a new constitution. The political and economic crises continued, however, and demonstrations broke out in Maseru in May. General elections first promised in 1992 were finally held in March 1993. The BCP returned to power under the leadership of Ntsu Mokhehle as prime minister. He appointed a commission in July 1994 to examine the circumstances surrounding the dethronement of King Moshoeshoe II in 1990. King Letsie's attempt to dismiss the BCP government in August 1994 proved unsuccessful, and Moshoeshoe was reinstated as king in January 1995. Less than a year later, Moshoeshoe died, and Letsie reassumed the throne.

Lesotho was heavily affected by developments in South Africa during the mid-1990s and by its own internal political instability. When the international community removed its economic sanctions against South Africa, Lesotho lost its advantage of being within South Africa but not part of it. This, together with the reduced South African demand for Sotho labourers, produced more unemployed and underemployed in Lesotho and increased political volatility and lawlessness there. Severe riots aimed mostly at Asian-owned businesses caused serious setbacks for foreign investment.

In 1997 the BCP dismissed Mokhehle as leader, and he eventually formed his own party, the Lesotho Congress of Democrats (LCD). The LCD overwhelmingly won the general elections of May 1998, and, upon Mokhehle's resignation, Pakalitha Mosisili became prime minister. Although claims of voting fraud were raised, the election was declared free and fair by many international observers. Opposition parties protesting in Maseru were joined in August by large numbers of jobless youths. The protesters obtained arms, and looting and arson broke out in Maseru and the surrounding towns; much of the capital was left in ruins.

Faced with an insurrection, the government asked the Southern African Development Community (SADC) to send troops to Lesotho from South Africa and Botswana to quell the disturbances. Eventually, SADC forces restored order, but not before the majority of businesses and government offices had been sacked or destroyed. In response, South Africa imposed an agreement that called for new elections. Stability was restored, and SADC forces withdrew from the country in May 1999. Although the government that took power in May 1998 was headed by Mosisili and the LCD, representatives from the SADC forced Lesotho to create an Interim Political Authority (IPA), which contained representatives from the country's major political parties and was charged with preparing for the 2000 elections.

CHALLENGES IN THE 21ST CENTURY

The IPA was inaugurated in late 1998 and immediately became embroiled in contentious debate regarding the type of electoral system to embrace. Because of the dissent, the IPA was not able to establish an electoral schedule in time for elections to be held in 2000, and they were postponed. In 2002, when the elections were finally held, the LCD again won the majority of parliamentary seats, and Mosisili was named to a second term as prime minister. In 2006, dissension within the LCD resulted in one of the party's prominent ministers, Thomas Thabane, leaving to form the All Basotho Convention (ABC); many other LCD ministers followed Thabane to the ABC. Nevertheless, the LCD managed to maintain control of the parliament after early elections were called in February 2007. Although the elections were generally viewed as free and fair by international observers, the ABC contested the results but to no avail.

Meanwhile, local government elections were held in 2005—the first such elections since independence—but were clouded by low voter turnout (less than one-third of eligible voters participated). Later that year the government made an ambitious effort to address the country's growing HIV/AIDS pandemic by offering free HIV testing to the entire population. Although the objective was to reach every household by the end of 2007, the program fell short of its goal, stymied by such factors as a lack of necessary medical staff and the logistics of reaching the many rural and mountainous locations in the country.

Lesotho also faced other problems in the early 21st century. The continued decline in agricultural production—caused in part by endemic soil erosion in the already limited arable land, as well as by repeated droughts and the impact of the HIV/AIDS pandemic on the workforce—resulted in chronic food shortages, and widespread poverty and unemployment plagued the country.

CHAPTER 7

MALAWI

M alawi is a landlocked country in southeastern Africa. A
former British protectorate, it gained independence in
1964. Lilongwe is the capital.

EARLY HISTORY

The paleontological record of human cultural artifacts
in Malawi dates back more than 50,000 years, although
known fossil remains of early *Homo sapiens* belong to the
period between 8000 and 2000 BCE. These prehistoric fore-
bears have affinities to the San people of Southern Africa
and were probably ancestral to the Twa and Fulani, whom
Bantu-speaking peoples claimed to have found when they
invaded the Malawi region between the 1st and 4th centuries
CE. From then to about 1200 CE, Bantu settlement patterns
spread, as did ironworking and the slash-and-burn method
of cultivation. The identity of these early Bantu-speaking
inhabitants is uncertain. According to oral tradition, names
such as Kalimanjira, Katanga, and Zimba are associated
with them.

   With the arrival of another wave of Bantu-speaking peoples between the 13th and 15th centuries CE, the recorded
history of the Malawi region began. These peoples migrated
into the region from the north, and they interacted with and
assimilated the earlier pre-Bantu and Bantu inhabitants. The

descendants of these peoples maintained a rich oral history, and, from 1500, written records were kept in Portuguese and English.

Among the notable accomplishments of the last group of Bantu immigrants was the creation of political states, or the introduction of centralized systems of government. They established the Maravi Confederacy about 1480. During the 16th century the confederacy encompassed the greater part of what is now central and southern Malawi, and, at the height of its influence, in the 17th century, its system of government affected peoples in the adjacent areas of present-day Zambia and Mozambique. North of the Maravi territory, the Ngonde founded a kingdom about 1600. In the 18th century a group of immigrants from the eastern side of Lake Malawi created the Chikulamayembe state to the south of the Ngonde.

The precolonial period witnessed other important developments. In the 18th and 19th centuries, better and more productive agricultural practices were adopted. In some parts of the Malawi region, shifting cultivation of indigenous varieties of millet and sorghum began to give way to more intensive cultivation of crops with a higher carbohydrate content, such as corn (maize), cassava (manioc), and rice.

The independent growth of indigenous governments and improved economic systems was severely disturbed by the development of the slave trade in the late 18th century and by the arrival of foreign intruders in the late 19th century. The slave trade in Malawi increased dramatically between 1790 and 1860 because of the growing demand for slaves on Africa's east coast.

Swahili-speaking people from the east coast and the Ngoni and Yao peoples entered the Malawi region between 1830 and 1860 as traders or as armed refugees fleeing the Zulu states to the south. All of them eventually created spheres of influence within which they became the dominant ruling class. The Swahili speakers and the Yao also played a major role in the slave trade.

Islam spread into Malawi from the east coast. It was first introduced at Nkhotakota by the ruling Swahili-speaking slave traders, the Jumbe, in the 1860s. Traders returning from the coast in the 1870s and '80s brought Islam to the Yao of the Shire Highlands. Christianity was introduced in the 1860s by David Livingstone and by other Scottish missionaries who came to Malawi after Livingstone's death in 1873. Missionaries of the Dutch Reformed Church of South Africa and the White Fathers of the Roman Catholic Church arrived between 1880 and 1910.

Christianity owed its success to the protection given to the missionaries by the colonial government, which the British established after occupying the Malawi region in the 1880s and '90s. British colonial authority was welcomed by the missionaries and some African

Missionary David Livingstone is credited with first bringing Christianity to the area in Africa that would become Malawi. Rischgitz/Hulton Archive/Getty Images

societies but was strongly resisted by the Yao, Chewa, and others.

COLONIAL RULE

In 1891 the British established the Nyasaland Districts Protectorate, which was called the British Central Africa Protectorate from 1893 and Nyasaland from 1907. Under the colonial regime, roads and railways were built, and the cultivation of cash crops by European settlers was introduced. On the other hand, the colonial administration did little to enhance the welfare of the African majority, because of commitment to the interests of European settlers. It failed to develop

Hastings Kamuzu Banda, 1960. Encyclopædia Britannica, Inc.

African agriculture, and many able-bodied men migrated to neighbouring countries to seek employment. Furthermore, between 1951 and 1953 the colonial government decided to join the colonies of Southern and Northern Rhodesia and Nyasaland in the Federation of Rhodesia and Nyasaland, against bitter opposition from their African inhabitants.

These negative features of colonial rule prompted the rise of a nationalist movement. From its humble beginnings during the period between the World Wars, African nationalism gathered momentum in the early 1950s. Of special impetus was the imposition of the federation, which nationalists feared as an extension of colonial power. The full force of nationalism as an instrument of change became evident after 1958 under the leadership of Hastings Kamuzu Banda, who had returned to the country that year after having been abroad to study and practice medicine. The federation was dissolved in 1963, and Malawi became independent as a member of the Commonwealth of Nations on July 6, 1964.

POSTINDEPENDENCE MALAWI

Banda retained the post of prime minister after the country achieved independence and later became president. He played an important role in Malawi during the next three decades before ultimately agreeing to step down and allow a peaceful transfer of power.

HASTINGS KAMUZU BANDA

(b. c. 1898, near Kasungu, British Central Africa Protectorate [now Malawi]—d. Nov. 25, 1997, Johannesburg, S.Af.)

Hastings Kamuzu Banda was the first president of Malawi (formerly Nyasaland) and the principal leader of the Malawi nationalist movement. He governed Malawi from 1963 to 1994, combining totalitarian political controls with conservative economic policies.

Banda's birthday was officially given as May 14, 1906, but he was believed to have been born before the turn of the century. He was the son of subsistence farmers and received his earliest education in a mission school. After working in Southern Rhodesia (now Zimbabwe) and South Africa, in 1925 he went to the United States, where he received a B.A. (1931) and a medical degree (1937) at the University of Chicago and Meharry Medical College in Tennessee, respectively. In order to achieve the qualifications needed to practice in the British Empire, Banda then continued his studies at the University of Edinburgh (1941) and subsequently practiced in northern England and London from 1945 to 1953.

Banda first became involved in his homeland's politics in the late 1940s, when white settlers in the region demanded the federation of the Rhodesias and Nyasaland. Banda and others in Nyasaland strongly objected to this extension of white dominance, but the Federation of Rhodesia and Nyasaland was nevertheless established in 1953. In 1953–58 Banda practiced medicine in Ghana, but from 1956 he was under increasing pressure from Nyasa nationalists to return. He finally did so, to a tumultuous welcome, in 1958. As president of the Nyasaland African Congress, he toured the country making antifederation speeches, and the colonial government held him partly responsible for increasing African resentment and disturbances. In March 1959 a state of emergency was declared, and he was imprisoned by the British colonial authorities. He was released in April 1960, and a few months later he accepted British constitutional proposals granting Africans in Nyasaland a majority in the Legislative Council. Banda's party won the general elections held in August 1961. He served as minister of natural resources and local government in 1961–63, and he became prime minister in 1963, the year the federation was finally dissolved. He retained the post of prime minister when Nyasaland achieved independence in 1964 under the name of Malawi.

Shortly after independence, some members of Banda's governing cabinet resigned in protest against his autocratic methods and his accommodation with South Africa and the Portuguese colonies. In 1965 a rebellion broke out, but it failed to take hold in the countryside. Malawi became a republic in 1966, with Banda as president. He headed an austere, autocratic one-party regime, maintained firm control over all aspects of the government, and jailed or executed his opponents. He was declared president for life in 1971. Banda concentrated on building up his country's infrastructure and increasing agricultural productivity. He established friendly trading relations with minority-ruled South Africa (to the disappointment of other African leaders) as well as with other countries in the region through which landlocked Malawi's overseas trade had to pass. His foreign-policy orientation was decidedly pro-Western.

Widespread domestic protests and the withdrawal of Western financial aid forced Banda to legalize other political parties in 1993. He was voted out of office in the country's first multiparty presidential elections, held in 1994.

THE BANDA REGIME (1963–94)

Soon after independence, a serious dispute arose between Banda, the prime minister, and most of his cabinet ministers. In September 1964 three ministers were dismissed and three others resigned in protest. Henry Chipembere, one of these ministers, escaped from house arrest and defied attempts at recapture, becoming the focus for antigovernment opinion until his death in 1975. On July 6, 1966, Malawi became a republic, and Banda was elected president; in 1971 he was made president for life.

Malawi's 1966 constitution established a one-party state under the Malawi Congress Party (MCP), which in turn was controlled by Banda, who consistently and ruthlessly suppressed any opposition. From independence the MCP government became a conservative, pro-Western regime, supported by a bicameral National Assembly whose members were elected within the single-party system.

Banda's government improved the transport and communication systems, especially the road and railway networks. There was also much emphasis on cash crop production and food security; the estate sector (which produced tobacco, tea, and sugar) met expectations, but smallholder production was not as successful, mainly because of the low prices offered by the Agricultural Development and Marketing Corporation (ADMARC), the state organization that had the monopoly on marketing smallholder produce. In addition, the cost of fertilizer, all of which was imported and also dominated by ADMARC, rendered smallholder agriculture expensive.

For more than 10 years, Malawi was able to prosper economically before being felled by a confluence of external factors. In 1980, in an effort to improve the country's economic situation and broaden regional ties, Malawi joined the Southern African Development Coordination Conference (later the Southern African Development Community), a union of black majority-ruled countries near minority-ruled South Africa that wished to reduce their dependence on that country. Banda refused to sever formal diplomatic ties with the discriminatory apartheid regime in South Africa, however—a decision that was not popular with the other leaders in the region.

On March 8, 1992, a pastoral letter written by Malawian Catholic bishops expressing concern at—among other things—the poor state of human rights, poverty, and their effects on family life was read in churches throughout Malawi. This act served to encourage underground opposition groups that had long waited for an opportunity to mount an open and vigorous campaign for multiparty democracy; exile groups also intensified their demands for political reform. Additional pressure was applied by international donors, who withheld financial aid. By the end of 1992, two internally based opposition parties, the Alliance for Democracy and the United Democratic Front (UDF), had emerged, and Banda agreed to hold a national referendum to determine the need for reform. Advocates for change won an overwhelming victory, and in May 1994 the first free elections in more than 30 years took place. Banda was defeated by Bakili Muluzi of the UDF by a substantial margin, and the UDF won a majority of seats in the National Assembly.

MALAWI SINCE 1994

A new constitution, officially promulgated in 1995, provided the structure for transforming Malawi into a democratic society. Muluzi's first term in office brought the country greater democracy and freedoms of speech, assembly, and association—a stark contrast to life under Banda's regime. Muluzi's administration also promised to root out government corruption and reduce poverty and food shortages in the country, although this

campaign met with limited success. Muluzi pursued good relations with a number of Arab countries, toward most of which Banda had been particularly cool; he also sought to play a more active role in African affairs than his predecessor. Muluzi was reelected in 1999, but his opponent, Gwandaguluwe Chakuamba, challenged the results. The aftermath of the disputed election included demonstrations, violence, and looting. During Muluzi's second term, he drew domestic and international criticism for some of his actions, which were viewed as increasingly autocratic.

Malawi's international standing was bolstered in 2000, when the country's small air force responded quickly to the flooding crisis in the neighbouring country of Mozambique, rescuing upward of 1,000 people. However, the country was not as quick to respond to a severe food shortage at home, first noted in the latter half of 2001. By February 2002 a famine had been declared, and the government was scurrying to find enough food for its citizens. Unfortunately, much international aid was slow to arrive in the country—or was withheld entirely—because of the belief that government mismanagement and corruption contributed to the food shortage. In particular, some government officials were accused of selling grain from the country's reserves at a profit to themselves prior to the onset of the famine.

Muluzi was limited to two terms as president, despite his efforts to amend the constitution to allow further terms. In

Malawians unload corn donated by the United States to combat a food shortage in 2002. Drought and suspected government mismanagement were blamed for the ensuing famine. Ami Vitale/ Getty Images

2004 his handpicked successor, Bingu wa Mutharika of the UDF, was declared the winner of an election tainted by irregularity and criticized as unfair. Mutharika's administration quickly set out to improve government operations by eliminating corruption and streamlining spending. To that end, Mutharika dramatically reduced the number of ministerial positions in the cabinet and initiated an investigation of several prominent UDF party officials accused of corruption, leading to several arrests. His actions impressed international donors, who resumed the flow of foreign aid previously withheld in protest of the financial mismanagement and corruption of Muluzi's administration.

By that time the country had been negatively affected by the HIV/AIDS crisis and the lack of such requisites as economically viable resources, an accessible and well-utilized educational system, and an adequate infrastructure—issues that continued to hamper economic and social progress. However, Mutharika's administration showed potential for leading Malawi on a path of meaningful political reform, which in turn promised to further attract much-needed foreign aid.

As his term progressed, Mutharika faced a number of political challenges, including conflicts with his predecessor and the UDF. In February 2005 Mutharika left the UDF, of which Muluzi was chairman, and announced shortly thereafter his intention to form a new party, the Democratic Progressive Party. In June the UDF brought an impeachment motion against Mutharika before the National Assembly, which in October voted to begin proceedings against him; although appeals to Mutharika's opponents by donor countries and neighbouring leaders asking that they reconsider were largely unsuccessful, the motion was finally withdrawn in early 2006. In July of that year, Muluzi was arrested on charges of corruption, although the charges were soon dropped because of lack of evidence. He was again arrested in mid-2008, in connection with an alleged plot to overthrow Mutharika, and again in February 2009, when he was accused of embezzling millions of dollars' worth of donor funding. Muluzi denied the charges and claimed they were part of a political conspiracy against him as well as an attempt to keep him from standing in the upcoming presidential election.

His desire to run for president was hindered by another factor: whether the two terms he had previously served made him ineligible for a third. The Malawi Electoral Commission felt they did and barred him from standing in the election, but Muluzi appealed, arguing that the potential third term would be nonconsecutive with his previous terms and therefore would not violate the two-term limit stipulated in the constitution. His appeal was denied by a Malawian court just days before the election, and he threw his support behind the primary opposition candidate John Tembo of the MCP.

In the presidential and parliamentary elections held on May 19, 2009, Mutharika soundly defeated the other candidates, but many people, including Tembo, alleged that voting irregularities were widespread. International monitors stated that Mutharika had an unfair advantage leading up to the election, noting that the state-controlled media did not provide fair and balanced coverage of all candidates.

CHAPTER 8

MOZAMBIQUE

Mozambique is located on the southeastern coast of Africa. A former Portuguese colony, it gained independence in 1975. The capital is Maputo.

PRECOLONIAL PERIOD

During the colonial era Mozambique's history was written as though it had begun with the arrival of the Portuguese, but the people of this region had developed complex communities based on agriculture, cattle raising, mining, crafts, and trade long before the first small groups of Portuguese settlers arrived in the 16th century.

EARLY SETTLEMENT

From at least the 3rd century CE, Iron Age people who practiced agriculture and kept both cattle and small livestock moved into Mozambique as part of the migration of Bantu speakers from west-central Africa toward the south and east. These people had mastered iron technology and combined the cultivation of some grains with knowledge of root and tree crops. In the process they created such sustained population growth that they needed to expand their territory. In a slow but fairly steady process, one branch of Bantu speakers moved east toward the Indian Ocean and then south along the coast, and another moved more directly south-southeast

An ancient grindstone and grinder found at Mapungubwe, an archaeological site in Southern Africa, believed to be similar to those used in the early settlements of Mozambique. Shem Compion/Gallo Images/Getty Images

into the Zimbabwe plateau and highlands of western Mozambique.

The characteristic social unit was the extended patrilineal household headed by an elder male and consisting of his wives, their unmarried children, adult sons, and the sons' families. Although both social and labour organization varied throughout the area, women were usually responsible for child care, cultivation, gathering of food crops, and food preparation, whereas men were involved in cattle keeping, hunting, toolmaking, and a range of crafts.

Toward the end of the 1st millennium CE, groups of households called *nyika* had emerged in south-central Mozambique as social units under the authority of a chief and chiefly household. In the 10th century a settlement known as Mapungubwe, which incorporated many *nyika*, developed in the upper reaches of the Limpopo River. It was the earliest of the settlements featuring stone enclosures, or *zimbabwe*s.

THE RISE OF THE ZIMBABWE CIVILIZATIONS

The groups on the Zimbabwe plateau expanded their herds and moved between the plateau and the surrounding Mozambican lowlands in pursuit of seasonal pastures, although the tsetse fly, which causes sleeping sickness, was present in the region. The region's economy was rooted in agriculture and cattle keeping, but its social and political organization became more complex with the development of local industries and trade, specifically the mining of gold, copper, and iron ore and the development of salt pans, tool forges, and potting industries. The civilization of Great Zimbabwe, which dominated the region politically from the mid-13th to the mid-15th century, controlled mining and trade.

The *zimbabwe* settlement at Manekweni, about 30 miles (50 km) from the Indian Ocean in southern Mozambique, replicated in miniature the social and settlement patterns of the highland interior. Manekweni was a centre for agriculture, cattle keeping, and the gold trade from about the 12th to the 18th century.

From roughly the 10th to the 18th century, Great Zimbabwe and the area of Central Africa around Lake Kisale (in the southern area of the Democratic Republic of the Congo) were the region's centres of production and intra-African trade. Beginning in at least the 1st millennium, however, people of this region traded with various non-Africans. The earliest and most important external trade link for Mozambique was with Middle Eastern and South Asian peoples who traded beads and cloth for gold across the Red Sea and the Indian Ocean.

By the 14th century, African Arab, or Swahili, trade cities were flourishing along the coast from Somalia in the north to Kilwa in what is now southern Tanzania. Smaller Swahili sultanates developed along the northern coast of Mozambique as far south as Angoche. A series of markets had arisen throughout the region by the 16th century, sustained by intraregional trade in raw materials and long-distance trade in gold, copper, ivory, and slaves.

ARRIVAL OF THE PORTUGUESE

The voyage of Vasco da Gama around the Cape of Good Hope into the Indian Ocean in 1498 marked the European entry into trade, politics, and society in the Indian Ocean world. The Portuguese gained control of the Island of Mozambique and the port city of Sofala in the early 16th century, and by the 1530s small groups of Portuguese had pushed their way into the interior, where they set up garrisons and trading posts at Sena and Tete on the Zambezi River and tried to gain exclusive control over the gold trade. The Portuguese attempted to legitimate and consolidate their trade and settlement positions through the creation of *prazos* (land grants) tied to European occupation. While *prazos* were originally developed to be held by Europeans, through intermarriage they became African Portuguese or African Indian centres defended by large African slave armies known as Chikunda. Most *prazos* had declined by the mid-19th century, but several of them survived and strongly resisted Portuguese domination until the last quarter of the 19th century.

The Portuguese were able to wrest much of the coastal trade from Arabs between 1500 and 1700, but, with the Arab seizure of Portugal's key foothold at Fort Jesus on Mombasa (now in Kenya) in 1698, the pendulum began to swing in the other direction. During the 18th and 19th centuries the Mazrui and Omani Arabs reclaimed much of the Indian Ocean trade, forcing the Portuguese to retreat south. During the 19th century other European powers, particularly the British and the French, became increasingly involved in the trade and politics of the region.

SLAVES AND TRADE

By the 18th century, slaves had become an increasingly important part of Mozambique's overall export trade from the East African coast. Yao traders developed slave networks from the Marave area around the tip of Lake Nyasa to Kilwa and the Island of Mozambique. *Prazo* traders along the Zambezi sold gold and slaves from Zumbo, Tete, and Manica to Portuguese merchants at Quelimane, and Tsonga ivory traders developed routes from the Transvaal region of South Africa and from the Zimbabwe plateau to coastal entrepôts at Inhambane and Maputo. During the 19th century, Mozambicans were sold as slaves in the Portuguese and Brazilian South Atlantic trade, the Arab trade from the Swahili coast, and the French trade to the sugar-producing islands of the Indian Ocean and Madagascar. Although the trade in slaves declined as a result of the mid-19th-century slave-trade agreements between Portugal and Britain, clandestine trade—particularly from central and northern Mozambique—continued into the 20th century.

During the first three decades of the 19th century, the proliferation of military and raiding groups from the conflicts in the northern Nguni heartland southwest of Mozambique had an important impact on southern and west-central Mozambique. Several military groups, offshoots of the emerging Zulu state, invaded Mozambican territory, seizing cattle, hostages, and food as they went. The waves of armed groups disrupted both trade and day-to-day production throughout the area. Two groups, the Jere under Zwangendaba and the Ndwandwe (both later known as Ngoni) under Soshangane, swept through Mozambique. Zwangendaba's group continued north across the Zambezi, settling to the west of contemporary Mozambique, but Soshangane's group crossed the Limpopo into southern Mozambique, where it eventually consolidated itself into the Gaza state. In the 1860s a succession struggle between the sons of Soshangane caused enormous suffering in the region and weakened the Gaza state.

COLONIAL MOZAMBIQUE

By the 1880s the Portuguese controlled trade and collected tribute in coastal enclaves from Ibo in the north to Lourenço Marques in the south, but their ability to control events outside those areas was quite limited. That situation, however, was about to change.

CONSOLIDATION OF PORTUGUESE CONTROL

Increasingly, as neighbours of the Gaza state were raided periodically for refusing to pay tribute, they began to ally themselves with the Portuguese, which the Portuguese both encouraged and exploited. In the 1890s a coalition of Portuguese troops and African armies marched against the state. When the Gaza leadership was finally defeated in 1897, southern Mozambique passed into Portuguese control. Two decades later the Portuguese, who had mounted dozens of military campaigns by that time, directly controlled the Barue of central Mozambique, the African Portuguese of the Zambezi and Maganja da Costa *prazos*, the Yao of Mataka, the northern Makua chiefdoms, and the northern coastal sheikhdoms of Angoche.

Trade in ivory, gold, slaves, rubber, oilseeds, and a broad range of European goods continued throughout the 19th century. However, European economic interest and influence in the region changed rapidly by mid-century in response to developments in both Africa and Europe. African labour was needed on the sugar plantations and at South African ports and mines after diamonds (at Kimberley in the 1860s) and gold (at Witwatersrand in the 1880s) were discovered. Because of the need for labour, Europeans were determined to gain greater control over tracts of land and their inhabitants at the expense of African leadership. The combined struggle for access to mineral-bearing lands and the labour force to work them fueled the so-called "scramble" in Southern Africa.

Portugal claimed a swath of territory from present-day Mozambique to Angola. Although the Germans, whose territory bordered Mozambique to the north, accepted the Portuguese claims—establishing Mozambique's northern boundary—British claims to the region contradicted those of Portugal, leading to prolonged negotiations. However, the Portuguese crown was heavily in debt to British financiers, and the small country was no match for Britain's military. In 1891, Portugal was forced to accept Britain's definition of Mozambique's western and southern boundaries.

Portugal had little hope of developing the entire region on its own, and so it turned to its familiar colonial strategy of leasing large tracts of land to private companies. Chartered companies were granted the privilege of exploiting the lands and peoples of specific areas in exchange for an obligation to develop agriculture, communications, social services, and trade. The Mozambique Company, the Niassa

Company, and the Zambezia Company were all established in this manner in the 1890s. Any economic development and investment in infrastructure was related directly to company interests and usually undertaken at African expense. Sugar, copra, and sisal plantations depending largely on conscripted labour and railways linking Beira with the British South Africa Company territory and British Nyasaland to the west and northwest were all developed and built at a high cost to the African workforce.

The Portuguese government eventually terminated the charters of the major concession companies, bringing all of Mozambique under direct Portuguese rule. Between the 1890s and the 1930s, Portuguese rule in Mozambique was characterized by the exploitation of African people and resources by private parties, whether they were foreign company shareholders or colonial bureaucrats and settlers. The most egregious colonial abuses—forced labour, forced crop cultivation, high taxes, low wages, confiscation of the most promising lands—occurred regardless of which group of Europeans was in control.

MOZAMBIQUE UNDER THE NEW STATE REGIME

The 1926 coup in Portugal created a Portuguese regime that came to be known as the "New State" (Estado Novo). Although most of the former abuses in Mozambique continued and in some cases were intensified, the New State consolidated the profit into fewer hands and promoted conditions that would favour capital accumulation by Portugal and the Portuguese over all others. While the administrative and educational systems in Mozambique were unified and developed more coherently under the New State, they were still principally directed toward settlers.

Colonial investment patterns began to change in the early 1950s, when Portugal set forth a series of development plans designed to extend and upgrade Mozambique's transportation and communications infrastructure. Portuguese who had exploited monopolies and incentives to great profit were encouraged to invest in, expand, and diversify their undertakings. The generally favourable prices for tropical commodities in the post-World War II era fueled the trend, and the colonial economy expanded vigorously. At the same time, the New State retained tight control over the economic and physical mobility of the Africans, and thousands of Portuguese settlers arrived in the 1950s and '60s to take advantage of employment and business opportunities denied to Africans. But in promoting these policies, Portuguese colonial authorities antagonized Africans of all social classes.

The African leadership that emerged in the late 1950s represented a broad cross section of the population and was able to channel considerable discontent against colonial power. Because the New State dealt with any form of political dissent with imprisonment, deportation, or

SAMORA MACHEL

(b. Sept. 29, 1933, Chilembene, Mozam.—d. Oct. 19, 1986, Mbuzini, S.Af.)

Samora Machel was one of the leaders who fought for independence when Mozambique was still a Portuguese colony. He later served as the first president of independent Mozambique (1975–86).

Born more than 200 miles north of Maputo, the capital of Mozambique, Machel received his education through mission schools. He refused to enter a seminary for higher education and instead became a nurse in Maputo.

Samora Machel. Agence France Presse/Hulton Archive/Getty Images

The experience radicalized him, and, after 10 years in the profession, he joined the clandestine Mozambique Liberation Front (Frelimo), which sent him to Algeria for military training. He rose quickly through the leadership ranks and became Frelimo's leader in 1970, after the 1969 assassination of Eduardo Mondlane.

Machel claimed that his radical political stance came originally not from reading Marx but from the experiences of his family; his parents were forced to grow cotton for the Portuguese and were displaced from their land in the 1950s in favour of Portuguese settlers. After Mozambique became independent in 1975, Machel became president. Frelimo followed Marxist ideology by nationalizing many institutions and supported Robert Mugabe in his fight to end white domination of his country, Zimbabwe. Machel, however, did sign the Nkomati Accord with South Africa in 1984, under which each country agreed not to support the other country's opposition movements, and thereby maintained an economic relationship with that country's white minority government. His charisma and personal style kept his government in power despite the droughts and floods of the early 1980s and the ongoing civil war with the Mozambique National Resistance (Renamo).

In 1986 Machel was returning to Mozambique from Zambia when his plane crashed in South Africa. It was believed by many that the South African government was somehow responsible for the crash, although it strongly denied a connection. Machel's widow, Graça, who married South African Pres. Nelson Mandela in 1998, gave evidence to South Africa's Truth and Reconciliation Commission that supported the involvement of the minority South African government. A memorial to Machel was erected in 1999 at the site of the crash.

execution, the formal political challenge to the regime developed among African workers and students living outside Mozambique. In 1962 Mozambican representatives from exiled political groups met in Tanganyika (now Tanzania) and formed the socialist Mozambique Liberation Front (Frente de Libertação de Moçambique; Frelimo), with Eduardo Mondlane as its first president.

Frelimo's strategy was not immediately clear, but, after serious internal debate, the ascendant leadership committed itself to an armed challenge. Frelimo's guerrilla forces, which had been trained and armed by African and Soviet-bloc supporters, attacked targets in northern Mozambique in September 1964, and the war for independence was launched. Portugal, faced with similar challenges in other African territories (Angola, Guinea-Bissau, and Cape Verde), responded with enormous military effort. Mondlane was killed in 1969, but the leadership of Frelimo was ably assumed by Samora Machel, and the Portuguese remained frustrated and militarily ineffectual against Frelimo's small-scale guerrilla engagements. By 1974 Frelimo forces could move about most of the north in relative freedom and had infiltrated central Mozambique, although the cities, most of the south, and the coastal areas as far north as Nacala remained in Portuguese hands.

INDEPENDENCE

In April 1974 the military in Portugal staged a coup, which was welcomed by those Portuguese who were unhappy with the New State regime, its African wars, and its ideology. Frelimo took advantage of its military position to insist on a ceasefire, which confirmed its right to assume power in an independent Mozambique. A quickly aborted countercoup attempt in Maputo in September and some rioting in October were the only overt challenges to Frelimo's authority.

Within a year of the Portuguese coup, most of the settler population had left Mozambique. On June 25, 1975, Mozambique became an independent, single-party state led by Frelimo, with Machel serving as president.

MOZAMBIQUE AS A ONE-PARTY STATE

Frelimo's solidarity with other African guerrilla groups fighting for political rights in the region strongly shaped events after it controlled the entire country. Mozambicans widely supported Frelimo's decisions to close the border with Rhodesia (now Zimbabwe), to implement international sanctions against the country, and to allow its guerrilla forces to develop bases in Mozambique, but these decisions proved costly when Mozambique suffered major losses of revenue and lives and the destruction of key infrastructure. Frelimo's support for the African National Congress (ANC) brought similar economic and military retribution from the white regime in South Africa.

Frelimo had mixed success with its social and economic policies during its first decade of rule. Forced cultivation, forced labour, and ethnic discrimination were ended, but the party's commitment to communal, cooperative, and state-run agriculture antagonized many African farmers, who had hoped to see land returned to their families. By 1985 Frelimo recognized the failure of its agricultural policy of moving farmers into communal villages. Under pressure from international creditors, it began de-emphasizing state ownership and control of markets in favour of the family agricultural sector.

The government's extensive investment in education, health care, and services for the majority population was initially highly successful. Within a decade of independence, however, these gains had been totally undermined by the actions of the Mozambique National Resistance (Resistência Nacional Moçambicana; Renamo), an insurgency group trained, supplied, and supported by Rhodesia, South Africa, former Portuguese settlers, and Mozambicans opposed to Frelimo. Renamo began economic sabotage and a campaign of terror against the rural population shortly after independence. In 1984 the governments of Mozambique and South Africa signed the Nkomati Accord, under which each country would no longer support the other country's opposition movement (ANC in South Africa and Renamo in Mozambique). Because this agreement did little to curb Renamo's activity and was violated by South Africa, Frelimo continued attempts to end the conflict

through negotiation. The leaders of Frelimo and Renamo finally accepted a peace agreement in October 1992, whereby Frelimo's leadership agreed to change the constitution and to open the political process to competing parties in exchange for Renamo's promise to end the war. Issues between the two groups were not totally resolved until 1994.

Peace in Mozambique

The multiparty elections that finally took place in October 1994 were the culmination of years of effort to reach a peaceful end to the war between Frelimo and Renamo. Frelimo, once a self-described Marxist-Leninist vanguard party and still progressive if not clearly socialist, made several important concessions to the peace process. Mozambique joined the World Bank and the International Monetary Fund in 1984 and adopted their demands to privatize the economy under a structural-adjustment program. Several years later Joaquim Chissano, who had become Mozambique's president when Machel died in a plane crash in 1986, introduced a new constitution that ended Frelimo's one-party rule and Mozambique's identity as a socialist country. That constitution allowed for multiparty elections, though other goals had to be met before elections could be held.

Renamo changed its image as an international pariah known for burning schools and health clinics and became a legitimate political party. Renamo's leader, Afonso Dhlakama, met with international political leaders and was accepted as a presidential candidate. During the election campaign the United Nations provided military and civilian police, who supervised the activities of their Mozambican counterparts, while the European Union supplied election materials. Although Frelimo and Renamo were the main contenders in the elections, many other smaller parties also emerged, including several founded by Mozambican businessmen who had been in exile for years. There were a dozen presidential candidates and a similar number of parties fielding candidates for the National Assembly. The elections were considered free and fair by international observers, with Frelimo president Chissano garnering the majority of the votes. Renamo, however, was strongly represented in the national government and the National Assembly.

The new government faced the lingering effects of the war, notably the presence of up to two million land mines in the countryside. An international operation has cleared some areas of mines, especially along roads, but many rural areas remain endangered. The effort to demobilize both Frelimo and Renamo forces and form a new, unified military also met with delays and difficulties, and in the mid-1990s soldiers waiting in demobilization camps for weeks without food, money, or prospects for work staged scattered violent uprisings.

In the early 21st century, Mozambique suffered several natural disasters, including drought, an earthquake, and devastating floods. The country's economic growth, though adversely affected by these events, was bolstered by significant debt relief and by economic reform measures enacted by the government. The new century also ushered in a change in leadership: in 2001 Chissano announced that he would not stand in the next presidential election. Frelimo, however, maintained control of the presidency when its candidate, Armando Guebuza, was victorious in the 2004 presidential election. He was reelected with 75 percent of the vote in 2009.

CHAPTER 9

NAMIBIA

Namibia is located on the southwestern coast of Africa. During the colonial era it was initially ruled by Germany and later by neighbouring South Africa until independence was achieved in 1990. The capital is Windhoek.

EARLY HISTORY AND THE BEGINNING OF THE COLONIAL ERA

The history of Namibia is not well chronicled. Its isolated geographic position limited contact with the outside world until the 19th century. Explorer, missionary, trader, conqueror, and settler sources are neither comprehensive, notable for accuracy, nor unbiased. Professional historiography is a post-1960 development in the country, and the political events of the years since then have coloured most of the written history.

The earliest Namibians were San, nomadic peoples with a survival-oriented culture based on hunting and gathering. Their clans were small and rarely federated, and their military technology was so weak that, even before the arrival of the Europeans, they had been pushed back to the desert margins. Rock paintings and engravings at Twyfelfontein, in northwest Namibia, have shed light on the early San hunter-gatherers who once inhabited the area. Stone artifacts, human figures, and animals such as giraffes, rhinoceroses, and zebras are depicted. Twyfelfontein was designated a UNESCO World Heritage site in 2007.

Sand dunes and vegetation at Sossusvlei in the Namib desert, Namibia. © Digital Vision/Getty Images

The first conquerors in southern Namibia were the Nama. They had a larger clan system, with interclan alliances, and a pastoral economy. Closely linked (usually in a dependent role) were the Damara, a people from central Africa whose culture combined pastoralism, hunting, and copper smelting. In northeastern and central Namibia the Herero (a pastoral people from central Africa) built up interlocked clan systems eventually headed by a paramount chief. The unity of the Herero nation, however, was always subject to splintering. In the north the Ovambo people developed several kingdoms on both sides of the Kunene River. They were mixed farmers (largely because of a more hospitable environment for crops) and also smelted and worked copper. To the east the related Kavango peoples had a somewhat similar but weaker state system. On the margins of Namibia—i.e., the Caprivi Strip in the far east and on the margins of the Kalahari—the local peoples and groupings were spillovers from southern Zambia (Barotse) and Botswana (Tswana).

Until the 1860s, European contact and penetration were slight. Diogo Cão and Bartolomeu Dias touched on the Namibian coast in 1486 and 1488, respectively, en route to and returning from the Cape of Good Hope, but there was virtually no contact until the 1670s. Afrikaner explorers after 1670 and Afrikaner traders and settlers about 1790 came to Namibia and eventually reached the southern boundaries of the Ovambo kingdoms, notably at the Etosha Pan. They—together with German missionaries, explorers of varied nationality, British traders, and Norwegian whalers—did not play a dominant role before 1860. Instead, they created the first avenues for trade (ivory and later cattle) and introduced firearms.

The latter heightened the destructiveness of conflicts among the various clans and peoples. So did the arrival, after the first quarter of the 19th century, of the Oorlam-Nama from the Cape. Their

BASTERS

Basters (from Afrikaans baster, *"bastard," or "half-breed") are members of an ethnically mixed group in Namibia and northwestern South Africa, most of whom are descendants of 17th- and 18th-century Dutch and French men and indigenous Nama (Khoekhoe) women of southwestern Africa. They speak a language that is primarily Afrikaans and follow a Western way of life. In the early 21st century they numbered about 40,000.*

The Basters were originally seminomadic pastoralists and hunters who gradually settled as pioneers in the northwestern frontier areas north of the Cape Colony. Largely through missionary work during the 19th century, they coalesced into fiercely independent, autonomous communities that maintained their identities even after being incorporated into the Cape Colony. Others moved farther north into what is now Namibia in the late 1860s because of pressure from Boer settlers and eventually established a settlement that became known as Rehoboth. With the independence of Namibia, the Basters (who had relatively privileged status under South African rule) sought greater autonomy, but they were unsuccessful. Nevertheless, they maintain a strong sense of group identity.

The Rehoboth community remains the largest group of Basters. They practice subsistence farming and keep cattle and sheep, but they also rely heavily on the remittances of migrants who work in Windhoek as skilled artisans, in Walvis Bay as labourers or fishermen, and in the diamond mines near the Orange River mouth at the South African border.

military technology (which included horses, guns, and a small mobile commando organizational pattern) was modeled on that of the Afrikaners. They came to dominate the resident Nama (Red Nation) and Damara. In the middle of the 19th century, a kingdom ruled by the Oorlam but partly Herero and supported by the Red Nation and Damara was established near Windhoek by the Oorlam chief Jonker Afrikaner.

Central Namibia was then an area of conflict between the southward-moving Herero and the northward-migrating Nama. In 1870 a peace treaty was signed with the Germans on the border of Herero country. Meanwhile, largely as a result of war pressures, Maherero had emerged as the Herero paramount chief. At this time a South African Creole ("Coloured") community, the Rehoboth Basters, had immigrated to a territory south of Windhoek, where they served as a buffer between the Herero and the Germans. Like the Oorlam, they were Europeanized in military technology as well as civil society and state organization, which were copied from the Afrikaners.

THE GERMAN CONQUEST

In the 1870s, British annexation of Namibia appeared imminent. A treaty with the Herero and the raising of the

British flag over Walvis Bay were seen as forerunners of the northward expansion of the Cape Colony. However, London proved reluctant to take on added costs in an apparently valueless area, and the way was left open for Germany's annexation of the area as South West Africa in the 1880s. The acquisitions, by exceedingly dubious "treaties" and more naked theft, did not go smoothly, despite the employment of so-called "divide and rule" tactics within and between peoples. The first major resistance—by the Herero in 1885—forced the Germans back to Walvis Bay until British troops were sent out.

By the turn of the century, German settlers had arrived, copper was minable, railway building from Swakopmund and Lüderitz was under way, and diamonds were soon discovered near Lüderitz. But from 1904 to 1907 a great war of resistance broke out, nearly expelling the Germans before it was quelled with extreme savagery by tactics including extermination, hangings, and forced detention in concentration camps.

The first phase of the war was fought between the Germans and the Herero (with a single Ovambo battle at Fort Namutoni near the Etosha Pan). It reached a climax when Lieut. Gen. Lothar von Trotha defeated the main Herero army at the Battle of Waterburg and, taking no prisoners, drove them into the Kalahari, where most died. By 1910 the loss of life by hanging, battle, or starvation and thirst—plus the escape of a few to the Bechuanaland protectorate—had reduced the Herero people by about 85 percent (about 75 percent dead, 5–10 percent in exile). The Nama resistance war came late because a key letter from Maherero's son and successor, Samuel Maherero, to the Oorlam chief Hendrik Witbooi that proposed joint action had been intercepted. The resistance was finally crushed in 1907, and Nama survivors were herded into concentration camps. War, starvation, and conditions in the camps claimed the lives of about half of the Nama.

The Germans allocated about half of the usable—and apparently all of the best—ranchland (except that of the Rehoboth Basters) to settlers and restricted Africans to reserves. The Tsumeb copper and zinc mines opened in 1906, and diamond mining (more accurately, sand sifting) began near Lüderitz in 1908 and at the main fields at the mouth of the Orange River (Oranjemund) a few years later. Railways linked Lüderitz, Keetmanshoop, and Windhoek as well as Swakopmund, Windhoek, and Tsumeb.

German direct rule never extended to the north. The "red line" delimited the southern two-thirds of South West Africa in which the German were able to establish effective European-style police control—known as the Police Zone—from the Ovambo and Kavango areas. In the latter, the near extinction of elephants, a rinderpest epidemic, and the rising consumption habits of the kings led to a migration of single male contract labourers to work in the mines and ranches and in construction. The "contract labour system"—which was to provide the cheap

German soldiers stationed in what is now Namibia in the early 1900s. German troops were assigned with putting down a revolt by the indigenous Herero. Three Lions/Hulton Archive/ Getty Images

labour for the colonial economy and later provided the national communication and solidarity links to build the liberation movements of 1960–90—had begun.

THE SOUTH AFRICAN CONQUEST

In 1914–15 South African troops invaded and captured South West Africa as part of the World War I conquest of the German colonies in Africa. Except for diamond mines, most property—including Tsumeb—found its way back into German hands. The rising De Beers colossus bought Oranjemund and the balance of the diamond-producing area to bolster its world domination. It was used as a market-balancing mine (that is, its production was varied to control the price of diamonds, and it was totally closed for more than two years in the 1930s), a role it played into the 1980s. Afrikaner settlers were encouraged to come to South West Africa for security reasons—to hold the inhabitants in check—at least as much as for economic reasons.

The League of Nations awarded a Class C mandate (meaning no real targets for development of the people toward independence were intended) to the crown of Great Britain to be exercised by the Union of South Africa authorities. That "sacred trust" was read as justifying settlement, greater exploitation, and no rights for black (and precious few for Coloured) Africans, plus a creeping annexation into South Africa as a "fifth province." The rail system was extended to Walvis Bay (the one good natural port) and south to the South African border and to Cape Town to tie South West Africa's economy to South Africa's on both the import and export sides.

South Africa extended direct rule to the Kunene and Okavango rivers—parallel to a Portuguese push south to the Angola-Namibia border. Resistance there and elsewhere in South West Africa flared into violence repeatedly until the 1930s, while trade union organizing and political as well as economic resistance began in the 1920s. Until 1945 South West Africa was not a productive colony—cattle and karakul (sheep) were in oversupply, diamond output was held low, and export prices for base metals were not attractive. Governance, security, and settler survival all had to be financed in large part from Pretoria.

THE POLITICAL ECONOMY OF A COLONIAL BOOM

The European enclave boomed. The situation was quite different for the other 90 percent of the people. Rising population was eroding productive capacity—per capita and absolutely by ecological damage—in African areas. Until the late 1970s, contract labour paid only enough to support a single person at subsistence level. Black nurses, teachers, and secretaries, as well as semiskilled workers, began to be trained and employed on a significant scale only in the mid-1970s. Land reallocations increased contract labour. A body called the Odendaal Commission organized separate development, which led to the creation of "homeland" authorities that benefited a new black elite—as in the 1980s did government wages and salaries for teachers, nurses, and black-area administrators and troops, and a wage increase by large employers in mining and finance. A rising proportion of black Namibians—two-thirds by the late 1980s—was left in abject poverty. Further, contract labour eroded the social and civil structures, giving rise to numerous and usually very poor female-headed households in the "homelands" and the urban peripheries.

FROM RESISTANCE TO LIBERATION STRUGGLE

From 1947, Namibians (initially via intermediaries) had begun to petition the United Nations (UN) against South African rule. A series of cases before the International Court of Justice (World Court)—the last, in 1971, declaring the mandate forfeiture by the United Nations in 1966 to be valid—led to a de jure UN assumption of sovereignty and de facto support via publicity, negotiation, and training for Namibian liberation.

In South West Africa the churches (numbering at least 80 percent of black Namibians in their membership) took an early lead in petitioning the UN and South Africa, and created a climate of black social and civil opinion favourable to the liberation struggle. However, they were slow to endorse its armed phase. From the 1950s to the '70s the churches

had become increasingly national in staff and outlook, in some cases after severe conflicts with the overseas "parent" bodies and local missionaries.

Black trade union activity (illegal until the mid-1980s) began to revive as well and focused rather more on political than on economic mobilization. The major strike of 1971–72 was against contract labour, the implementation of apartheid (the policy that sanctioned racial segregation and political and economic discrimination against non-whites), and the 1966 failure of the initial World Court case as much as it was for wage increases per se.

From 1958 to 1960 the political focus turned from resistance to liberation, and leadership passed from traditional chiefs to party leaders. SWAPO (nominally South West Africa People's Organization, although only the acronym has been used since 1980) was founded as the Ovamboland People's Organization in 1958; it achieved a national following as SWAPO in 1960. In 1959 SWANU (South West Africa National Union) was formed, largely by Herero intellectuals. Within a decade, SWAPO had become the dominant party and had grown beyond its Ovambo roots. The presence of Ovambo throughout the nation due to contract labour was used to forge a national communication system and mobilizing capacity.

The parties had been formed because petitioning seemed ineffective. The forced removal (with violence and deaths) of black Namibians from a part of

Windhoek known as the Old Location to the outlying township of Katatura in the late 1950s was perhaps the key catalytic event. Until 1966 the parties sought—in the face of increasing repression—to press for redress of grievances from South Africa and via the United Nations. Indeed, until the 1970s the armed struggle, then largely across the border from Zambia, was only a minor nuisance to South Africa.

The 1971–72 strike marked a turning point in terms of national solidarity and nationwide participation in the struggle. This greatly alarmed South Africa. A rising crescendo of trials and summary imprisonment and torture was pursued, though this process had already begun when Herman Toivo ja Toivo and most other SWAPO leaders not already in exile were tried for terrorism and imprisoned on Robben Island in 1968. From 1969 SWAPO had operated along almost all of the northern border—an operation that was easier after Angolan independence in 1975—and in the north-central farming areas around Grootfontein. Although set back by an internal leadership crisis and division among fighting cadres in 1976, the armed struggle had become militarily damaging and economically costly to South Africa by the end of the 1970s.

THE ROAD TO NAMIBIA

From 1977 through 1988 the economy of Namibia stagnated overall and fell by more than 3 percent per year per capita. Five factors influenced this: six years of drought, decline in fishing yields (because of overfishing), serious worsening of import-export price ratios, the slow growth and mismanagement of the South African economy, and the impact of the war on the budget and on both domestic and foreign investor confidence. For white residents, real incomes (except in ranching) stagnated or rose slowly. For blacks, they rose for perhaps one-sixth of households in wage employment with government or large enterprises and declined rapidly for others, especially for residents of the northern "operational area" (war zone).

For South Africa, Namibia turned from an economic asset to a millstone (with a war bill by the late 1980s on the order of $1 billion a year—comparable to Namibia's gross domestic product). Capital stock was run down, and output of all major products—beef, karakul, fish, base metals, uranium oxide, and diamonds—fell.

On the domestic side, a long series of South African attempts to build up pro-South African parties with substantial black support failed even when trade unions were legalized, wages raised, and petty apartheid laws (including abolition of the contract labour and residence restrictions) relaxed. Indeed, after the failure of the alliance between moderate black Bishop Abel Muzorewa and white Prime Minister Ian Smith in the Zimbabwe independence elections, South Africa's internal political maneuvers looked increasingly desperate and lacking in conviction.

SAM NUJOMA

Sam Nujoma. Trevor Samson/AFP/Getty Images

(b. May 12, 1929, Owambo, South West Africa [now Namibia])

Sam Nujoma was one of the leaders in the fight against South Africa for the independence of his homeland, South West Africa. He served as the first president of the newly independent country—which had been renamed Namibia—from 1990 to 2005.

Nujoma was born Samuel Shafiihuma Nujoma to a peasant family in the remote Ongandjera region of Owambo (Ovamboland) and spent his early years tending the family's few cattle and goats. His primary education began at night school, and he left school at age 16 to become a railway dining-car steward. After a fellow worker was sent home without compensation following a serious injury, Nujoma tried to form a trade union for railway men but was discharged. He subsequently worked as a clerk and a store assistant.

In the late 1950s he helped found the Ovamboland People's Organization, the forerunner of the South West Africa People's Organization (SWAPO). He went into exile in 1960 and was named president of SWAPO after it was founded on April 19 of that year. After several years of fruitlessly petitioning the United Nations to compel South Africa to release control of South West Africa, SWAPO embarked on an armed struggle in 1966. Although its guerrilla force, the People's Liberation Army of Namibia (PLAN), failed to liberate any territory, it succeeded in focusing international attention on Namibia. In 1973 the UN General Assembly recognized SWAPO as the sole legitimate representative of the Namibian people, and in 1978 the Security Council adopted Resolution 435, which set out terms for eventual Namibian independence and which was finally accepted by South Africa in 1988. In September 1989, after nearly 30 years in exile, Nujoma returned to Namibia to lead SWAPO to victory in the UN-supervised November elections. On the day of Namibia's independence, March 21, 1990, Nujoma was sworn in as president.

Although often accused of being a Marxist, Nujoma professed himself drawn more to the pragmatism of Scandinavian democratic socialism. In 1994 he was reelected president, and in 1998 the SWAPO-controlled parliament agreed to amend the constitution, allowing Nujoma to run for a third term. The move drew international and domestic criticism, but Nujoma easily won reelection in 1999. He later announced that he would not run for a fourth term, and in 2005 he stepped down from office, allowing for a peaceful transfer of power to his democratically elected successor, Hifikepunye Pohamba (SWAPO). Nujoma stepped down from his position as president of SWAPO in 2007.

Internationally and militarily, decline was slower and less apparent. While the UN Security Council had passed resolutions (notably resolution 435) demanding independence for Namibia, South Africa skillfully and repeatedly protracted negotiations and played on U.S. fears of communism and paranoia about Cuba, whose troops had defeated the 1975 South African invasion of Angola and remained there to augment the defense against South Africa and its Angolan allies or proxies.

Through 1986 about 2,500 South African soldiers had died, a figure proportionally higher per capita than the U.S. death toll in the Vietnam War. However, the South African government skillfully disguised the high casualty rate as well as the fiscal burden of the Namibian occupation and policy in Angola. The war, like the negotiations, appeared stalemated.

The turning point came in 1988. South African forces, which had invaded Angola the previous year, were defeated near Cuito-Cuanavale. Air control was lost, and the Western Front defenses were tumbled back to the border (by a force consisting largely of units of SWAPO's People's Liberation Army of Namibia [PLAN] under Angolan command). By June South Africa had to negotiate a total withdrawal from Angola to avoid a military disaster, and by the end of December it had negotiated a UN-supervised transition to elections, a new constitution, and independence for Namibia.

INDEPENDENCE

The United Nations Transition Assistance Group (UNTAG) opened operations in April 1989. After a disastrous start—in which South African forces massacred PLAN forces seeking to report to UNTAG to be confined to designated areas—UNTAG slowly gained control over the registration and electoral process in most areas.

The election of 1989, held under the auspices of the UN, gave SWAPO 57 percent of the vote and 60 percent of the seats. Sam Nujoma, the longtime leader of SWAPO, became president. With two-thirds majorities needed to draft and adopt a constitution, some measure of reconciliation was necessary to avoid deadlock. In fact, SWAPO and the business community—as well as many settlers—wanted a climate of national reconciliation in order to achieve a relatively peaceful initial independence period.

As a result, a constitution emphasizing human, civil, and property rights was adopted unanimously by the end of 1990, and reconciliation with settlers and (to a degree) with South Africa became the

dominant mood. For the new government, the costs of reconciliation included
retaining about 15,000 unneeded white
civil servants, deferring the landownership and mineral-company terms
issues, and offering de facto amnesty for
all pre-independence acts of violence
(including those of SWAPO against suspected spies and dissidents in Angola
in the late 1980s). The benefits were the
takeover of a functioning public administration and economy (with growth
rising to 3 percent in 1990) and grudg-
ing but real South African cooperation
on fishing and use of Walvis Bay. Above
all, South Africa abstained from mounting destabilization measures or creating
proxy armed forces.

On March 21, 1990, the South African
flag was lowered and Namibia's raised
at the National Stadium. Namibia subsequently joined the Commonwealth,
the UN, and the Organization of
African Unity (now the African Union).
Diplomatic relations were established
with many countries. The Namibian
Defense Force—which included members
of PLAN as well as the former South West
African Territory Force—was created with
the assistance of British military advisers.

South Africa agreed to a transition to
Namibian sovereignty over Walvis Bay,
which was effected in 1994. It also agreed
to a revised boundary along the Orange
River, giving Namibia riparian rights; the
earlier border had been placed on the
north bank and thus left Namibia without
water rights. Namibia remained a member
of the Southern African Customs Union.

The political climate was calm. The
main opposition party, the Democratic
Turnhalle Alliance (heir to South Africa's
puppet government efforts and ben-
eficiary of considerable South African
funds for campaign financing), held
almost one-third of the seats in the legislature but was neither particularly
constructive nor totally obstructive. In
the 1994 national elections, SWAPO consolidated its hold on power, surpassing
the two-thirds majority needed to revise
the constitution—which it did in 1998,
passing an amendment that allowed
President Nujoma to run for a third term.
Despite widespread disapproval of the
amendment, Nujoma was easily reelected
in 1999.

SWAPO maintained its hold on power
in the country's 1999 elections, in the face
of allegations from the opposition—now
headed by a SWAPO splinter party, the
Congress of Democrats—that the government was engaging in authoritarian
practices. Opponents also questioned
the government's 1998 decision to dispatch troops to the Democratic Republic
of the Congo to support the government
of Congolese Pres. Laurent Kabila during
that country's civil war. The government
generated even greater controversy in
1999 when it granted the Angolan government permission to pursue Angolan
rebels into Namibian territory, leading to
unrest along the border that did not sub-
side until 2002.

At the beginning of the 21st century
and after its first decade of independence, Namibia stood apart from many

other African countries as a model of political and economic stability. Nevertheless, the country still had serious matters to address. As in much of Africa, the spread of AIDS was a concern: by 2000 one in five adult Namibians was infected. Another issue at the forefront was land reform—the government program of purchasing farmland owned by the white minority and redistributing it to the historically disadvantaged and landless black Namibians. The controversy surrounding land reform continued to escalate in the first decade of the new century as the slow progress of the program frustrated many, and the threat of forcible seizures of farmland loomed.

The new millennium also saw the democratic transfer of power in the country. After leading Namibia since the country gained independence, Nujoma stepped down from office at the end of his third term. Fellow SWAPO member Hifikepunye Pohamba prevailed in the November 2004 presidential elections and was inaugurated the next year. In the presidential and parliamentary elections of November 2009, Pohamba was reelected, and SWAPO maintained its hold on the majority of parliamentary seats. Several opposition groups, however, refused to accept the results of the election, claiming that the country's electoral laws were violated. International observers, while noting that some aspects of electoral procedures needed improvement, declared that the elections were largely transparent and fair.

CHAPTER 10

SOUTH AFRICA

South Africa is the southernmost country on the African continent. Four British colonies formed the Union of South Africa, a dominion within the British Commonwealth that came into existence in 1910. In 1961 it withdrew from the British Commonwealth and declared itself the independent Republic of South Africa. There are three cities that serve as capitals: Pretoria (executive), Cape Town (legislative), and Bloemfontein (judicial).

PREHISTORY

The prehistory and history of South Africa span nearly the entire known existence of human beings and their ancestors—some three million years or more. The earliest creatures that can be identified as ancestors of modern humans are classified as australopithecines (literally "southern apes"). The first specimen of these hominins to be found (in 1924) was the skull of a child from a quarry site at Taung in what is now the North West province. Subsequently more australopithecine fossils were discovered in limestone caves farther northeast at Sterkfontein, Swartkrans, and Kromdraai (collectively designated a UNESCO World Heritage site in 1999), where they had originally been deposited by predators and scavengers.

South Africa's prehistory has been divided into a series of phases based on broad patterns of technology. The primary distinction is between a reliance on chipped and flaked stone implements (the Stone Age) and the ability to work iron (the Iron Age). Spanning a large proportion of human history, the Stone Age in Southern Africa is further divided into the Early Stone Age, or Paleolithic Period (about 2,500,000–150,000 years ago), the Middle Stone Age, or Mesolithic Period (about 150,000–30,000 years ago), and the Late Stone Age, or Neolithic Period (about 30,000–2,000 years ago). The simple stone tools found with australopithecine fossil bones fall into the earliest part of the Early Stone Age.

THE EARLY STONE AGE

Most Early Stone Age sites in South Africa can probably be connected with the hominin species known as *Homo erectus*. Simply modified stones, hand axes, scraping tools, and other bifacial artifacts had a wide variety of purposes, including butchering animal carcasses, scraping hides, and digging for plant foods. Most South African archaeological sites from this period are the remains of open camps, often by the sides of rivers and lakes, although some are rock shelters, such as Montagu Cave in the Cape region.

Change occurred slowly in the Early Stone Age. For more than a million years and over a wide geographic area, only slight differences existed in the forms of stone tools. The slow alterations in hominins' physical appearance that took place over the same time period, however, have allowed physical anthropologists to recognize new species in the genus *Homo*. An archaic form of *H. sapiens* appeared about 500,000 years ago. Important specimens belonging to this physical type have been found at Hopefield in Western Cape province and at the Cave of Hearths in Mpumalanga province.

THE MIDDLE STONE AGE

The long episode of cultural and physical evolution gave way to a period of more rapid change about 200,000 years ago. Hand axes and large bifacial stone tools were replaced by stone flakes and blades that were fashioned into scrapers, spear points, and parts for hafted, composite implements. This technological stage, now known as the Middle Stone Age, is represented by numerous sites in South Africa.

Open camps and rock overhangs were used for shelter. Day-to-day debris has survived to provide some evidence of early ways of life, although plant foods have rarely been preserved. Middle Stone Age bands hunted medium-sized and large prey, including antelope and zebra, although they tended to avoid the largest and most dangerous animals, such as the elephant and the rhinoceros. They also ate seabirds and marine mammals that could be found along the shore and sometimes collected tortoises and ostrich eggs in large quantities. The rich archaeological deposits of Klasies River Mouth, on the Cape coast west of Port Elizabeth, have preserved the first known instance of shellfish being used as a food source.

Klasies River Mouth has also provided important evidence for the emergence of anatomically modern humans. Some of the human skeletons from the lower levels of this site, possibly 115,000 years old, are decidedly modern in form. Fossils of comparable age have been excavated at Border Cave, in the mountainous region between KwaZulu-Natal province and Swaziland.

THE LATE STONE AGE

Basic toolmaking techniques began to undergo additional change about 40,000 years ago. Small finely worked stone implements known as microliths became more common, while the heavier scrapers and points of the Middle Stone Age appeared less frequently. Archaeologists refer to this technological stage as the Late Stone Age. The numerous collections of stone tools from South African archaeological sites show a great degree of variation through time and across the subcontinent.

The remains of plant foods have been well preserved at such sites as Melkhoutboom Cave, De Hangen, and

San art etched in stone in uKhahlamba-Drakensberg Park, South Africa. Experts suggest these drawings were created by shamans, which means they may have served as talismans. Ariadne Van Zandbergen/Lonely Planet Images/Getty Images

Diepkloof in the Cape region. Animals were trapped and hunted with spears and arrows on which were mounted well-crafted stone blades. Bands moved with the seasons as they followed game into higher lands in the spring and early summer months, when plant foods could also be found. When available, rock overhangs became shelters; otherwise, windbreaks were built. Shellfish, crayfish, seals, and seabirds were also important sources of food, as were fish caught on lines, with spears, in traps, and possibly with nets.

Dating from this period are numerous engravings on rock surfaces, mostly on the interior plateau, and paintings on the walls of rock shelters in the mountainous regions, such as the Drakensberg and Cederberg ranges. The images were made over a period of at least 25,000 years. Although scholars originally saw the South African rock art as the work of exotic foreigners such as Minoans or Phoenicians or as the product of primitive minds, they now believe that the paintings were closely associated with the work of medicine men, shamans who were involved in the well-being of the band and often worked in a state of trance. Specific representations include depictions of trance dances, metaphors for trance such as death and flight, rainmaking, and control of the movement of antelope herds.

PASTORALISM AND EARLY AGRICULTURE

New ways of living came to South Africa about 2,000 years ago. Until that time,

human communities had survived by gathering plant foods and by hunting, trapping, and scavenging for meat, but with the introduction of agriculture—arguably the single most important event in world history—people began to make use of domesticated animals and plants. This in turn led to a slow but steady rise in population and to more-complex political and religious organizations, among other things. Crops could be grown and cattle, sheep, and goats herded near permanent villages and towns in the east, where rainfall was adequate. In the more arid west, domestic livestock were kept by nomadic pastoralists, who moved over wide territories with their flocks and herds.

Although the origin of nomadic pastoralism in South Africa is still obscure, linguistic evidence points to northern Botswana as a probable source. The linguistic evidence is supported by finds of sheep bones and pottery from Bambata Cave in southwestern Zimbabwe that have been dated to about 150 BCE. Whether new communities moved into South Africa with their flocks and herds or whether established hunter-gatherer bands took up completely new ways of living remains unclear. In any case, the results of archaeological excavations have shown that sheep were being herded fairly extensively by the first few centuries CE in eastern and western parts of the Cape and probably in the northern Cape as well.

While traces of ancient herding camps tend to be extremely rare, one of the best-preserved finds is at Kasteelberg, on the southwest coast near St. Helena Bay. Pastoralists there kept sheep, hunted seals and other wild animals, and gathered shellfish, repeatedly returning to the same site for some 1,500 years. Such communities were directly ancestral to the Khoekhoe (also spelled Khoikhoi) herders who encountered European settlers at the Cape of Good Hope in the mid-17th century.

The archaeological traces of farmers in the eastern regions of South Africa are more substantial. The earliest sites date to the 3rd century CE, although farming was probably already well established by this time. Scatters of potsherds with distinctive incised decoration mark early village locations in Mpumalanga and parts of KwaZulu-Natal.

THE IRON AGE

Because the first farmers had knowledge of ironworking, their archaeological sites are characterized as Iron Age (c. 200 CE). New groups of people arriving in South Africa at that time had strong connections to East Africa. They were directly ancestral to the Bantu-speaking peoples who form the majority of South Africa's population today.

IRON AGE SITES

Early Iron Age farmers grew crops, cutting back the vegetation with iron hoes and axes, and herded cattle and sheep. They heavily supplemented farming by gathering wild plant foods, engaging in some hunting, and collecting shellfish if they lived near enough to the coast. Where conditions for agriculture were favourable, such as in the Tugela River valley in the east, villages grew to house several hundred people. Some trade existed between groups of farmers—evidence for specialization in salt making has been found in the northeast—and with the hunter-gatherer bands that continued to occupy most parts of South Africa. Finely made life-size ceramic heads found near the city of Lydenburg (now Mashishing) in eastern South Africa and dated to the 7th century CE are all that remains of the people who once inhabited this region.

Early Iron Age villages were built in low-lying areas, such as river valleys and the coastal plain, where forests and savannas facilitated shifting (slash-and-burn) agriculture. From the 11th century, however, in the period conventionally known as the Late Iron Age, farming communities began to settle the higher-lying grasslands. It has not been established whether these new communities were inhabited by invaders or reflected the diffusion of new knowledge to existing populations. In many areas the new communities started making different forms of pottery and built villages out of stone. Most probably these and other changes in patterns of behaviour reflect the increasing importance of cattle in economic life.

FIRST URBAN CENTRES

Other changes came in the north. Arab traders established small settlements on the Tanzanian and Mozambican coasts in their search for ivory, animal skins, and other exotica. The trade beads they offered in return began to reach villages in the interior, the first indications that the more complex economic and social structures associated with long-distance trade were developing. The arid Limpopo River valley, avoided by the earliest farmers, developed as a trade route. Sites such as Pont Drift (c. 800–1100) and Schroda (dated to the 9th century) show that their occupants were wealthy in both livestock and trade beads.

The Limpopo River valley was also the setting in which Bambandyanalo and Mapungubwe developed as South Africa's first urban centres during the 11th century. Starting as a large village like Schroda and Pont Drift, Mapungubwe rapidly developed into a town of approximately 10,000 people. Differences in status were clearly demarcated: the elite lived and were buried at the top of the stark sandstone hill at the town's centre, while the rest of the population lived in the valley below. Hilltop graves contained lavish burial goods, including a carefully crafted gold rhinoceros and evidence of specialized crafts such as bone and ivory working. Bambandyanalo and Mapungubwe were abandoned after the 13th century after having been occupied for several hundred years. The trade connections that the Limpopo valley offered were taken over by Great Zimbabwe, farther to the north.

EUROPEANS IN SOUTH AFRICA

The first Portuguese ships rounded the Cape of Good Hope in 1488, their occupants intent on gaining a share of the lucrative Arab trade with the East. Over the following century, numerous vessels made their way around the South African coast, but the only direct African contacts came with the bands of shipwreck survivors who either set up camp in the hope of rescue or tried to make their way northward to Portuguese settlements in present-day Mozambique. Both the British and the Dutch challenged the Portuguese control of the Cape sea route from the early 17th century. The British founded a short-lived settlement at Table Bay in 1620, and in 1652 the Dutch East India Company set up a small garrison under the slopes of Table Mountain for provisioning their fleets.

SETTLEMENT OF THE CAPE COLONY

The Dutch East India Company, always mindful of unnecessary expense, did not intend to establish more than a minimal presence at the southernmost part of Africa. Because farming beyond the shores of Table Bay proved necessary, however, nine men were released from their contracts with the company and granted land along the Liesbeek River in 1657. The company made it clear that the Khoekhoe were not to be enslaved, so, beginning in that same year, slaves arrived in the Cape from West and East Africa, India, and the Malay Peninsula. By the end of the century, the imprint of Dutch colonialism in South Africa was clear, with settlers, aided by increasing numbers of slaves, growing wheat, tending vineyards, and grazing their sheep and cattle from the Cape peninsula to the Hottentots Holland Mountains some 30 miles (50 km) away. A 1707 census of the Dutch at the Cape listed 1,779 settlers owning 1,107 slaves.

In the initial years of Dutch settlement at the Cape, pastoralists had readily traded with the Dutch. However, as the garrison's demand for cattle and sheep continued to increase, the Khoekhoe became more wary. The Dutch offered tobacco, alcohol, and trinkets for livestock. Numerous conflicts followed, and, beginning in 1713, many Khoekhoe communities were ravaged by smallpox. At the same time, colonial pastoralists—the Boers, also called trekboers—began to move inland beyond the Hottentots Holland Mountains with their own herds. The Khoekhoe chiefdoms were largely decimated by the end of the 18th century, their people either dead or reduced to conditions close to serfdom on colonial farms. The San—small bands of hunter-gatherers—fared no better. Pushed back into marginal areas, they were forced to live by cattle raiding, justifying in colonial eyes their systematic eradication. The men were slaughtered, and the women and children were taken into servitude.

The trekboers constantly sought new land, and they and their families spread northeast as well as north, into the grasslands that long had been occupied by African farmers. For many generations these farmers had lived in settlements concentrated along the low ridges that

break the monotony of the interior plateau. While it is difficult to make population estimates, it is thought that some of the larger villages could have housed several hundred people. Cattle were held in elaborately built stone enclosures, the ruins of which survive today across a large part of Free State province and in the higher areas north of the Vaal River. Extensive exchange networks brought iron for hoes and spears from specialized manufacturing centres in the Mpumalanga Lowveld and the deep river gorges of KwaZulu-Natal.

Thus, by the closing decades of the 18th century, South Africa had fallen into two broad regions: west and east. Colonial settlement dominated the west, including the winter rainfall region around the Cape of Good Hope, the coastal hinterland northward toward the present-day border with Namibia, and the dry lands of the interior. Trekboers took increasingly more land from the Khoekhoe and from remnant hunter-gatherer communities, who were killed, were forced into marginal areas, or became labourers tied to the farms of their new overlords. Indigenous farmers controlled both the coastal and valley lowlands and the Highveld of the interior in the east, where summer rainfall and good grazing made mixed farming economies possible.

Cape Town was developing into South Africa's major urban centre, although it took many years for it to equal the size that Mapungubwe had attained some five centuries earlier. The initial grid of streets had been expanded and linked the company's garden to the new fortress that overlooked Table Bay. Houses featuring flat roofs, ornate pediments, and symmetrical facades sheltered officials, merchants, and visitors en route between Europe and the East. A governor and council administered the town and colony. While the economy was in principle directed by the interests of the Dutch East India Company, in practice corruption and illegal trading were dominant forces. Both the town and the colony existed in large part because of slaves, who by now outnumbered their owners.

GROWTH OF THE COLONIAL ECONOMY

From 1770 to 1870 the region became more fully integrated into the world capitalist economy. Trekboers, who were weakly controlled by the Dutch East India Company, advanced across the semidesert Karoo of the central Cape and collided with African agricultural peoples along a line running from the lower Vaal and middle Orange river valleys to the sea around the Gamtoos River (west of modern Port Elizabeth). These agriculture-based African societies proved resilient but, even at their height in the 1860s, were unable to unite completely enough to expel the Europeans.

The decisive moment for the colony occurred in 1806 when Britain seized Cape Colony during the Napoleonic Wars. Initially the colony's importance was related to its function as a strategic base to protect Britain's developing empire in India. In the next few years, however, it also served as a market, a source of raw materials, and an outlet for emigration from Britain.

African societies after the 1760s were increasingly affected by ivory and slave traders operating from Delagoa Bay, Inhambane, and the lower Zambezi River in the northeast as well as by traders and raiders based in the Cape to the south. In response to these invasions, the farming communities created a number of sister states different in structure, scale, and military capacity from anything that had existed before. The Pedi and Swazi in the eastern Highveld, the Zulu south of the Pongola River, the Sotho to the east of the Caledon River valley, the Gaza along the lower Limpopo, and the Ndebele in present-day southwestern Zimbabwe proved to be the most successful.

The areas of the western Cape with the longest history of settlement by Europeans had evolved an agricultural economy based on wheat farming and viticulture, worked by imported slave labour. Slaves were treated harshly, and punishments for slaves who assaulted Europeans were brutal—one of the most heinous being death by impalement. Escaped slaves formed groups called Maroons—small self-sufficient communities—or fled into the interior. Because slave birth rates were low and settler numbers were increasing, in the 1780s the Dutch stepped up the enserfment of surviving Khoe (also spelled Khoi; pejoratively called Hottentots) to help run their farms. Those Khoe who could escape Dutch subjugation joined Xhosa groups in a major counteroffensive against colonialism in 1799–1801, and there were slave rebellions in the outskirts of Cape Town in 1808 and 1825.

The Dutch refusal to grant citizenship and land rights to the "Coloured" offspring of unions between Europeans and Khoe or slaves produced an aggrieved class of people, known as Basters (or Bastards), who were Christian, spoke Dutch, and had an excellent knowledge of horses and firearms. Many fled north toward and over the Orange River in search of land and trading opportunities. After merging with independent Khoe groups, such as the Kora, they formed commando states under warlords, three of the more successful being the Bloem, Kok, and Barends families, who were persuaded by missionaries in the early 19th century to change their name to Griqua. By the 1790s they were trading with and raiding local African communities such as the Rolong, Tlhaping, Hurutshe, and Ngwaketse. For self-defense some of these African communities formed larger groupings who competed against each other in their quest to control trade routes going south to the Cape and east to present-day Mozambique.

The Portuguese and also some British, French, Americans, and Arabs traded beads, brass, cloth, alcohol, and firearms along the southeast coast in return for ivory, slaves, cattle, gold, wax, and skins. During the late 18th century, large volumes of ivory were exported annually from Delagoa Bay, and slaves were taken from the Komati and Usutu (a major tributary of the Maputo) river regions and sent to the Mascarene Islands in the Indian Ocean and to Brazil to work on sugarcane and coffee plantations. By 1800 trade routes linked Delagoa Bay and coastal trade routes with the central interior.

European trade precipitated structural transformation within societies inland of Delagoa Bay. Warlords reorganized military institutions to hunt elephants and slaves. Profits from this trade enhanced the warlords' ability to disperse patronage, attract followers, and raise military potential and, in turn, their capacity to dominate land, people, and cattle. Near the bay, Tembe and Maputo were already powerful states by the 1790s. To the west of the coastal lowlands emerged the Maroteng of Thulare, the Dlamini of Ndvungunye, and the Hlubi of Bhungane. Between the Pongola and Tugela rivers evolved the Mthethwa of Dingiswayo south of Lake St. Lucia, the Ndwandwe of Zwide, the Qwabe of Phakatwayo, the Chunu of Macingwane, and, south of the Tugela, the Cele and Thuli. Several groups—for example, the Mthethwa, Ndwandwe, and Qwabe—later merged with the Zulu. These groups competed to dominate trade and became more militarized the closer they were to the Portuguese base.

INCREASED EUROPEAN PRESENCE (C. 1810–35)

The Cape Colony had spawned the subcolonies of Natal, the Orange Free

State, and the Transvaal by the 1860s. European settlement advanced to the edges of the Kalahari region in the west, the Drakensberg and Natal coast in the east, and the tsetse-fly- and mosquito-ridden Lowveld along the Limpopo River valley in the northeast. Armed clashes erupted over land and cattle, such as those between the Boers and various Xhosa groups in the southeast beginning in the 1780s, and Africans lost most of their land and were henceforth forced to work for the settlers. The population of European settlers increased from some 20,000 in the 1780s to about 300,000 in the late 1860s. Although it is difficult to accurately estimate the African population, it probably numbered somewhere between two and four million.

BRITISH OCCUPATION OF THE CAPE

When Great Britain went to war with France in 1793, both countries tried to capture the Cape so as to control the important sea route to the East. The British occupied the Cape in 1795, ending the Dutch East India Company's role in the region. Although the British relinquished the colony to the Dutch in the Treaty of Amiens (1802), they reannexed it in 1806 after the start of the Napoleonic Wars. The Cape became a vital base for Britain prior to the opening of the Suez Canal in 1869, and the Cape's economy was meshed with that of Britain. To protect the developing economy there, Cape wines were given preferential access to the British market until the mid-1820s. Merino sheep were introduced, and intensive sheep farming was initiated in order to supply wool to British textile mills.

The infrastructure of the colony began to change: English replaced Dutch as the language of administration; the British pound sterling replaced the Dutch rix-dollar; and newspaper publishing began in Cape Town in 1824. After Britain began appointing colonial governors, an advisory council for the governor was established in 1825, which was upgraded to a legislative council in 1834 with a few "unofficial" settler representatives. A virtual freehold system of landownership gradually replaced the existing Dutch tenant system, under which European colonists had paid a small annual fee to the government but had not acquired land ownership.

A large group of British settlers arrived in 1820. This, together with a high European birth rate and wasteful land usage, produced an acute land shortage, which was alleviated only when the British acquired more land through massive military intervention against Africans on the eastern frontier. Until the 1840s the British vision of the colony did not include African citizens (referred to pejoratively by the British as "Kaffirs"), so, as Africans lost their land, they were expelled across the Great Fish River, the unilaterally proclaimed eastern border of the colony.

The first step in this process included attacks in 1811–12 by the British army on the Xhosa groups, the Gqunukhwebe and

Ndlambe. An attack by the Rharhabe-Xhosa on Graham's Town (Grahamstown) in 1819 provided the pretext for the annexation of more African territory, to the Keiskamma River. Various Rharhabe-Xhosa groups were driven from their lands throughout the early 1830s. They counterattacked in December 1834, and Governor Benjamin D'Urban ordered a major invasion the following year, during which thousands of Rharhabe-Xhosa died. The British crossed the Great Kei River and ravaged territory of the Gcaleka-Xhosa as well. (The Gcaleka chief, Hintsa, invited to hold discussions with British military officials, was held hostage and died trying to escape.) The British colonial secretary, Lord Glenelg, who disapproved of D'Urban's policy, halted the seizure of all African land east of the Great Kei. D'Urban's initial attempt to rule conquered Africans with European magistrates and soldiers was overturned by Glenelg. Instead, for a time, Africans east of the Keiskamma retained their autonomy and dealt with the colony through diplomatic agents.

The British had chronic difficulties procuring enough labour to build towns and develop new farms. Indeed, though Britain abolished its slave trade in 1807 and pressured other countries to do the same, the British in Southern Africa continued to import some slaves into the Cape after that date, but in numbers insufficient to alleviate the labour problem. A ban in 1809 on Africans crossing into the Cape aggravated the labour shortage, and so the British, like the Dutch before them, made the Khoe serfs through the Caledon (1809) and Cradock (1812) codes.

Anglo-Boer commandos provided another source of African labour by illegally capturing San women and children (many of the men were killed) as well as Africans from across the eastern frontier. Griqua raiding states led by Andries Waterboer, Adam Kok, and Barend Barends captured more Africans from among people such as the Hurutshe, Rolong, and Kwena. Other people, such as those known as the Mantatees, were forced to become farmworkers, mainly in the eastern Cape. European farmers also raided for labour north of the Orange River.

Cape authorities overhauled their policy in 1828 in order to facilitate labour distribution and to align the region with the growing imperial antislavery ethos. Ordinance 49 permitted black labourers from east of the Keiskamma to go into the colony for work if they possessed the proper contracts and passes, which were issued by soldiers and missionaries. This was the beginning of the pass laws that would become so notorious in the 20th century. Ordinance 50 briefly ended the restrictions placed on the Khoe, including removing the requirement for passes, and allowed them to choose their employers, own land, and move more freely. Because an insufficient labour force still existed, Anglo-Boer armies (supported by Khoe, Tembu, Gcaleka, and Mpondo auxiliaries) acquired their own workers by attacking the Ngwane east of the

Great Kei at Mbolompo in August 1828. The formal abolition of slavery took place in 1834–38, and control of African labourers became stricter through the Masters and Servants Ordinance (1841), which imposed criminal penalties for breach of contract and desertion of the workplace and increased the legal powers of settler employers.

THE DELAGOA BAY SLAVE TRADE

While events were unfolding at the Cape, the slave trade at Delagoa Bay had been expanding since about 1810 in response to demands for labour from plantations in Brazil and on the Mascarene Islands. During the late 1820s, slave exports from the Delagoa Bay area reached several thousand a year, in advance of what proved to be an ineffective attempt to abolish the Brazilian trade in 1830. After a dip in the early 1830s, the Bay slave trade peaked in the late 1840s.

The impact of the slave trade was increasing destabilization of hinterland societies as populations were forcibly removed. The Gaza, Ngoni, and other groups became surrogate slavers and joined the Portuguese soldiers in inland raiding. Along the Limpopo and Vaal river networks, Delagoa Bay slavers competed with Griqua slavers in supplying the Cape. After slavers burned crops and famines became common, many groups—including the Ngwane, Ndebele, and some Hlubi—fled westward into the Highveld mountains during the 1810s and '20s. The Kololo, on the other hand,

moved east out of Transorangia, where they ran into Bay slavers, and migrated west into Botswana. In 1826 they were attacked by an alliance of Ngwaketse and European mercenaries and ended up in Zambia in the 1850s exporting slaves themselves to the Arabs and Portuguese.

EMERGENCE OF THE EASTERN STATES

Four main defensive African state clusters had emerged in eastern South Africa by the 1820s: the Pedi (led by Sekwati) in the Steelpoort valley, the Ngwane (led by Sobhuza) in the eastern Transvaal, the Mokoteli (led by Moshoeshoe) in the Caledon River region, and the Zulu (led by Shaka) south of the Swart-Mfolozi River. The Pedi received refugees from the Limpopo and coastal plains, and the Mokoteli absorbed eastern Transorangian refugees, which enabled them to defeat the Griqua and Korana raiders by the mid-1830s. By 1825 Shaka had welded the Chunu, Mthethwa, Qwabe, Mkhize, Cele, and other groups into a large militarized state with fortified settlements called *amakhanda*. Zulu *amabutho* (age sets or regiments) defended against raiders, provided protection for refugees, and, apparently, began to trade in ivory and slaves themselves.

From 1824 the Zulu began to clash with Cape colonists who came to Port Natal (renamed Durban in 1835) and organized mercenary armies. These groups were comparable to the Portuguese *prazero* armies along the Zambezi and to the warlord state set up by the Portuguese trader João Albasini in the eastern Transvaal in the 1840s, but they operated on a smaller scale. During the 1820s European raiders joined Zulu *amabutho* in attacking areas north of the Swart-Mfolozi River and south of the Mzimkulu River, where in the mid-1820s French ships exported slaves. Francis Farewell's raiders, in alliance with Zulu groups, seized women and children in the same area in 1828.

Conflicts split the Zulu elite into rival factions and led to Shaka's assassination in 1828. Shaka's half brother Dingane became the Zulu leader, but his succession was accompanied by civil wars and by increasing interference in the Delagoa Bay trading alliances. By the mid-1830s a coalition of Cape merchants had begun planning for the formal colonization of Natal, with its superb agricultural soils and temperate climate. The British left the less-desirable malaria-ridden Delagoa Bay region to the Portuguese, who traded slaves out of Lourenço Marques (now Maputo, Mozam.) for another half century.

THE EXPANSION OF EUROPEAN COLONIALISM (C. 1835–70)

European colonialism in the region expanded for a number of reasons, including the desires to claim more land and search for greater economic opportunities. The impact of this expansion was far-reaching.

THE GREAT TREK

A few Boer settlers had moved north of the Orange River before 1834, but after that the number increased significantly, a migration later known as the Great Trek. The common view that this was a bid to escape the policies of the British—i.e., the freeing of slaves—is difficult to sustain, as most of the former slave owners did not migrate (most trekkers came from the poorer east Cape), and the earlier labour shortage had been alleviated by 1835. Instead, the trek was more of an explosive culmination of a long sequence of colonial labour raids, land seizures, punitive commando raids, and commercial expansions. Europeans, who possessed technologically advanced weaponry, also had instructive examples of how small groups of raiders in Natal and Transorangia could cause disruption over large areas. Thus, the trekkers should not be seen as backward feudalists escaping the modern world, as some historians have maintained, but as energized people extending their frontier.

Several thousand Boers migrated with their families, livestock, retainers, wagons, and firearms into a region already destabilized and partially depopulated by Griqua and coastal raiders. They did encounter some Africans (such as the Ndebele), who in the early 1830s had moved from the southeastern to the western Transvaal. The Boers and their Rolong, Taung, and Griqua allies, however, crushed the Ndebele during

1837, taking their land and many cattle, women, and children. The remaining Ndebele fled north, where they resettled in southern Zimbabwe.

The trekkers had penetrated much of the Transvaal by the early 1840s. A grouping of commando states emerged based at Potchefstroom, Pretoria, and, from 1845, Ohrigstad-Lydenburg in the eastern Transvaal. Andries Hendrik Potgieter, Andries Pretorius, Jan Mocke, and others competed for followers, attacked weaker African chiefdoms, hunted elephants and slaves, and forged trading links with the Portuguese. Other Boers turned east into Natal and allied themselves with the resident British settlers. Farms developed slowly and, as had been the case in the Cape prior to the 1830s, depended on forced labour. Until the 1860s the Pedi and Swazi in the east and even the Kwena and Hurutshe in the west were strong enough to avoid being conscripted as labour and thus limited the labour supply.

THE BRITISH IN NATAL

The appearance of thousands of British settlers in Natal in the 1840s and '50s meant that for the first time Africans and European settlers lived together—however uneasily—on the same land. The Boers began to carve out farms in Natal as they had done along the eastern frontier, but further slave and cattle raids on the Bhaca south of the Mzimkulu provided the pretext for British annexation of Natal in 1843. Theophilus Shepstone received an appointment in 1845 as a diplomatic agent (later secretary for native affairs), and his position served as a prototype for later native commissioners. The Harding Commission (1852) set aside reserves for Africans, and missionaries and pliant chiefs were brought in to persuade Africans to work. After 1849 Africans became subject to a hut tax intended to raise revenue and drive them into labour. Roads were built, using forced labour, and Africans were obliged to pay rent on state land and European farms. To meet these burdens some African cultivators grew surplus crops to sell to the growing towns of Pietermaritzburg and Durban.

The British were reluctant, though, to annex the Transorangian interior, where no strategic interests existed. Boer trade links with Delagoa Bay posed little threat because Portugal was virtually a client state of Britain. To the Boers fell the tasks of eroding African resistance and developing the land, although the policy never received clear enunciation or much financial backing. Britain halfheartedly attempted to protect some of its African client states, such as that of the Griqua and the Sotho state led by Moshoeshoe. However, after further fighting with the Rharhabe-Xhosa on the eastern frontier in 1846, Governor Colonel Harry Smith finally annexed, over the next two years, not only the region between the Great Fish and the Great Kei rivers (establishing British Kaffraria) but also a large area between the Orange and Vaal rivers, thus establishing the Orange River Sovereignty. These moves provoked further warfare in 1851–53 with the Xhosa (joined once more by many Khoe), with a few British politicians ineffectively trying to influence events.

A striking feature of this period was the capacity of the Sotho people to fend off military conquest by the British and Boers. After defeating and absorbing the rival Tlokwa in 1853–54, Moshoeshoe became the most powerful African leader south of the Vaal-Pongolo rivers. His soldiers utilized firearms and, in the cold Highveld, horses—which proved to be the keys to political and military survival there.

ATTEMPTS AT BOER CONSOLIDATION

Faced with these unprofitable conflicts, the British temporarily withdrew from the Southern African interior, and the Transvaal and Orange Free State Boers gained independence through the Sand River and Bloemfontein conventions (1852 and 1854, respectively). Both Boer groups wrote constitutions and established *Volksraade* (parliaments), although their attempts at unification failed. For more than a decade, civil wars and the struggle with the environment hampered consolidation among the Boers. Nevertheless, the Orange Free State's economy grew rapidly, and by the 1860s the Boers were exporting significant amounts of wool via Cape ports.

THE CAPE ECONOMY

Capitalist infrastructure came earlier to the Cape than to the Boer regions because of its older colonial history and its seacoast links to the British Empire. Banks, insurance companies, and limited-liability companies arose in the 1840s and '50s, and a class of prosperous colonial shopkeepers, financiers, traders, and farmers emerged as Cape Town grew to more than 30,000 people in the 1850s. Port Elizabeth, established in 1820, also became an important trading centre and harbour. The British government granted the Cape settlers what was termed "representative government" in March 1853 (the Legislative Assembly had elected members, with an executive appointed from London) and "responsible government" in 1872 (the assembly appointed the executive). Franchise qualifications were relatively low, and even some Africans could vote, although their small number had no political impact. These nominal rights were reduced later in the century and abolished outright in 1936.

Between 1811 and 1858 colonial aggression deprived Africans of most of their land between the Sundays and Great Kei rivers and produced poverty and despair. From the mid-1850s British magistrates held political power in British Kaffraria, destroying the power of the Xhosa chiefs. Following a severe lung sickness epidemic among their cattle in 1854–56, the Xhosa killed many of their remaining cattle and in 1857–58 grew few crops in response to a millenarian prophecy that this would cause their ancestors to rise from the dead and destroy the whites. Many thousands of Xhosa starved to death, and large numbers of survivors

Missionaries walk across a suspension bridge over the Orange River in South Africa. European missionaries infiltrated South Africa starting in the early 19th century, introducing western goods as well as Christianity to native peoples. Imagno/Hulton Archive/Getty Images.

were driven into the Cape Colony to work. British Kaffraria fused with the Cape Colony in 1865, and thousands of Africans newly defined as Fingo resettled east of the Great Kei, thereby creating Fingoland. The Transkei, as this region came to be known, consisted of the hilly country between the Cape and Natal. It became a large African reserve and grew in size when those parts that were still independent were annexed in the 1880s and '90s (Pondoland lost its independence in 1894).

European missionaries and their African catechists worked unremittingly from the 1820s to Christianize indigenous communities and to introduce them to European manufactured goods they had previously done well without. Whatever intentions the missionaries may have had, their efforts undermined African worldviews and contributed to the destruction of traditional African communities throughout South Africa. For a time nevertheless, a small number of African peasant farmers used plows, paid rents and taxes, produced for the market, and sold surplus grain to the towns in competition with colonial farmers. The difficulty they encountered obtaining capital, however, as well as the legal and political discrimination they faced, drove most of them out of business in the decades following the South African War of 1899–1902.

The Cape economy, narrowly based on wine and wool, was not particularly prosperous. Wool exports, though soaring to some 6,000 tons in 1855, lagged far behind those of Australia and remained susceptible to drought and market slumps. African labour built roads, but only a few miles of railway were constructed before 1870. Various alternatives that would broaden the economic base were explored. Accumulations of guano (droppings of gannets and cormorants used as fertilizer) were exploited on off-coast islands; copper mining began in the southwestern party of the country; hunters operating as far north as the Zambezi sent back large quantities of ivory; and traders, hunters, missionaries, and full-time prospectors surveyed and sampled the rocks. The most potentially rewarding commodities were diamonds discovered in the Vaal valley and gold found in the Tati valley and in the northern and eastern Transvaal between 1866 and 1871.

DISPUTES IN THE NORTH AND EAST

To the north, colonial communities and African states alternately cooperated and competed with each other, with the advantage slowly moving to the colonists. The Swazi and Gaza supplied slaves both to the Transvaal Boers and to the Portuguese. During the 1850s the Swazi overran much of the Lowveld, where they absorbed many groups and exchanged captured children for firearms and horses with the Transvaal settlers. After the death of Soshangane (leader of the Gaza state) in 1856, a Gaza civil war broke out that also involved the

Swazi, Boers, and Portuguese. After the Swazi gained control of land almost to Maputo in 1864, the Gaza (under the victorious Mzila) migrated northward into the Buzi River area of present-day eastern Zimbabwe.

Farther south the Zulu competed with the Swazi and the Boers to dominate the Pongolo and Ngwavuma valleys and with the Boers to control the Buffalo (Mziniathi) River area. The colonial administrator, Theophilus Shepstone, interfered not only in Zulu politics but also in Ndebele succession dispute (1869–72), attempting to oust the eventual leader (Lobengula) in favour of a pretender. Marthinus Pretorius, the Transvaal leader, annexed huge areas, at least on paper. To the irritation of settler farmers and plantation owners, few Zulu went south to work in Natal. Instead, a supply of Mozambican indentured labourers (some of them forced) entered the region. This eventually evolved into a steady flow of migrant workers in the following decades, but, because not enough labour appeared initially in the early 1860s, indentured labourers from India were brought in to work on the new sugar plantations.

The Sotho continued their tenacious hold on their lands along the Caledon River and for a time supplied the Boers of the Orange Free State with grain and cattle. The Sotho mobilized a force of 10,000 and defeated the Boers in 1858. The Boers, however, coveted the fertile Caledon valley and defeated the Sotho eight years later after the Boers regained their unity. The Sotho were forced to sign the Treaty of Thaba Bosiu (1866), and only British annexation of Sotho territory in 1868 prevented their complete collapse.

THE ZULU AFTER SHAKA

The Zulu, although initially successful at repelling the Europeans, were, like the Ndebele, eventually overpowered by them in clashes such as the Battle of Blood (Ncome) River in 1838. Boer attacks on the Zulu between 1838 and 1839 precipitated a Zulu civil war between Dingane and Mpande. The latter allied himself with the Boer invaders and so split the kingdom. Between 1839 and 1840 the Boers seized large parts of the Zulu kingdom, including the area between the Tugela and the Swart-Mfolozi. When the British in turn evicted the Boers and annexed Natal in 1843, the southern region to the Tugela was restored to the Zulu. Mpande (reigned 1840–72), a formidable ruler, controlled territory between the Tugela in the south and, roughly, the Pongolo in the north, boundaries that were not seriously disturbed until 1879.

In 1856 the primary conflict in the Zulu civil war (the Battle of Ndondakasuka on the lower Tugela River, close to the sea) elevated Mpande's younger son, Cetshwayo, over Mpande's older son, Mbuyazi. Although Cetshwayo formally became ruler of Zululand only upon his father's death in 1872, he had in fact effectively ruled the kingdom since the early 1860s.

By the late 1870s, colonial officials had identified the Zulu kingdom as a major obstacle to confederation, and in January 1879 British and colonial troops invaded Zululand. During his rule Mpande had expanded Zulu military capacity, and Cetshwayo used this effectively against the British invaders at Isandhlwana in 1879. The annihilation of a large British force at Isandhlwana slowed the invasion, but imperial firepower ultimately prevailed. For the Zulu, political dismemberment followed military defeat. British divide-and-rule policies precipitated

CETSHWAYO

(b. *c.* 1826, near Eshowe, Zululand [now in South Africa]—d. Feb. 8, 1884, Eshowe)

Cetshwayo (also spelled Cetewayo) was the last great king of the independent Zulus (reigned 1872–79), whose strong military leadership and political acumen restored the power and prestige of the Zulu nation, which had declined during the reign of his father, Mpande (Panda). As absolute ruler of a rigidly disciplined army of 40,000 men, Cetshwayo was considered a threat to British colonial interests. The Anglo-Zulu War (1879) and subsequent destruction of Zulu power removed that threat.

Cetshwayo distinguished himself early in life, taking part in the 1838 Zulu attempt to evict the invading Boers from Natal, and in the early 1850s he was involved in fighting between the Zulu and the Swazi for control of the Pongola region. Cetshwayo was widely regarded as the de facto heir to Mpande, and from about 1861, as his father aged, Cetshwayo effectively ruled Zululand. After his father's death in 1872, Cetshwayo's position as ruler was formalized. His sovereignty was also recognized by the neighbouring British administration, which controlled the colony of Natal to the immediate south of the Zulu kingdom.

In 1877 the British annexed the Boer republic of Transvaal, an event that fostered a drive to federate the Southern African white colonies and to destroy the autonomy of the independent Southern African kingdoms. The British took over preexisting Boer claims to parts of western Zululand, and in early 1878 Sir Theophilus Shepstone, the Transvaal administrator, and Sir Bartle Frere, the high commissioner of the Cape, began a propaganda campaign against Cetshwayo and the Zulu.

In December 1878 Frere issued an ultimatum to Cetshwayo that was designed to be impossible to satisfy: the Zulu were, among other things, to dismantle their "military system" within 30 days. As expected, the ultimatum was not met, and in January 1879 the British attacked Zululand. Cetshwayo was eventually captured in August 1879 and subsequently exiled to Cape Town.

In July 1882 Cetshwayo was permitted to travel to the United Kingdom to seek support from British politicians for the restoration of the Zulu monarchy. Permission was granted, but the ensuing plan ensured the permanent emasculation of the monarchy. Cetshwayo returned in January 1883 and became embroiled in a Zulu civil war. He later fled to the British Zulu Native Reserve, where he died at the British administrative centre of Eshowe in February 1884. The official cause of his sudden death was given as a heart attack, though the Zulu believed he had been poisoned. Cetshwayo's grave, in the Nkandla forest, is considered sacred and is guarded by the Zulu.

another civil war in 1883, and Zululand was annexed in 1887.

THE DECLINE OF THE AFRICAN STATES

As the 1860s came to an end, the great African states began to weaken. Not only did many important African leaders die during this period (Soshangane in 1858, Sekwati of the Pedi in 1861, Mswati in 1865, Mzilikazi in 1868, Moshoeshoe in 1870, and Mpande in 1872), but, increasingly, Europeans were determined to exploit Africans as a source of labour and to acquire the last large fertile areas controlled by them.

Colonial troops tipped the balance decisively against societies that had previously withstood attempts to bring them under the settlers' control. A century of military conflict on the Cape frontier ended with the Cape-Xhosa war of 1877–78. Between 1878 and 1881 the Cape Colony defeated rebellions in Griqualand West, the Transkei, and Basutoland. Sir Bartle Frere, governor of the Cape and high commissioner from March 1877, rapidly decided that independent African kingdoms had to be tamed in order to facilitate political and economic integration of the region.

Governor George Grey had already proposed a federated South Africa in 1858, and in the late 1860s the discovery of gold and diamonds reactivated this idea. The annexation of Basutoland in 1868 began a series of movements toward consolidation that included the British seizure of the diamond fields from the competing Griqua, Tlhaping, and Boers in 1871 (the Keate Award), Colonial Secretary Lord Carnarvon's more determined federation plan of 1875, Shepstone's invasion of the Transvaal in 1877, and the British invasions of Zululand and Pediland in 1879. British troops also took part in an 1879 campaign that crushed Pedi military power in the northern Transvaal. With the collapse of Zulu resistance in the 1880s, the invasions of the Gaza and Ndebele kingdoms in 1893–96, and the crushing of Venda resistance in 1898, by 1900 no autonomous African societies remained in the region.

DIAMONDS, GOLD, AND IMPERIALIST INTERVENTION (1870–1902)

South Africa experienced a transformation between 1870, when the diamond rush to Kimberley began, and 1902, when the South African War ended. Midway between these dates, in 1886, the world's largest goldfields were discovered on the Witwatersrand. As the predominantly agrarian societies of European South Africa began to urbanize and industrialize, the region evolved into a major supplier of precious minerals to the world economy; gold especially was urgently needed to back national currencies and ensure the continued flow of expanding international trade. British colonies, Boer republics, and African kingdoms all came under British control. These dramatic changes were propelled by two linked forces: the development of a capitalist mining industry and a sequence of imperialist interventions by Britain.

DIAMONDS AND CONFEDERATION

A chance find in 1867 had drawn several thousand fortune seekers to alluvial diamond diggings along the Orange, Vaal, and Harts rivers. Richer finds in "dry diggings" in 1870 led to a large-scale rush. By the end of 1871 nearly 50,000 people lived in a sprawling polyglot mining camp that was later named Kimberley.

Initially, individual diggers, black and white, worked small claims by hand. As production rapidly centralized and mechanized, however, ownership and labour patterns were divided more starkly along racial lines. A new class of mining capitalists oversaw the transition from diamond digging to mining industry as joint-stock companies bought out diggers. The industry became a monopoly by 1889 when De Beers Consolidated Mines (controlled by Cecil Rhodes) became the sole producer. Although some white diggers continued to work as overseers or skilled labourers, from the mid-1880s the workforce consisted mainly of black migrant workers housed in closed compounds by the companies (a method that had previously been used in Brazil).

The diamond zone was simultaneously claimed by the Orange Free State, the South African Republic, the western Griqua under Nicolaas Waterboer, and southern Tswana chiefs. At a special hearing in October 1871, Robert W. Keate (then lieutenant governor of Natal) found in favour of Waterboer, but the British persuaded him to request protection against his Boer rivals, and the area was annexed as Griqualand West.

The annexation of the diamond fields signaled a more progressive British policy under a Liberal ministry but fell short of the ambitious confederation policy pursued by Lord Carnarvon, the colonial secretary in Benjamin Disraeli's 1874 Conservative government. He sought to unite the republics and colonies into a self-governing federation in the British Empire, a concept inspired by Theophilus Shepstone, who, as secretary for native affairs in Natal, urged a coherent regional policy with regard to African labour and administration.

Carnarvon concentrated at first on persuading the Cape and the Free State to accept federation, but a conference in London in August 1876 revealed how unreceptive these parties were to the proposal. With his southern gambit frustrated, Carnarvon embarked on a northern strategy. The South African Republic (Transvaal), virtually bankrupt, had suffered military humiliation at the hands of the Pedi, and support for Pres. Thomas F. Burgers had declined because of this. Carnarvon commissioned Shepstone to annex the Transvaal, and, after encountering only token resistance at the beginning of 1877, he proclaimed it a British colony a few months later.

The new possession proved difficult to administer as empty coffers and insensitivity to Afrikaner resentments led to a clash over tax payments, and, under a triumvirate of Paul Kruger, Piet Joubert, and Marthinus Wessel Pretorius, the Transvaal Boers opted to fight for independence. British defeats, especially at Majuba in 1881, ended British insistence on the concept of confederation. By the London Convention of 1884, republican self-government was restored, subject to an imprecise British "suzerainty" over external relations.

AFRIKANER AND AFRICAN POLITICS IN THE CAPE

The white population in the Cape numbered 240,000 by the mid-1870s and constituted about one-third of the colony's population. Cape revenues accounted for three-fourths of the total income in the region's four settler states in 1870, as the diamond discoveries created more revenue that could be used to build railways and public works. Although by this time some two-thirds of the settler population spoke Dutch or Afrikaans, political power rested largely with an English-speaking elite of merchants, lawyers, and landholders.

The conflict between Afrikaners and English speakers led to the establishment of the Afrikaner Bond in 1879. The Bond initially represented poorer farmers and espoused an anti-British Pan-Afrikanerism in the Cape and beyond, but, after its reorganization a few years later under Jan Hendrik Hofmeyr, the group began to champion the Cape's commercial interests and

acquired a new base of support—mainly wealthier farmers and urban professionals. When Hofmeyr threw his support behind Cecil Rhodes in 1890, he enabled Rhodes to become prime minister of the Cape; their alliance stemmed from a mutual desire for northward economic expansion. A major cleavage, however, opened up between Bond politicians and the English-speaking voters loosely defined as Cape liberals. The latter, particularly those in constituencies in the eastern Cape that had a significant percentage of black male voters, were tactically friendly to the small enfranchised stratum of fairly prosperous black peasants, whereas the Bond and most English-speaking white voters were hostile toward the black farmers growing cash crops and pursued more-restrictive franchise qualifications.

The number of blacks in the colony greatly increased between 1872 and 1894 as heretofore independent territories were annexed to the Cape. As black farmers became more prosperous and as more blacks became literate clerks and teachers, many individuals qualified to vote. The rise of the Afrikaner Bond and new laws affecting franchise qualifications and taxes also stimulated more-vigorous black participation in electoral politics after 1884. New political and educational bodies came into existence in the eastern Cape, as did the first black newspapers and black-controlled churches. The period also witnessed the first political organizations among Coloureds in the Cape and Indians in Natal and the Transvaal.

GOLD MINING

Prospectors established in 1886 the existence of a belt of gold-bearing reefs 40 miles (60 km) wide centred on present-day Johannesburg. The rapid growth of the gold-mining industry intensified processes started by the diamond boom: immigration, urbanization, capital investment, and labour migrancy. By 1899 the gold industry attracted investment worth £75 million, produced almost three-tenths of the world's gold, and employed more than 100,000 people (the overwhelming majority of them black migrant workers).

The world's richest goldfield was also the most difficult to work. Although the gold ore was abundant, the layers of it ran extremely deep, and the ore contained little gold. To be profitable, gold mining had to be intensive and deep-level, requiring large inputs of capital and technology. A group system, whereby more than 100 companies had been arranged into nine holding companies, or "groups," facilitated collusion between companies to reduce competition over labour and keep costs down. The gold mines rapidly established a pattern of labour recruitment, remuneration, and accommodation that left its stamp on subsequent social and economic relations in the country. White immigrant miners, because of their skills, scarcity, and political power, won relatively high wages. In contrast, the more numerous unskilled black migrants from throughout Southern Africa, especially from present-day Mozambique, earned low pay (at century's end about one-ninth the wage of white miners). Migrant miners were housed in compounds, which facilitated their control and reduced overhead costs.

THE ROAD TO WAR

Even before the discovery of gold, the South African interior was an arena of tension and competition. Germany annexed South West Africa in 1884. The Transvaal claimed territory to its west. Britain countered by designating the territory the Bechuanaland protectorate and then annexed it as the crown colony of British Bechuanaland. Rhodes secured concessionary rights to land north of the Limpopo River, founded the British South Africa Company, and in 1890 dispatched a pioneer column to occupy what became known as Rhodesia.

While these forces jostled for position in the region at large, the domestic politics of the Transvaal became unsettled. Paul Kruger's government made strenuous efforts to accommodate the mining industry, but it was soon at loggerheads with Britain, the mine magnates, and the British and other non-Afrikaner Uitlander ("Outlander") immigrants. British policy makers expressed concern about the Transvaal's potential as an independent actor, and deep-level-mine owners chafed at mine bosses' corruption and inefficiency. The grievances of the Uitlanders, largely excluded from the vote, provided both cause and cover for a conspiracy between British officials and mining capitalists. An Uitlander uprising in Johannesburg was to be supported by an armed invasion from Bechuanaland, headed by Leander Starr Jameson, Rhodes's lieutenant, who would intervene to "restore order."

The plot was botched. The Uitlander rising did not take place, but Jameson went ahead with his incursion in December 1895, and within days he and his force had been rounded up. While Rhodes had to resign as prime minister of the Cape, British Colonial Secretary Joseph Chamberlain managed to conceal his complicity. The Jameson Raid polarized Anglo-Boer sentiment in South Africa, simultaneously exacerbating republican suspicions, Uitlander agitation, and imperial anxieties.

In February 1898 Kruger was elected to a fourth term as president of the Transvaal. He entered a series of negotiations with Sir Alfred Milner (who became high commissioner and governor of the Cape in 1897) over the issue of the Uitlander franchise. Milner declared in private early in 1898 that "war has got to come" and adopted intransigent positions. The Cape government, headed by William P. Schreiner, attempted to mediate, as did Marthinus Steyn, the president of Free State, even while he attached his cause to Kruger's. In September 1899 the two Boer republics gave an ultimatum to

Britain, and, when it expired on October 11, Boer forces invaded Natal.

THE SOUTH AFRICAN WAR (1899–1902)

While the government of Lord Salisbury in Britain went to war to secure its hegemony in Southern Africa, the Boer republics did so to preserve their independence. The expensive and brutal colonial war lasted two and a half years and pitted almost 500,000 imperial troops against 87,000 republican burghers, Cape "rebels," and foreign volunteers. The numerical weakness of the Boers was offset by their familiarity with the terrain, support from the Afrikaner populace, and the poor leadership and dated tactics of the British command. Although often styled a "white man's war," both sides used blacks extensively as labour, and at least 10,000 blacks fought for the British.

In the first phase of the war, Boer armies took the offensive and punished British forces at Colenso, Stormberg, and Magersfontein in December 1899 ("Black Week"). During 1900 Britain rushed reinforcements to the front, relieved sieges at Ladysmith, Kimberley, and Mafeking, and took Bloemfontein, Johannesburg, and Pretoria. In the third phase, Boer commandos avoided conventional engagements in favour of guerrilla warfare. The British commander, Lord Kitchener, devised a scorched-earth policy against the commandos and the rural population supporting them, in which he

Men guard South African railway tracks during the conflict known as the South African War. British troops outnumbered Boer forces five to one, yet the conflict lasted more than two years. Popperfoto/Getty Images

destroyed arms, blockaded the countryside, and placed the civilian population in concentration camps. Some 25,000 Afrikaner women and children died of disease and malnutrition in these camps, while 14,000 blacks died in separate camps. In Britain the Liberal opposition vehemently objected to the government's methods for winning the war.

Boer forces, which at the end consisted of about 20,000 exhausted and demoralized troops, sued for peace in May 1902. The Treaty of Vereeniging reflected the conclusive military victory of British power but made a crucial concession. It promised that the "question of granting the franchise to natives [blacks]" would be addressed only after self-government had been restored to the former Boer republics. The treaty thus allowed the white minority to decide the political fate of the black majority.

RECONSTRUCTION, UNION, AND SEGREGATION (1902–29)

The Union of South Africa was born on May 31, 1910, created by a constitutional convention (in Durban in 1908) and an act of the British Parliament (1909). The infant state owed its conception to centralizing and modernizing forces generated by mineral discoveries, and its character was shaped by eight years of "reconstruction" between 1902 and 1910. During that period, efficient administrative structures were created, and a relationship developed between Afrikaner politicians and mining capitalists that consolidated the economic dominance of gold. Reconstruction also ensured that settler minorities would prevail over the black majority. Black societies were policed and taxed more effectively, and the new constitution excluded blacks from political power. Racial segregation was further developed through policies proposed during reconstruction and solidified after 1910.

Both Afrikaner and black nationalism utilized new political vehicles. Syndicalist white workers and Afrikaner republican diehards fought against employers and government, their clashes culminating in the Rand Revolt of 1922. Black protests against the new order ranged from genteel lobbying and passive resistance to armed rural revolt, strikes, and mass mobilization.

MILNER AND RECONSTRUCTION

High Commissioner Milner transferred his headquarters from Cape Town to Pretoria in 1902. The move symbolized the centrality of the Transvaal to his mission of constructing a new order in South Africa. When Milner departed in 1905, his vision of a country politically dominated by English-speaking whites had failed. Schemes to flood the rural Transvaal with British settlers yielded only a trickle, and, worse yet, compulsory Anglicization of education only intensified feelings of Afrikaner nationalism. Opposition to "Milnerism" defined the emergent political groups led by former Boer generals Louis Botha, Jan Smuts, and J.B.M. (Barry) Hertzog. Milner had hoped to withhold self-rule from whites in South Africa until "there are three men of British race to two of Dutch." But, when Henry Campbell-Bannerman's Liberal ministry granted responsible government to the former republics in 1907, Afrikaner parties won elections in the Transvaal.

Yet, if Milner's political design failed to take shape, he did largely realize his blueprint for economic and social engineering. Served by a group of handpicked young administrators, he made economic recovery a priority because it was imperative to restore the mines to profitability. He lowered rail rates and tariffs on imports and abolished the expensive concessions granted by the Kruger regime. Milner also made strenuous efforts to ensure cheap labour to the mines. To achieve this goal, he authorized the importation of some 60,000 Chinese indentured labourers when black migrants resisted wage cuts. Chinese miners, who would mostly return home by 1910, performed only certain tasks, but their employment set a precedent for a statutory colour bar in the gold mines. Although this experiment provoked political outcries in the Transvaal and in Britain, it succeeded in undercutting the bargaining power of black workers. The value of gold production swelled from £16 million in 1904 to £27 million by 1907.

The administration worked to remodel the Transvaal as a stable base for agricultural, industrial, and finance capital, spending some £16 million to return Afrikaners to their farms and equip them. It established a land bank, promoted scientific farming methods, and developed more-efficient tax-collection methods, which increased pressures on black peasants to work for white farmers. Especially on the Witwatersrand, the young administrators tackled town planning, public transport, housing, and sanitation, and in each of these spheres a new urban geography proceeded from the principle of separating white and black workers.

The South African Native Affairs Commission (SANAC) was appointed to provide comprehensive answers to "the native question." Its report (1905) proposed territorial separation of black and white landownership, systematic urban segregation by the creation of black "locations," the removal of black "squatters" from white farms and their replacement by wage labourers, and the segregation of blacks from whites in the political sphere. These (and other SANAC recommendations) provided the basis for laws passed between 1910 and 1936.

CONVENTION AND UNION

Concern in London over the electoral victory by the Afrikaner party Het Volk evaporated as soon as it became clear that both Botha and Smuts understood the economic preeminence of mining capital. A policy of reconciliation between Afrikaans- and English-speaking whites was also promoted.

A national convention, which met in Durban in 1908–09, drafted a constitution. Afrikaner leaders and Cape Premier John X. Merriman opted for a unitary state with Dutch and English as official languages and with parliamentary sovereignty. Executive authority was vested in a governor-general who would be advised by a cabinet from the governing party. Two "entrenched" clauses, on language and franchise, could be amended only by a two-thirds majority vote in Parliament. While Cape delegates favoured a colour-blind franchise, those from the Transvaal and Orange Free State demanded an exclusively white electorate. A compromise simply confirmed existing electoral arrangements. The former republics retained white male adult suffrage and did not consider female suffrage (white women finally won the right to vote in 1930). In 1910, 85 percent of Cape voters were white, 10 percent Coloured, and 5 percent black. Representation was further limited on racial lines: even in the Cape, only whites could stand for Parliament.

BLACK, COLOURED, AND INDIAN POLITICAL RESPONSES

The South African War occurred at a time when many black communities suffered under great hardship. During the 1890s, drought and cattle disease (particularly rinderpest) impoverished pastoralists, while competition increased for black land and labour. During the war, most black South Africans identified with the British cause because imperial politicians assured them that "equal laws, equal liberty" for all races would prevail after a Boer defeat.

However, the Treaty of Vereeniging withdrew such promises, and a sense of betrayal stimulated political protest, especially among mission-educated blacks. Various organizations arose to counter the impending union of white-ruled provinces by ethnically and regionally uniting blacks. In response to the constitutional convention, blacks held their own (the South African Native Convention) in Bloemfontein. This provided an important step toward the formation of a permanent national black political organization. Such an organization was finally founded on Jan. 8, 1912, when the South African Native National Congress (from 1923 the African National Congress; ANC) came into existence. Not all black protest occurred through the new middle-class organizations, however. Some black farmers from Natal refused to pay a poll tax in 1906, and their resistance developed into an armed rising led by Bambatha, a Zulu chief. At the end of this "reluctant rebellion," between 3,000 and 4,000 blacks had been killed and many thousands imprisoned.

Parallel developments took place among politically conscious Coloureds and Indians. Their first nationally based organization was the African Political (later People's) Organization, founded in Cape Town in 1902. Under the presidency of Abdullah Abdurahman, this body lobbied for Coloured rights and had links at times with other black political groups. Indians in the Transvaal, led by Mohandas K. Gandhi, also resisted discriminatory legislation. Gandhi spent the years 1893 to 1914 in South Africa as a legal agent for Indian merchants in Natal and the Transvaal. Between 1906 and 1909, in protest against a Transvaal registration law requiring Indians to carry passes, Gandhi first implemented the methods of satyagraha (nonviolent noncompliance), which he later used with great effect in India.

UNION AND DISUNITY

Supported by the majority party in each province and by the British government, Louis Botha formed the first union government in May 1910. The Botha administration entered a period of continuous change and violent conflict as tensions arose from issues left unresolved by the constitution, from rapid but uneven economic growth, and from the

AFRICAN NATIONAL CONGRESS (ANC)

The African National Congress is a South African political party and black nationalist organization. Founded in 1912 as the South African Native National Congress, it had as its main goal the maintenance of voting rights for Coloureds (persons of mixed race) and black Africans in Cape Province. It was renamed the African National Congress in 1923. From the 1940s it spearheaded the fight to eliminate apartheid, the official South African policy of racial separation and discrimination.

In the late 1920s the ANC's leaders split over the issue of cooperation with the Communist Party, and the ensuing victory of the conservatives left the party small and disorganized through the 1930s. In the 1940s, however, the ANC revived under younger leaders who pressed for a more militant stance against segregation in South Africa. The ANC Youth League, founded in 1944, attracted such figures as Walter Sisulu, Oliver Tambo, and Nelson Mandela, who galvanized the movement and challenged the moderate leadership. Under the presidency of Albert Luthuli, the ANC after 1952 began sponsoring nonviolent protests, strikes, boycotts, and marches against the apartheid policies that had been introduced by the National Party government that came to power in 1948. Party membership grew rapidly. A campaign against the pass laws (blacks were required to carry passes indicating their status) and other government policies culminated in the Defiance Campaign of 1952. In the process ANC leaders became a target of police harassment: in 1956 many of its leaders were arrested and charged with treason.

In 1960 another group, the Pan-Africanist Congress (PAC), organized massive demonstrations against the pass laws, during which police killed 69 unarmed demonstrators at Sharpeville (south of Johannesburg). At this point the National Party banned, or outlawed, both the ANC and the PAC. Denied legal avenues for political change, the ANC first turned to sabotage and then began to organize outside of South Africa for guerrilla warfare. In 1961 an ANC military organization, Umkhonto we Sizwe ("Spear of the Nation"), with Mandela as its head, was formed to carry out acts of sabotage as part of its campaign against apartheid. Mandela and other ANC leaders were sentenced to life imprisonment in 1964 (the Rivonia Trial). Although the ANC's campaign of guerrilla warfare was basically ineffective because of stringent South African internal security measures, surviving ANC cadres kept the organization alive in Tanzania and Zambia under Tambo's leadership. The ANC began to revive inside South Africa toward the end of the 1970s, following the Soweto uprising in 1976, when the police and army killed more than 600 people, many of them children.

The administration of F.W. de Klerk lifted the ban on the ANC in 1990, and its leaders were released from prison or allowed to return to South Africa. Mandela succeeded Tambo as ANC president in 1991 and led the group in negotiations (1992–93) with the government over transition to a government elected by universal suffrage. In April 1994 the party swept to power in the country's first such election. Mandela stepped down as ANC president in 1997 and was succeeded by Thabo Mbeki, who, in turn, was succeeded by Jacob Zuma in 2007.

legacy of conquest and dispossession of the indigenous peoples.

One source of conflict was the relationship between employers and organized white workers. The Chamber of Mines and miners' trade unions on the Witwatersrand engaged in combat for a decade and a half. Whenever violent confrontations flared up—as they did in 1907, 1913, and 1914—the government deployed troops to end the strikes. White workers suspended strike action during World War I, but militancy returned in 1919, this time fueled by inflation. The Chamber of Mines announced in December 1921 that, because of rising costs and a falling gold price, it planned on replacing semiskilled white workers with lower-paid blacks. A miners' protest stoppage in January 1922 became a general strike, and in March it developed into an armed rising, with strikers organized as commandos. Jan Smuts, prime minister since Botha's death in 1919, used artillery and aircraft to crush what became known as the Rand Revolt, at a cost of some 200 lives. This intense conflict between white unions and employers ended with the passage of the Industrial Conciliation Act in 1924, which set up new state structures for regulating industrial conflicts.

Black workers also engaged in sporadic strikes before, during, and after World War I, giving rise to the first black trade unions. More than 70,000 African gold miners halted production for a week when they struck for higher wages in February 1920. Soldiers and police broke the strike, but not before 11 miners died and more than 100 were injured. This strike was part of a wave of protest in several cities as inflation eroded the real wages of black workers.

AFRIKANER REBELLION AND NATIONALISM

When Britain declared war on Germany in 1914, South Africa's dominion status meant that it was automatically at war, and its troops mobilized to invade German South West Africa. This sparked a rebellion led by former Boer generals, who held high-ranking positions as officers in the Union Defence Force. Some 10,000 soldiers, mainly poverty-stricken rural Afrikaners, joined the rising. The government used 32,000 troops to suppress it, and more than 300 men lost their lives in the fighting.

The rebellion, though, was an atypical episode in the rise of Afrikaner nationalism as a political force. More-telling responses came from those Afrikaners who had been profoundly affected by economic change, war, and reconstruction. After 1902, thousands of landless families streamed into the cities, indicating the extent to which the prewar rural social order had crumbled. One response to the threat of further disintegration was a "second language movement" spearheaded by teachers, clergymen, journalists, and lawyers who felt deeply threatened by the cultural dominance of English speakers. It succeeded in its immediate aim when

Afrikaans replaced Dutch as an official language in 1925.

J.B.M. Hertzog founded the National Party in 1914, with support mainly from "poor whites" and militant intellectuals. The general election of 1915 gave the National Party 30 percent of the vote, with Afrikaners deserting the South African Party led by Botha and Smuts. Hertzog's party won a majority of both seats and votes in 1920 on a platform of republicanism and separate school systems for Afrikaans- and English-speaking whites. The June 1924 election propelled Hertzog to the position of prime minister

J.B.M Hertzog. Hulton Archive/Getty Images

through a coalition between the National and Labour parties known as the Pact government.

SEGREGATION

In the first two decades of the union, segregation became a distinctive feature of South African political, social, and economic life as whites addressed the "native question." Blacks were "retribalized" and their ethnic differences highlighted. New statutes provided for racial separation in industrial, territorial, administrative, and residential spheres. This barrage of legislation was partly the product of reactionary attitudes inherited from the past and partly an effort to regulate class and race relations during a period of rapid industrialization when the black population was growing steadily.

The 1911 Mines and Works Act and its 1926 successor reserved certain jobs in mining and the railways for white workers. The Natives' Land Act of 1913 defined less than one-tenth of South Africa as black "reserves" and prohibited any purchase or lease of land by blacks outside the reserves. The law also restricted the terms of tenure under which blacks could live on white-owned farms. The Native (Urban Areas) Act of 1923 segregated urban residential space and created "influx controls" to reduce access to cities by blacks. Hertzog proposed increasing the reserve areas and removing black voters in the Cape from the common roll in 1926, aims that were finally realized through the Representation of

Natives Act (1936). Blacks now voted on a separate roll to elect three white representatives to the House of Assembly.

THE PACT YEARS (1924–33)

Hertzog's Pact government strengthened South Africa's autonomy, aided local capital, and protected white workers against black competition. Hertzog also played a leading role at the Imperial Conference in London that issued the Balfour Report (1926), establishing autonomy in foreign affairs for the dominions. When he returned from Britain, Hertzog turned his attention to creating the symbols of nationalism—flag and anthem. Economic nationalism included protective tariffs for local industry, subsidies to facilitate agricultural exports, and a state-run iron and steel industry. White trade unions grew more bureaucratic and less militant, although their members enjoyed at best modest material gains. Unskilled and nonunionized whites who received support through sheltered employment in the public sector and through prescribed minimum wages in the private sector gained more directly. Although the overall level of white poverty remained high, through these policies the manufacturing sector absorbed white labour nearly twice as fast as black.

Blacks gained little during this period and continued to lose earlier benefits. For them, segregation meant restricted mobility, diminished opportunities, more-stringent controls, and a general sense of exclusion. Economic conditions in the reserves continued to deteriorate, the terms of tenancy became more onerous on white-owned farms, and the urban slums provided a harsh alternative for those who left the land.

The first mass-based black political organization, the Industrial and Commercial Workers Union (ICU), flourished in response to deteriorating conditions. Until 1926 the ICU was a Cape-based organization with black and some Coloured members drawn mainly from urban areas. As a broadly based vehicle of rural protest, it had many thousands of supporters among black tenants on white farms. The ICU linked innumerable local rural grievances with a generalized call for land and liberation, but by 1929 its influence had declined. However, other organizations built on its base. The Communist Party of South Africa (CPSA), founded in 1921, was at first active almost solely within white trade unions, but from 1925 it recruited black members more energetically, and in 1928–29 it called for black majority rule and closer cooperation with the ANC. Its connection to the ANC occurred most prominently with Josiah Gumede (president 1927–30), whose political views moved leftward in the late 1920s. This led to a split in the ANC in 1930 as the more moderate members expelled the more radical ones.

The 1929 general election reflected the political challenges to white supremacy. For the first time since union, questions of "native policy" dominated white electoral politics. Afrikaner nationalists made "black peril" and "communist menace" their rallying cries. It was not to be the last such occasion.

THE APARTHEID YEARS

The Hertzog government achieved a major goal in 1931 when the British Parliament passed the Statute of Westminster, which removed the last vestiges of British legal authority over South Africa. Three years later the South African Parliament secured that decision by enacting the Status of the Union Act, which declared the country to be "a sovereign independent state." These actions also laid the groundwork for segregationist policies to flourish in South Africa.

THE INTENSIFICATION OF APARTHEID IN THE 1930S

Although Hertzog's National Party held a majority of the seats in the House of Assembly and dominated the South African cabinet in the early 1930s, its mismanagement of problems created by the Great Depression led him to form a coalition with his rival Smuts in 1933. Smuts was the leader of the South African Party, whose support came from the major industrialists and which was the party of most of the English-speaking whites (who made up less than half of the white population). In contrast, the National Party derived its main support from Afrikaner farmers and intellectuals. By 1934 the two organizations had merged to form the United Party, with Hertzog as prime minister and Smuts his deputy. The two parties and the two leaders had a common interest in favouring the enfranchised population, nearly all of whom were white, over the unenfranchised, all of whom were black. They agreed to provide massive support for white farmers, to assist poor whites by providing them with jobs protected from black competition, and to curb the movement of blacks from the reserves into the towns. Meanwhile, National Party member Daniel F. Malan disagreed with the merger of the parties and chose to keep the National Party functioning.

The earnings from South Africa's gold exports increased sharply after Britain and the United States abandoned the gold standard in the early 1930s. White farmers prospered, new secondary industries were established, and South Africans of all races continued to flock to the towns. South Africa changed from a predominantly rural country that exported raw materials and imported manufactured consumer goods into a country with a diverse economy. Although the standard of living for most whites improved greatly from this expansion, the lives of Coloureds, blacks, and Indians were hardly affected. The government did add some land to the reserves in 1936, but it never exceeded 13 percent of the area of the country. Until the end of apartheid, almost nine-tenths of South Africa—including the best land for agriculture and the bulk of the mineral deposits—belonged exclusively to whites. Unsurprisingly, conditions on the native reserves became progressively worse through overpopulation and soil erosion. The government attempted to resolve these problems through a series of programs called Betterment Schemes, which involved keeping tight control over land use in the reserves, often drastically culling cattle, and enforcing the building of contour ridges to reduce soil erosion. Overcrowding in the reserves made it necessary for a high proportion of the men to work for wages elsewhere—on white farms or in the towns, where they lived in a hostile world. Black and Coloured farm labourers, scattered in small groups throughout the agricultural areas, were isolated, and in the towns life was insecure and wages low. In the gold-mining industry the real wages of blacks declined by about one-seventh between 1911 and 1941; white miners received 12 times the salary of blacks.

Education for blacks was left largely to Christian missions, whose resources, even when augmented by small government grants, enabled them to enroll only a small proportion of the black population. Missionaries did, however, run numerous schools, including some excellent high schools that took a few pupils through to the university level, and were the dominant influence at the South African Native College at Fort Hare (founded 1916), which included degree courses. These institutions educated a small but increasing number of blacks, who secured teaching jobs and positions in the lower reaches of the civil service or functioned as clergy (especially in the

independent churches that had broken away from mainstream white churches).

Educated blacks were frustrated by the fact that whites did not treat them as equals, and some of them took part in opposition politics in the ANC. However, the ANC and two parallel movements—the African Political Organization (a Coloured group) and the South African Indian Congress—had little popular support and exerted little influence during this period. Their leaders were mission-educated men who had liberal goals and used strictly constitutional methods, such as petitions to the authorities. The radical African ICU had collapsed by 1930, and the CPSA made little headway among blacks.

WORLD WAR II

When Britain declared war on Germany on Sept. 3, 1939, the United Party split. Hertzog wanted South Africa to remain neutral, but Smuts opted for joining the British war effort. Smuts's faction narrowly won the crucial parliamentary debate, and Hertzog and his followers left the party, many rejoining the National Party faction Malan had maintained since 1934. Smuts then became the prime minister, and South Africa declared war on Germany.

South Africa made significant contributions to the Allied war effort. Some 135,000 white South Africans fought in the East and North African and Italian campaigns, and 70,000 blacks and Coloureds served as labourers and transport drivers. South African platinum, uranium, and steel became valuable resources, and, during the period that the Mediterranean Sea was closed to the Allies, Durban and Cape Town provisioned a vast number of ships en route from Britain to the Suez.

The war proved to be an economic stimulant for South Africa, although wartime inflation and lagging wages contributed to social protests and strikes after the end of the war. Driven by reduced imports, the manufacturing and service industries expanded rapidly, and the flow of blacks to the towns became a flood. By the war's end, more blacks than whites lived in the towns. They set up vast squatter camps on the outskirts of the cities and improvised shelters from whatever materials they could find. They also began to flex their political muscles. Blacks boycotted a Witwatersrand bus company that tried to raise fares, they formed trade unions, and in 1946 more than 60,000 black gold miners went on strike for higher wages and improved living conditions.

Although the 1946 strike was brutally suppressed by the government, white intellectuals did propose a series of reforms within the segregation framework. The government and private industry made a few concessions, such as easing the industrial colour bar, increasing black wages, and relaxing the pass laws, which restricted the right of blacks to live and work in white areas. The government, however, failed to discuss these problems with black representatives.

Afrikaners felt threatened by the concessions given to blacks and created a series of ethnic organizations to promote their interests, including an economic association, a federation of Afrikaans cultural associations, and the Afrikaner Broederbond, a secret society of Afrikaner cultural leaders. During the war many Afrikaners welcomed the early German victories, and some of them even committed acts of sabotage.

The United Party, which had won the general election in 1943 by a large majority, approached the 1948 election complacently. While the party appeared to take an ambiguous position on race relations, Malan's National Party took an unequivocally pro-white stance. The National Party claimed that the government's weakness threatened white supremacy and produced a statement that used the word *apartheid* to describe a program of tightened segregation and discrimination. With the support of a tiny fringe group, the National Party won the election by a narrow margin.

THE NATIONAL PARTY AND APARTHEID

After its victory the National Party rapidly consolidated its control over the state and in subsequent years won a series of elections with increased majorities. Parliament removed Coloured voters from the common voters' rolls in 1956. By 1969 the electorate was exclusively white: Indians never had any parliamentary representation, and the seats for white representatives of blacks and Coloureds had been abolished.

One plank of the National Party platform was for South Africa to become a republic, preferably outside the Commonwealth. The issue was presented to white voters in 1960 as a way to bring about white unity, especially because of concern with the problems that the Belgian Congo was then experiencing as it became independent. By a simple majority the voters approved the republic status. The government structure would change only slightly: the governor-general would be replaced by a state president, who would be chosen by Parliament. At a meeting in London in March 1961, South Africa had hoped to retain its Commonwealth status, but, when other members criticized it over its apartheid policies, it withdrew from the organization and on May 31, 1961, became the Republic of South Africa.

The government vigorously furthered its political goals by making it compulsory for white children to attend schools that were conducted in their home language, either Afrikaans or English (except for the few who went to private schools). It advanced Afrikaners to top positions in the civil service, army, and police and in such state corporations as the South African Broadcasting Corporation. It also awarded official contracts to Afrikaner banks and insurance companies. These methods raised the living standard of Afrikaners closer to that of English-speaking white South Africans.

Following a recession in the early 1960s, the economy grew rapidly until the late 1970s. By that time, owing to the efforts of public and private enterprise, South Africa had developed a modern infrastructure, by far the most advanced in Africa. It possessed efficient financial institutions, a national network of roads and railways, modernized port facilities in Cape Town and Durban, long-established mining operations producing a wealth of diamonds, gold, and coal, and a range of industries. De Beers Consolidated Mines and the Anglo American Corporation of South Africa, founded by Ernest Oppenheimer in 1917, dominated the private sector, forming the core of one of the world's most powerful networks of mining, industrial, and financial companies and employing some 800,000 workers on six continents. State corporations (parastatals) controlled industries vital to national security. South African Coal, Oil, and Gas Corporation (SASOL) was established in 1950 to make South Africa self-sufficient in petroleum resources by converting coal to gasoline and diesel fuel. After the United Nations (UN) placed a ban on arms exports to South Africa in 1964, Armaments Corporation of South Africa (Armscor) was created to produce high-quality military equipment.

The man who played a major part in transforming apartheid from an election slogan into practice was Hendrik F. Verwoerd. Born in the Netherlands, Verwoerd immigrated with his parents to South Africa when he was a child. He became minister of native affairs in

1950 and was prime minister from 1958 until 1966, when Dimitri Tsafendas, a Coloured man, assassinated him in Parliament. (Tsafendas was judged to be insane and was confined to a mental institution after the murder.) Verwoerd's successor, B.J. Vorster, had been minister of justice, police, and prisons, and he shared Verwoerd's philosophy of white supremacy. In Verwoerd's vision, South Africa's population contained four distinct racial groups—white, black, Coloured, and Asian—each with an inherent culture. Because whites were the "civilized" group, they were entitled to control the state.

The all-white Parliament passed many laws to legalize and institutionalize the apartheid system. The Population Registration Act (1950) classified every South African by race. The Prohibition of Mixed Marriages Act (1949) and the Immorality Act (1950) prohibited interracial marriage or sex. The Suppression of Communism Act (1950) defined communism and its aims broadly to include any opposition to the government and empowered the government to detain anyone it thought might further "communist" aims. The Indemnity Act (1961) made it legal for police officers to commit acts of violence, to torture, or to kill in the pursuit of official duties. Later laws gave the police the right to arrest and detain people without trial and to deny them access to their families or lawyers. Other laws and regulations collectively known as "petty apartheid" segregated South Africans in every sphere of life: in buses, taxis, and hearses, in cinemas, restaurants, and hotels, in trains and railway waiting rooms, and in access to beaches. When a court declared that separate amenities should be equal, Parliament passed a special law to override it.

"Grand apartheid," in contrast, related to the physical separation of the racial groups in the cities and countryside. Under the Group Areas Act (1950) the cities and towns of South Africa were divided into segregated residential and business areas. Thousands of Coloureds, blacks, and Indians were removed from areas classified for white occupation.

Blacks were treated like "tribal" people and were required to live on reserves under hereditary chiefs except when they worked temporarily in white towns or on white farms. The government began to consolidate the scattered reserves into 8 (eventually 10) distinct territories, designating each of them as the "homeland," or Bantustan, of a specific black ethnic community. The government manipulated homeland politics so that compliant chiefs controlled the administrations of most of those territories. Arguing that Bantustans matched the decolonization process then taking place in tropical Africa, the government devolved powers onto those administrations and eventually encouraged them to become "independent." Between 1976 and 1981 four accepted independence—Transkei, Bophuthatswana, Venda, and Ciskei—though none was ever recognized by a foreign government. Like the other homelands, however, they were

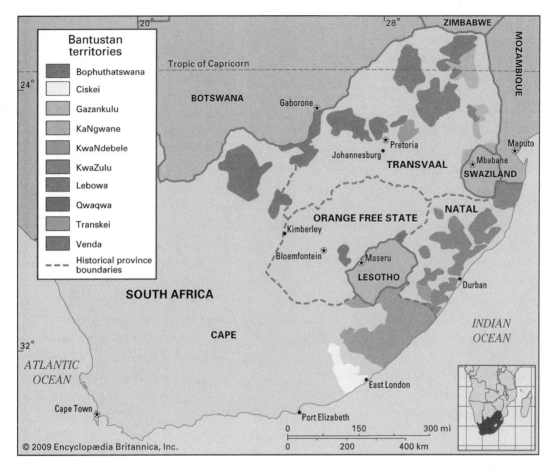

Bantustan territories (also known as black homelands or black states) in South Africa during the apartheid era.

economic backwaters, dependent on subsidies from Pretoria.

Conditions in the homelands continued to deteriorate, partly because they had to accommodate vast numbers of people with minimal resources. Many people found their way to the towns. Attempting to reverse this flood, the government strengthened the pass laws by making it illegal for blacks to be in a town for more than 72 hours at a time without a job in a white home or

business. A particularly brutal series of forced removals were conducted from the 1960s to the early '80s, in which more than 3.5 million blacks were taken from towns and white rural areas (including lands they had occupied for generations) and dumped into the reserves, sometimes in the middle of winter and without any facilities.

The government also established direct control over the education of blacks. The Bantu Education Act (1953) took black schools away from the missions, and more state-run schools—especially at the elementary level—were created to meet the expanding economy's increasing demand for semiskilled black labour. The Extension of University Education Act (1959) prohibited the established universities from accepting black students, except with special permission. Instead, the government created new ethnic university colleges—one each for Coloureds, Indians, and Zulus and one for Sotho, Tswana, and Venda students, as well as a medical school for blacks. The South African Native College at Fort Hare, which missionaries had founded primarily but not exclusively for blacks, became a state college solely for Xhosa students. The government staffed these ethnic colleges with white supporters of the National Party and subjected the students to stringent controls.

RESISTANCE TO APARTHEID

Apartheid imposed heavy burdens on most South Africans. The economic gap between the wealthy few, nearly all of whom were white, and the poor masses, virtually all of whom were black, Coloured, or Indian, was larger than in any other country in the world. While whites generally lived well, Indians, Coloureds, and especially blacks suffered from widespread poverty, malnutrition, and disease. Most South Africans struggled daily for survival despite the growth of the national economy.

After the ANC Youth League emerged in the early 1940s, the ANC itself came to life again under a vigorous president, Albert Luthuli, and three younger men—Walter Sisulu, Oliver Tambo, and Nelson Mandela (the latter two briefly had a joint law practice in Johannesburg). The South African Indian Congress, which had also been revitalized, helped the ANC organize a defiance campaign in 1952, during which thousands of volunteers defied discriminatory laws by passively courting arrest and burning their pass books. A mass meeting held three years later, called Congress of the People, included Indians, Coloureds, and sympathetic whites. The Freedom Charter was adopted, asserting that "South Africa belongs to all who live in it, black or white, and no Government can justly claim authority unless it is based on the will of the people." The government broke up the meeting, subsequently arrested more than 150 people, and charged them with high treason. Although the trial did not result in any guilty verdicts, it dragged on until 1961. To prevent further gatherings, the government passed the Prohibition of Political Interference Act (1968), which banned the formation and foreign financing of nonracial political parties.

Robert Sobukwe, a language teacher at the University of the Witwatersrand, led a group of blacks who broke away from the ANC in 1959 and founded the Pan-Africanist Congress (PAC) because they believed that the ANC's alliance with white, Coloured, and Indian organizations had impeded the struggle for black liberation. The PAC launched a fresh antipass campaign in March 1960, and thousands of unarmed blacks invited arrest by presenting themselves at police stations without passes. At Sharpeville, a black township near Johannesburg, the police opened fire on the crowd outside a police station. At least 67 blacks were killed and more than 180 wounded, most of them shot in the back. Thousands of workers then went on strike, and in Cape Town some 30,000 blacks marched in a peaceful protest to the centre of the city. Rebellion in rural areas such as Pondoland also erupted at this time against the controls of homeland authorities. The government reestablished control by force by mobilizing the army, outlawing the ANC and the PAC, and arresting more than 11,000 people under emergency regulations.

After Sharpeville the ANC and PAC leaders and some of their white sympathizers came to the conclusion that apartheid could never be overcome by peaceful means alone. PAC established an armed wing called Poqo, and the ANC set up its military wing, Umkhonto we Sizwe ("Spear of the Nation"), in 1961. Although their military units detonated several bombs in government buildings during the next few years, the ANC and PAC did not pose a serious threat to the state, which had a virtual monopoly on modern weaponry. By 1964 the government had captured many of the leaders, including Mandela and Sobukwe, and they were sentenced to long terms at the prison on Robben Island in Table Bay, off Cape Town. Other perpetrators of acts of sabotage, including John Harris (who was white), were hanged. Hundreds of others fled the country, and Tambo presided over the ANC's executive headquarters in Zambia.

ROBBEN ISLAND

Robben Island is located in Table Bay, part of the Western Cape province of South Africa. It is 5 miles (8 km) west of the mainland and 6 miles (10 km) north of Cape Town and has an approximate area of 5 square miles (13 square km). Its name is the Dutch word for "seals," once plentiful in the surrounding waters. The island was a common stopping point for passing ships in the 16th and early 17th centuries. After early efforts at settlement, it was made a Dutch and then a British penal colony. The island housed a leper colony from 1846 to 1931, and those judged insane were also sent there. A lighthouse was installed in 1864. Fortifications were erected during World War II, and from the mid-1960s to 1991 Robben Island served as South Africa's maximum-security prison. Most inmates, including Nelson Mandela, were black South Africans incarcerated for their resistance to apartheid. The last of these prisoners were released in 1991. The island continued to serve as a medium-security prison for criminal offenders until 1996. In 1997 it was turned into a museum and declared a national monument, and in 1999 it received designation as a UNESCO World Heritage site.

THE UNRAVELING OF APARTHEID

The government was successful at containing opposition for almost a decade, and foreign investment that had been briefly withdrawn in the early 1960s returned. Such conditions proved to be only temporary, however.

A new phase of resistance began in 1973 when black trade unions organized a series of strikes for higher wages and improved working conditions. Stephen Biko and other black students founded the Black Peoples Convention (BPC) in 1972 and inaugurated what was loosely termed the Black Consciousness movement, which appealed to blacks to take pride in their own culture and proved immensely attractive.

On June 16, 1976, thousands of children in Soweto, an African township outside Johannesburg, demonstrated against the government's insistence that they be taught in Afrikaans rather than in English. When the police opened fire with tear gas and then bullets, the incident initiated a nationwide cycle of protest and repression. Using its usual tactics, the government banned many organizations such as the BPC, and within a year the police had killed more than 500, including Biko. These events focused worldwide attention on South Africa. The UN General Assembly had denounced apartheid in 1973; four years later the UN Security Council voted unanimously to impose a mandatory embargo on the export of arms to South Africa.

The illusion that apartheid would bring peace to South Africa had shattered by 1978. Most of the homelands proved to be economic and political disasters: labour was their only significant export, and most of their leadership was corrupt and unpopular. The national economy entered a period of recession, coupled with high inflation, and many skilled whites emigrated. South Africa, increasingly isolated as the last bastion of white racial domination on the continent, became the focus of global denunciation.

At that time the leadership of the National Party passed to a new class of urban Afrikaners—business leaders and intellectuals who, like their English-speaking white counterparts, believed that reforms should be introduced to appease foreign and domestic critics. Pieter W. Botha succeeded B.J. Vorster as prime minister in August 1978, and his government introduced some reforms, but it also increased state controls. It repealed the bans on interracial sex and marriage, desegregated many hotels, restaurants, trains, and buses, removed the reservation of skilled jobs for whites, and repealed the pass laws. Provided that black trade unions registered, they received access to a new industrial court, and they legally could strike. A new constitution was promulgated that created separate parliamentary bodies for Indians and for Coloureds, but it also vested great powers in an executive president, namely Botha.

The Botha reforms, however, stopped short of making any real change in the distribution of power. The white parliamentary chamber could override the Coloured and Indian chambers on matters of national significance, and all blacks remained disenfranchised. The Group Areas Act and the Land Acts maintained residential segregation. Schools and health and welfare services for blacks, Indians, and Coloureds remained segregated and inferior, and most nonwhites, especially blacks, were still desperately poor. Moreover, Botha used the State Security Council, which was dominated by military officers, rather than the cabinet as his major policy-making body, and he embarked on a massive military buildup. Military service for white males, already universal, increased from nine months to two years and included annual reserve duty.

South Africa's black neighbours formed the Southern African Development Coordinating Conference in 1979 in an effort to limit South Africa's economic domination of the region, but it made little progress. Most of the export trade from the region continued to pass through the country to South African ports, and South Africa provided employment for some 280,000 migrant workers from neighbouring countries. Botha also used South Africa's military strength to restrain its neighbours from pursuing antiapartheid policies. The South African Defense Force (SADF) assisted the Renamo (Mozambique National Resistance) rebels in Mozambique and the UNITA (National Union for the Total Independence of Angola) faction in Angola's civil war. SADF troops entered Botswana, Swaziland, Zimbabwe, Lesotho, and Mozambique in order to make preemptive attacks on ANC groups and their allies in these countries. Botha kept what was then called South West Africa/Namibia under South African domination in defiance of the UN, which had withdrawn the mandate it had granted to South Africa over the region. The country even produced a few nuclear weapons, the testing of which was detected in 1979. Increasingly, South African dissidents from all race groups were harassed, banned, or detained in prison without necessarily being charged under renewable 90-day detention sentences.

During the 1980s the conservative administrations of Prime Minister Margaret Thatcher in Britain and Pres. Ronald Reagan in the United States faced increasingly insistent pressures for sanctions against South Africa. A high-level Commonwealth mission went to South Africa in 1986 in an unsuccessful effort to persuade the government to suspend its military actions in the townships, release political prisoners, and stop destabilizing neighbouring countries. Later that year American public resentment of South Africa's racial policies was strong enough for the U.S. Congress to pass—over a presidential veto—the Comprehensive Anti-Apartheid Act, which banned new investments and loans, ended air links, and prohibited the importation of many commodities. Other governments took similar actions.

The struggle intensified during the early 1980s and became further polarized. The new constitution of 1983 attempted to split the opposition to apartheid by meeting Indian and Coloured grievances while at the same time giving blacks no political rights except in the homelands. In response, more than 500 community groups formed the United Democratic Front, which became closely identified with the exiled ANC. Strikes, boycotts, and attacks on black police and urban councillors began escalating, and a state of emergency was declared in many parts of the country in 1985; a year later the government promulgated a nationwide state of emergency and embarked on a campaign to eliminate all opposition. For three years policemen and soldiers patrolled the black townships in armed vehicles. They destroyed black squatter camps and detained, abused, and killed thousands of blacks, while the army continued its forays into neighbouring countries. Rigid censorship laws tried to conceal those actions by banning television, radio, and newspaper coverage.

The brute force used by the government did not halt dissent. Longstanding critics such as Anglican Archbishop Desmond Tutu, the 1984 Nobel Peace Prize laureate, defied the government, and influential Afrikaner clerics and intellectuals withdrew their support. Resistance by black workers continued, including a massive strike by the National Union of Mineworkers, and saboteurs caused an increasing number of deaths and injuries. The economy suffered severe strain from the costs of sanctions, administering apartheid, and military adventurism, especially in Namibia and Angola. The gross domestic product decreased, annual inflation rose above 14 percent, and investment capital became scarce. Moreover, in 1988 the army suffered a military setback in Angola, after which the government signed an accord paving the way for the removal of Cuban troops that had been sent to Angola and for the UN-supervised independence of Namibia in 1990. Given these circumstances, many whites came to realize that there was no stopping the incorporation of blacks into the South African political system.

Government officials held several discussions with imprisoned ANC leader Mandela as these events unfolded, but Botha balked at the idea of allowing blacks to participate in the political system. National Party dissent against Botha in 1989 forced him to step down as both party leader and president. The National Party parliamentary caucus subsequently chose F.W. de Klerk, the party's Transvaal provincial leader, as his successor. More than 20 years younger than Botha, de Klerk exhibited more sensitivity to the dynamics of a world where, as democracy arose in eastern Europe and the former Soviet Union, the blatant racism that still existed in South Africa could no longer be tolerated. De Klerk announced a program of radical change in a dramatic address to Parliament on Feb. 2, 1990; nine days later Mandela was released from prison. During the next year Parliament repealed the basic apartheid laws, lifted the state of emergency, freed many political prisoners, and allowed exiles to return to South Africa. Mandela was elected president of the ANC in 1991, succeeding Tambo, who was in poor health and died two years later.

TRANSITION TO MAJORITY RULE

Mandela and de Klerk, who both wanted to reach a peaceful solution to South Africa's problems, met with representatives of most of the political organizations in the country, with a mandate to draw up a new constitution. These negotiations took place amid pervasive and escalating violence, especially in the southern Transvaal, the industrial heart of the country, and in Natal. Most of the conflicts in the Transvaal occurred between Zulu migrant workers, who were housed in large hostels, and the residents of the adjacent townships. The conflicts in Natal existed mainly between Zulu supporters of the ANC and members of the Inkatha Freedom Party (IFP), a Zulu movement led by Chief Mangosuthu Buthelezi, who was chief minister of the KwaZulu homeland.

As the bargaining continued, both Mandela and de Klerk made concessions, with the result that both of them ran the risk of losing the support of their respective constituencies. While whites were loath to forfeit their power and privileges, blacks had hoped to win complete control of the state. A majority of white voters endorsed the negotiating process in a referendum in 1992, but both white and black extremists tried to sabotage the process through various acts of terror.

Mandela and de Klerk finally reached a peaceful agreement on the future of South Africa at the end of 1993, an achievement for which they jointly received the 1993 Nobel Peace Prize. In addition, leaders of 18 other parties endorsed an interim constitution, which was to take effect immediately after South Africa's first election by universal suffrage, scheduled for April 1994. A parliament to be elected at that time would oversee the drafting of a permanent constitution for the country. The temporary constitution enfranchised all citizens 18 and older, abolished the homelands, and divided the country into nine new provinces, with provincial governments receiving substantial powers. It also contained a long list of political and social rights and a mechanism through which blacks could regain ownership of land that had been taken away under apartheid.

POSTAPARTHEID SOUTH AFRICA

In the April 1994 election the ANC won almost two-thirds of the vote, the National Party slightly more than one-fifth, and the IFP most of the rest; all three received proportional cabinet representation. The ANC also became the majority party in seven of the provinces, but the IFP won a majority in KwaZulu-Natal, and the National Party—supported by mixed-race (people formerly classified as "Coloured" under apartheid) as well as white voters—won a majority in Western Cape. Mandela was sworn in as president of the new South Africa on May 10 before a vast jubilant crowd that included the secretary-general of the UN, 45 heads of state, and delegations from many other countries. Thabo Mbeki, a top official in the ANC, and de Klerk both became deputy presidents.

THE MANDELA PRESIDENCY

The new, multiparty "government of national unity" aimed to provide Africans

Nelson Mandela being sworn in as president of South Africa in 1994. Walter Dhladhla/AFP/ Getty Images

with improved education, housing, electricity, running water, and sanitation. Recognizing that economic growth was essential for such purposes, the ANC adopted a moderate economic policy, dropping the socialist elements that had characterized its earlier programs. Mandela and his colleagues campaigned vigorously for foreign aid and investment, but capital investment entered the new South Africa slowly.

The government also had to grapple with a host of daunting institutional problems associated with the transition to a postapartheid society. Blacks joined the civil service, antiapartheid guerrillas became members of the police and the army, and new municipal governments that embraced both the old white cities and their black township satellites sprang into existence. Labour disputes, criminal violence, and conflict between Zulu factions, especially in KwaZulu-Natal, continued. The IFP (which supported a new provincial constitution that granted a sweeping autonomy to KwaZulu-Natal but was struck down by the Constitutional Court) refused to participate in the process that resulted in the creation of the new national constitution that Parliament passed in May 1996. Parliament revised the constitution in October after it was reviewed by the Constitutional Court; Mandela signed it

THE TRUTH AND RECONCILIATION COMMISSION

The most important domestic agency created during Mandela's presidency was the Truth and Reconciliation Commission (TRC), which was established to review atrocities committed during the apartheid years. It was set up in 1995 under the leadership of Archbishop Tutu and was given the power to grant amnesty to those found to have committed "gross violations of human rights" under extenuating circumstances.

The TRC was the target of widespread criticism; whites saw it as selectively targeting them, and blacks viewed its actions as a charade that allowed perpetrators of heinous crimes to go free. Former president P.W. Botha refused to answer a summons to give testimony to the commission and received a fine and a suspended sentence, although the sentence was later appealed and overturned. Nonetheless, the TRC uncovered information that otherwise would have remained hidden or taken longer to surface. For example, details of the murders of numerous ANC members were exposed, as were the operations of the State Counterinsurgency Unit at Vlakplaas. Its commander, Colonel Eugene de Kock, was subsequently sentenced to a long prison term. The commission also investigated those opposed to apartheid. One of the most prominent was Winnie Madikizela-Mandela, the former wife of Nelson Mandela, who served briefly as a deputy minister in 1994–95. The TRC report indicated that she had been involved in apartheid-era violence. The report also allowed many to finally learn the fate of relatives or friends who had "disappeared" at the hands of the authorities.

into law in December of the same year. Also in 1996, the National Party left the government to form a "dynamic but responsible" opposition.

SOUTH AFRICA SINCE MANDELA

Mbeki replaced Mandela as president of the ANC in December 1997 and became president of the country after the ANC's triumphant win in the June 1999 elections. Mbeki pledged to address economic woes and the need to improve the social conditions in the country. The ANC was again victorious in the April 2004 elections, and Mbeki was elected to serve another term. South Africa had entered the 21st century with enormous problems to resolve, but the smooth transition of power in a government that represented a majority of the people—something unthinkable less than a decade earlier—provided hope that those problems could be addressed peaceably.

In March 2005 deputy president Jacob Zuma—who was widely held to be Mbeki's successor as president of the ANC and, eventually, as president of the country—was dismissed by Mbeki amid charges of corruption and fraud; the next year Zuma stood trial for an unrelated charge of rape. He was acquitted of rape in May 2006, and the corruption charges were dropped later that year. Despite the repeated allegations of wrongdoing, which his supporters claimed were politically motivated, Zuma remained a

popular figure within the ANC and was selected over Mbeki to be party president at the ANC conference in December 2007, in what was one of the most contentious leadership battles in the party's history. Later that month Zuma was recharged with corruption and fraud, and additional charges were brought against him. All charges were eventually dismissed in September 2008 on a legal technicality, but prosecutors from the National Prosecuting Agency (NPA) vowed to appeal the ruling.

Ironically, it was perhaps Mbeki rather than Zuma who was most politically harmed by the controversy surrounding Zuma's corruption charges. Following an allegation by a High Court judge that there had been political interference (allegedly by Mbeki or at his behest) in Zuma's prosecution on corruption-related charges, on Sept. 20, 2008, Mbeki was asked by the ANC to resign from the South African presidency, which he agreed to do once the relevant constitutional requirements had been fulfilled. On September 25 he was succeeded by Kgalema Motlanthe, who was selected by the National Assembly to serve as interim president until elections could be held in 2009.

As the 2009 general election drew near, the spotlight was once again on the corruption-related charges against Zuma and the allegations of political interference, culminating in an announcement by the National Prosecuting Authority (NPA) on April

6, 2009, that the charges would be withdrawn. Although prosecutors stated that they felt the charges had merit, they noted evidence of misconduct in the handling of Zuma's case. Opposition parties condemned the announcement, alleging that the NPA bowed to pressure from the ANC to drop the charges before the election, and complained that the NPA's actions left the question of Zuma's innocence unresolved. The ANC, however, was unscathed by the pre-election drama. It finished far ahead of the other parties in the April 22 general election, winning almost 66 percent of the vote, and Zuma was poised to become the country's next president. He was officially elected to the presidency in a National Assembly vote, held on May 6; he was inaugurated on May 9.

CHAPTER 11

SWAZILAND

Swaziland is a landlocked country in southeastern Southern Africa. A former British protectorate, it gained independence in 1968. The capital is Mbabane.

EARLY HISTORY

The Swazi nation is a relatively recent political grouping, the main amalgamation of clans having taken place under Dlamini military hegemony about the middle of the 19th century. However, the record of human settlement in what is now Swaziland stretches far back into prehistory. The earliest stone tools, found on ancient river terraces, date back more than 250,000 years, and later stone implements are associated with evidence of *Homo sapiens* from perhaps as long ago as 100,000 years. By 42,000 years ago the inhabitants were quarrying red and black hematite ore for cosmetic purposes on the top of the Ngwenya massif (where in 1964 a large open-cut mining operation was developed to exploit the rich ore deposit). This ranks as one of the world's earliest mining and trading activities, and mining continued for many thousands of years after that. Much later—about 20,000 years ago—the archaeological record reveals occupation by the ancestors of the San hunter-gatherers, who created the distinctive rock paintings found throughout the western part of the country.

About 2,000 years ago groups of Bantu-speaking peoples (Nguni, Sotho, and Tswana) moved southward across the

Limpopo River. They cultivated crops, kept livestock (sheep and goats), used pottery, and smelted iron—hence their designation as Early Iron Age peoples. At a later date cattle were introduced. These people are recorded at Ngwenya, where the mining of iron ore has been dated to about 400 CE. During the following centuries the more attractive areas of Swaziland were settled by these ancestors of the Nguni and Sotho clans, whom the Swazi encountered in the late 18th and early 19th centuries.

The ancestors of the Dlamini clan were part of this southward movement, which reached the Delagoa Bay area (now Maputo) of Mozambique some considerable time before the arrival of the Portuguese in the early 16th century. There they settled as part of the Thembe-Tonga group of peoples until the mid-18th century, when, probably because of dynastic conflict, they moved southward along the coastal plain between the mountains and the Indian Ocean—"scourging the Lubombo," as a royal praise song puts it. Up to this time they called themselves Emalangeni. Later they moved westward through the Lubombo range and up the Pongola valley, where about 1770 under their king Ngwane III they established the first nucleus of the Swazi nation (bakaNgwane) near what is now Nhlangano.

EMERGENCE OF THE SWAZI NATION

This was a turbulent period in the history of southeastern Africa, when a number of major clan groupings were struggling for supremacy. Two of these, the Ndwandwe and the Zulu, located to the south of the new Ngwane homeland, constituted a serious threat to the Dlamini, who strove to establish their control over the clans among whom they had settled. Nevertheless, by the end of the century, they had achieved considerable success in assimilating some of these clans and in forging bonds with others to create a new political grouping.

However, this new power base was not strong enough to ward off aggression by their southern neighbours, so about 1820 under their new king—Sobhuza I, or Somhlohlo ("The Wonder")—they moved northward to establish a safer heartland in central Swaziland (the Middleveld). There the Dlamini consolidated their power under Sobhuza I and his son Mswati II. Part of this success must be attributed to Sobhuza's adoption of the Zulu age-group system of military organization, which created regiments across clan loyalties and which was at all times strictly disciplined. By 1860 they had extended their power through conquest and assimilation far beyond the boundaries of present-day Swaziland under Mswati II, whom later generations described as "their greatest fighting king" and who gave his name to the nation.

At the peak of their power, however, a new factor had emerged in the regional geopolitics, which over the next 40 years caused the gradual contraction of Swazi territorial and political authority. This was the competing pressure from the

SOBHUZA

(b. *c.* 1795—d. *c.* 1839, near Manzini, Swaziland)

Sobhuza I was the Southern African king (reigned from about 1815) who developed the chieftaincy that under his son, Mswati II, was to become the Swazi nation (now Swaziland).

Sobhuza was the son of the Ngwane chief Ndvungunye (of the Dlamini clan), whose chieftaincy was situated somewhere near the Pongola River, south of Delagoa Bay (the exact area is still uncertain). About 1820, after being attacked by warriors from the Ndwandwe chieftaincy under Zwide, Sobhuza began to migrate with his people north of the Usutu River, where he was attacked on several more occasions. After the destruction of the Ndwandwe in the mid-1820s (attributed to the Zulu under Shaka), Sobhuza returned south to the Ezulwini valley (southern Swaziland), where he established his village. He extended Dlamini-Ngwane influence over much of what is now central Swaziland. Although the Dlamini-Ngwane were raided by the Zulu in 1828 and 1836, Sobhuza's people survived during the 1830s. Sobhuza married Thandile, daughter of Zwide, and groomed his son, Mswati, as his heir.

expanding Boer republic of the Transvaal and from the growing British imperial presence, especially after the discovery in South Africa of diamonds in 1867 and gold in 1871.

The main destabilizing force was the stream into the country of European prospectors and concession hunters, which the Swazi were able to contain for a while but which became a flood after the kingship passed to Mbandzeni in 1875. By 1890 so many concessions had been granted for so many purposes (in addition to land and mineral rights) that practically the whole country was covered two, three, or even four deep in concessions of all kinds and for different periods. Although the Swazi maintained that these were all leasehold rights that would terminate at some future date, they had, as it later transpired, signed away their independence.

In 1888 the Swazi tried to regulate the new influences that the influx of Europeans had created by granting them a charter of conditional self-government subject to the royal veto. Behind the concessions scramble by individuals, however, lay the intrigue and conflict of the two white powers, the Boers and the British. The former needed a route to the sea, while the latter wanted to contain them. Swaziland stood in the way, as an obstacle to be manipulated by both.

Under a convention between the British government and one of the Boer states, the South African Republic (also known as the Transvaal), a provisional government consisting of representatives of the two powers and a representative of the Swazi people was set up in 1890. In 1893 the British government signed a new convention permitting the South

MSWATI II

(b. c. 1825, near Manzini [now in Swaziland]—d. August 1865, Swaziland)

Mswati II was a Southern African king and son of Sobhuza I. Mswati (also spelled Mswazi) was the greatest of the Dlamini-Ngwane kings, and the Swazi (as the Dlamini-Ngwane came to be called) take their name from him. Mswati extended his kingdom northward into Rhodesia (now Zimbabwe), including territory since lost by the Swazi.

Mswati was the son of Sobhuza I by his wife Thandile. He succeeded to the kingship on his father's death c. 1839, but he began his effective rule when he was circumcised (a rite of passage signifying attainment of maturity) in 1845. He dealt with internal rebellion, pressures resulting from Boer invasions into the eastern Transvaal, and land rivalries with Mpande's Zulu in the Ingwavuma River area. He expanded the control of Sobhuza's original chieftaincy to include much of modern Swaziland's Lowveld, creating one of the most powerful nations of Southern Africa. After the death of the Gaza king Soshangane (c. 1858–59), Mswati's people interfered in the Gaza succession in a long-running series of wars and clashes. By 1865 the Swazi were hegemonic in the lowlands to the west of Delagoa Bay. In August 1865, however, Mswati died prematurely at the height of his success. His successors, Ludvongo and, after 1874, Mbandzeni, were unable to preserve Swazi power against Boer land claims and pursuit of minerals. By 1890 Swaziland had virtually collapsed as an autonomous entity and was preserved from incorporation into the Union of South Africa in 1910 only by previous British annexation in the aftermath of the South African War (1899–1902).

African Republic to negotiate with the Swazi regent and her council for a proclamation allowing the republic to assume powers of jurisdiction, legislation, and administration without the incorporation of Swaziland into the republic. The Swazi refused to sign the proclamation, but in 1894 another convention was signed by the two powers, virtually giving unilateral effect to its terms. After the South African War of 1899–1902 all the rights and powers of the republic passed to Great Britain, and in June 1903, by an order in council under the Foreign Jurisdiction Act, the governor of the Transvaal was empowered to

administer Swaziland and to legislate by proclamation. In 1906 these powers were transferred to a high commissioner for Basutoland, Bechuanaland, and Swaziland.

COLONIAL ADMINISTRATION

The colonial years from 1906 to the late 1940s saw Swaziland drift into a backwater of the British Empire. A fundamental reason was that provision had been made in the South Africa Act of 1909 (which established the Union of South Africa as a British dominion) for the possible eventual transfer of Swaziland (and Basutoland

and Bechuanaland) to the union. While this possibility existed, no socioeconomic improvement took place, and it was difficult to distinguish Swaziland from the neighbouring rural areas of South Africa (there were no border posts). Politically, the situation was epitomized in the downgrading of the title of king to that of paramount chief and of his function to that of "native administration." Despite a number of requests from South Africa over the years, however, the imperial power declined to transfer Swaziland. This resolution was stiffened by events in South Africa after the 1948 election, which heralded the onset of apartheid, a policy of racial separation and discrimination. Also, from 1945 onward, Britain had begun to tackle socioeconomic problems. By the mid-1950s the issue of transfer was dead, though the grand apartheid design of separate homelands for Africans still included Swaziland.

From 1960 the economy forged ahead steadily, but sociopolitical progress followed more slowly. A constitution providing for limited self-government was promulgated in 1963, and in 1967 the country became a protected state under which the kingship was restored. This was followed by full independence on Sept. 6, 1968.

SWAZILAND SINCE INDEPENDENCE

King Sobhuza II of Swaziland was installed as the Ngwenyama of the Swazi nation in 1921. The king jealously

King Mswati III, during his 1986 coronation. His administration faced accusations of corruption and demands for democratization. Mswati approved a new national constitution in 2005. Walter Dhladhla/AFP/Getty Images

cherished and preserved Swazi traditions. Five years after independence, the king repealed the constitution designed by the British and restored the traditional system of government, in which all effective power remains in the royal capital. A system of local government, known as the *tinkhundla*, operates at the grass roots. Sobhuza's concession to modern government was to retain the cabinet system with a prime minister and other ministers, but all are chosen by the king. Under his firm but benevolent rule, Swaziland enjoyed a remarkable degree of political stability and economic progress. Emphasis was placed on education—which had been neglected in colonial times—on health, and on other human resource developments.

King Sobhuza's death on Aug. 21, 1982, was followed by a power struggle within the royal family, which was not finally resolved until 1986, when the teenage heir, Prince Makhosetive, was installed as King Mswati III. His rule, characterized as autocratic and rife with corruption and excess, was beset with demands for democratic reform. Demonstrations and strikes were held during the 1990s and 2000s to protest the slow pace of progress toward democratic change.

To appease his many critics, King Mswati III appointed a committee to draft a new constitution in 2001. Released for public comment in May 2003, it was criticized for falling short of democratic reform, as it banned opposition political parties and allowed the king to retain absolute governing powers. A revised version, which neither banned political parties nor acknowledged their existence, was signed by the king in July 2005 and went into effect in February 2006.

CHAPTER 12

ZAMBIA

Z ambia is a landlocked country in Southern Africa. A former British colony, it gained independence in 1964. The capital is Lusaka.

ARCHAEOLOGY AND EARLY HISTORY

Stone tools attributable to early types of humans have been found near Victoria Falls and in the far northeast, near Kalambo Falls. In 1921, excavations at Kabwe revealed the almost complete skull of *Homo sapiens rhodesiensis* ("Broken Hill Man"), which may be well over 100,000 years old. However, by 20,000 BCE the only surviving type of human throughout the Old World was the ancestor of modern humans, *Homo sapiens sapiens*, who developed the use of spears, the bow and arrow, game traps, and grindstones. Remains of such industries have been found in much of central and northern Zambia, sometimes near lakes and rivers but often in caves and rock-shelters.

During the 1st millennium CE, Zambia was occupied by migrants from farther north who probably spoke Bantu languages; they certainly cultivated crops and kept domestic stock. Traces of ironworking in central and western Zambia have been dated to the first five or six centuries CE. Iron tools and weapons greatly increased mastery over both man and nature and, together with food production, promoted population growth. Stone-using hunters and gatherers were liable to be overrun and absorbed by the food producers, though some survived on the edges of farming zones until a few centuries ago. The complex layers of paintings found in rock-shelters in northeastern Zambia indicate that the homes of stone-using hunters became the shrines of invading farmers.

In central Zambia, by the 6th century CE, the first food producers worked copper as well as iron. By about 1000 CE, copper ingots were being made at Kansanshi, at the western end of the Copperbelt, which implies that copper was being traded extensively and perhaps used as currency.

Early in the 2nd millennium CE, cattle keeping became more intensive on the Batoka Plateau of southern Zambia, while cotton spinning and pipe smoking were introduced. The associated pottery seems directly ancestral to that made locally in the 20th century. Similar evidence of cultural continuity over a long period has also been found in the resemblance between modern pottery in central, northern, and eastern Zambia and a kind of pottery that has been dated to the 12th century CE. The differences in pottery traditions have been ascribed to immigration. They also indicate thicker settlement of woodland through the adoption of *chitemene* cultivation, widespread in Zambia even today. This technique depends heavily on the use of iron axes, because seed is sown in the ashes of branches lopped from trees.

In southern Zambia, archaeology has thrown light on both the emergence of class distinctions and the beginnings of trade with the east coast. About the 14th century a few people were buried wearing ornaments of seashells and exotic glass beads near Kalomo and at Ingombe Ilede, near the confluence of the Zambezi and Kafue rivers. The latter burials also included gold beads, copper ingots, and iron bells of a kind later associated with chieftainship. These metals would have come from south of the Zambezi, but they were probably being reexported down the river by Muslim traders, either Arab or African.

The period between about 1500 and 1800 remains relatively obscure. This was when copper was most intensively mined at Kansanshi, but it is not known who was buying it. The main evidence for these centuries consists of oral traditions. In much of Zambia, from the upper Kafue to the Malawi border, there are legends of groups being founded by chiefly families who came from Luba country in what is now southeastern Democratic Republic of the Congo. Such stories should not be taken at face value. They dramatize prolonged processes of population drift and the spread of cultural influences. By the 18th century, small-scale chieftainship was probably widespread in northern and eastern Zambia, but few of the group names current today would have meant much; such names refer not to long-enduring communities but to changing perceptions of cultural and political differences. In the early 19th century, however, there were at least four areas in which the growth of kingdoms was strengthening the sense of group

COPPERBELT

The Copperbelt is a zone of copper deposits and associated mining and industrial development dependent upon them in Southern Africa. It extends about 280 miles (450 km) northwest from Luanshya, Zamb., into the southern region of the Democratic Republic of the Congo. The zone is up to 160 miles (260 km) in width and contains more than a tenth of the world's copper deposits, found mostly in Late Precambrian sedimentary deposits with the ore concentrated in zones indicative of hilltop and beach, or near-shore, environments. The Copperbelt forms the greatest concentration of industry in sub-Saharan Africa outside the Republic of South Africa.

Upon Zambia's independence in 1964, its thriving economy was heavily reliant on copper exports. In 1969 the Zambian government nationalized the copper-mining industry, which was then to be run by a parastatal organization, Zambian Consolidated Copper Mines. By the mid-1970s the price of copper on the world market had steeply dropped, resulting in a damaging economic decline. In the 1990s the mining industry began to be privatized, and most of the copper mines were sold.

identity: in the east, among the Chewa; in the northeast, among the Bemba; on the lower Luapula, among the Lunda (who had indeed invaded from the west about 1740); and on the upper Zambezi, among the Luyana (later called Lozi). In the Lunda and Luyana kingdoms a prosperous valley environment encouraged dense settlement and prompted the development of relatively centralized government.

EXTERNAL CONTACTS

Trade between Zambia and the Western world began with the Portuguese in Mozambique. Early in the 17th century, the Portuguese ousted Muslims from the gold trade of central Africa. Early in the 18th century, they founded trading posts at Zumbo and Feira, at the confluence of the Zambezi and Luangwa rivers. By 1762

they were regularly acquiring ivory and copper from Zambians in exchange for cotton cloth. During the later 18th century, slave-owning Goans and Portuguese mined gold and hunted elephants among the southern Chewa. Their activities were reported to Kazembe III, the Lunda king on the Luapula, by Bisa traders who exported his ivory and copper to the Yao in Malawi. Kazembe already had indirect access to European goods from the west coast; he now hoped to cut out his African middlemen. One Goan visited Kazembe and was warmly received, but, though the Portuguese government dispatched further expeditions in 1798 and 1831, they came to nothing, mainly because the Portuguese on the Zambezi were turning their attention to exporting slaves rather than ivory or gold. Western Zambia was also beginning to be enmeshed in the Portuguese slave trade, directed to Brazil.

From the early 19th century African traders from Angola bought slaves to the north of the Lozi kingdom, though the Lozi themselves kept servile labour for production at home.

During the second half of the 19th century Zambia was convulsed by traders, raiders, and invaders who came from all surrounding areas. From about 1840 to 1864 the Lozi kingdom was ruled by the Kololo, warrior-herdsmen who had fled north from Sotho country. In the 1860s and '70s the northern Chewa were conquered by a group of Ngoni, who had also come from the far south. Meanwhile, the Bemba and Kazembe's Lunda began selling ivory and slaves to Arabs and Africans from the east coast. At the same time, ivory and slaves were hunted in central Zambia by Chikunda adventurers armed with guns, and South African traders were buying ivory from the Lozi. A few rulers contrived to turn such trade to their own advantage, and the general rise in demand for goods stimulated local production of ironwork, salt, tobacco, and food. Indeed, several crops of American origin were introduced, such as corn (maize), cassava (manioc), peanuts (groundnuts), and sugarcane. Much of Zambia was devastated by marauders, however.

At the end of the 19th century Zambia came under British rule. British interest in the region had first been aroused by the missionary-explorer David Livingstone, who crossed Zambia during three great expeditions between 1853 and his death, near Lake Bangweulu, in 1873. Livingstone's reports of the expanding slave trade inspired other missionaries to come to central Africa and continue the struggle against it, but it was the mining magnate Cecil Rhodes who ensured that so much country north as well as south of the Zambezi came within a British sphere of influence during the "scramble for Africa." In 1889 the British government granted a charter to Rhodes's British South Africa Company (BSAC), bestowing powers of administration and enabling it to stake claims to African territory at the expense of other European powers. The unique butterfly shape of Zambia resulted from agreements in the 1890s between Britain and Germany, Portugal, and the Belgian king Leopold II, and these in turn rested on treaties, mostly stereotyped in form, between Rhodes's agents and African chiefs.

At this stage there was little resistance to white intrusion. The most immediate threat to African land and labour came in Ngoniland, thought by whites to be rich in gold, and the Ngoni duly fought company troops in 1898. The Bemba, however, faced no such challenge and in any case were deeply divided, while the Lozi king believed that alliance with the company would protect his empire against both the Portuguese and the Ndebele. It is also likely that disease and famine undermined the will to resist: there were smallpox epidemics in the early 1890s, widespread rinderpest in 1892–95, and locust plagues throughout the decade.

COLONIAL RULE

At first the BSAC administered its territory north of the Zambezi in two parts, North-Eastern and North-Western Rhodesia. In 1911 these were united to form Northern Rhodesia, with its capital at Livingstone, near Victoria Falls. Among a population of perhaps one million, there were about 1,500 white residents. Some had come to mine surface deposits of copper, and a few, mostly from South Africa, farmed on the plateau east of Livingstone. However, the BSAC regarded the country chiefly as a source of labour for gold and coal mines in Southern Rhodesia and for the copper mines in the southern region of the Belgian Congo, which in 1910 were linked by rail to Southern Rhodesia and the east-coast port of Beira, Mozam. By then company officials had been posted to most parts of Northern Rhodesia and levied taxes in order to force Africans to seek work. Such pressure sometimes provoked violent, but small-scale, resistance.

World War I bore heavily on the territory. For the campaign against the Germans in East Africa, 3,500 troops were recruited and 50,000 porters conscripted, mostly from the northeast; many never returned. Food supplies were requisitioned, yet food production was crippled. Women, as always, bore the brunt of sowing and harvesting, but, in the absence of men to cut trees and clear new land, farm plots were worked to exhaustion. Labour was also urgently needed for mining; war boosted the demand for base metals from Northern Rhodesia as well as Katanga. The Bwana Mkubwa mine exported copper from 1916 to 1918, and from 1917 to 1925 the country's main export was lead from Broken Hill (now Kabwe). African resentment of wartime hardship found expression in the millennial Watchtower movement, which inspired rebellion among the Mambwe in the northeast. More-effective opposition to BSAC rule came from white settlers, especially when an income tax was imposed in 1920. The company was ready to give up the increasingly costly burden of administering Northern Rhodesia and in 1924 handed over this responsibility to the Colonial Office in London, which soon set up a legislative council to which five members were elected by the white population, then about 4,000.

The British government hoped to increase white settlement as part of a wider strategy to strengthen British influence between South Africa and Kenya. Land was reserved for white ownership along the railway line, in the far north, and in the east. African reserves were marked out around these areas in 1928–30. This soon led to overcrowding, soil exhaustion, and food shortage, yet few whites took up the land available to them. By 1930 it was clear that copper was the country's most promising resource. Huge deposits had been located far beneath the headwaters of the Kafue and were mined by companies mostly financed from South Africa, through the Anglo American Corporation, and the United States, through the Rhodesian Selection Trust.

In 1930–31 prices for copper collapsed, partly as a result of the worldwide depression. However, the new mines enjoyed a comparative advantage, since they worked high-grade ores at relatively low cost. For skilled labour they depended on whites, who had to be paid what they might have earned in South Africa. African labour, however, was cheap and abundant, and employers accepted a high turnover rate to avoid providing the amenities that would encourage permanent African settlement in urban areas. From 1935 copper prices rose sharply, and by 1938 Northern Rhodesia contributed a substantial amount to the world's total output of copper.

Yet copper exports did not confer much prosperity. Near the railway both African and white farmers grew food for the mines, but most African farmers were too remote from the market to be able to earn a cash income. More than half the able-bodied male population worked for wages away from home, and as many of these worked outside the territory as within it. On the Copperbelt itself, low wages and poor conditions provoked Africans to strike at three mines in 1935. Nor were rising copper sales of much benefit to the government (whose capital was moved to Lusaka in 1935). The mineral rights were owned by the BSAC, which duly exacted royalties. Taxation was levied on what profits remained, but half was retained by the British government, which made only tiny grants for economic development. In 1938 these arrangements were criticized by a

visiting financial expert, Sir Alan Pim. In a report to the Colonial Office, he urged more public investment in roads, schools, and health services, for Africans as well as whites. Missionaries ran many primary schools, but in 1942 only 35 Africans were receiving secondary education.

When World War II broke out in 1939, Britain contracted to buy the whole output of the Copperbelt. British dependence on undisturbed copper production meant that white mine workers were allowed to maintain an industrial colour bar. Nonetheless, a second strike by African mine workers, in 1940, caused a revision of wage scales to take account of accumulating experience and skill. After the war the new Labour government in Britain began to promote the formation of African trade unions, and by 1949 half the African mine workers in Northern Rhodesia belonged to a single union. In the same year, new legislation confirmed that (in contrast to South Africa and Southern Rhodesia) African unions had the same bargaining rights as those of white workers. Meanwhile, between 1942 and 1946, African teachers, clerks, foremen, and clergy had formed welfare societies both in the mining towns and in rural areas; in 1948 these gave rise to the Northern Rhodesia Congress. Some of its members sat on the African Representative Council set up by the government in 1946. This body had no power, but it criticized political and social conditions, especially the informal colour bar, and from 1948 it elected two Africans to sit on the Legislative Council. In the countryside "indirect rule" through chiefs became more broadly representative.

In some respects, Africans made important advances in the first postwar years. On the other hand, these advances also strengthened white aspirations to settler self-government, as in Southern Rhodesia. Although whites formed less than 2 percent of the Northern Rhodesian population, their numbers rose between 1946 and 1951 from 22,000 to 37,000, partly because of immigration from Britain. The Legislative Council included eight elected white members, and in deference to them a large-scale development plan was drastically revised between 1947 and 1953 at the expense of African education.

Yet this was not enough. To many whites, the best hope of entrenching white supremacy seemed to lie in amalgamation with the south. This ambition gained support from British politicians and civil servants who feared that Southern Rhodesia would otherwise fall under the sway of the Afrikaner nationalists who had come to power in South Africa in 1948. In 1951 the British Labour government was replaced by Conservatives less concerned to avoid alienating African opinion. Despite widespread popular protest, in which chiefs and Congress combined, Northern and Southern Rhodesia and Nyasaland were brought together in the Central African Federation in 1953.

The federation was a curious and unstable compromise. Its government was based in Southern Rhodesia, which also dominated the federal parliament. It had wide powers over all three territories, though in the north Britain retained control over questions of African land, education, and political status. At first, African suspicions of federation were blunted in Northern Rhodesia by an economic boom. Copper prices had risen steeply following sterling devaluation in 1949 and the outbreak of war in Korea in 1950; the mining companies finally began to pay regular dividends, while the Northern Rhodesian government received a share of royalties. Following a major African strike in 1952, the real wages of African mine workers at last moved upward. The companies increased their use of machinery and African skills; in 1955 the industrial colour bar was breached, and a select minority of African workers were encouraged to live out their working lives in the mining areas. "Stabilized" labour began to replace oscillating migrant labour.

In 1956, however, the copper boom came to an end. Whites in Northern Rhodesia became increasingly aware of how far the federal tax system channeled copper profits into Southern Rhodesia. Many Africans were thrown out of work, while little had been done to help African farming or education, despite federal propaganda for "partnership." A new generation of leaders in Congress wanted Northern Rhodesia to become an independent African state, as Ghana had become in 1957. In 1958, led by Kenneth Kaunda, a former teacher and civil servant, these radicals split off from

Congress to found the Zambia African National Congress and its successor, the United National Independence Party (UNIP). Britain accepted that Africans would have to be given more power than the federal government was willing to concede. In 1962 UNIP organized a massive campaign of civil disobedience, but it agreed to take part in elections under a new constitution, and an election later that year gave Africans a majority in the legislature. The federation with Southern Rhodesia and Nyasaland was dissolved at the end of 1963.

INDEPENDENT ZAMBIA

Early in 1964 an election in Northern Rhodesia based on universal adult suffrage gave UNIP a decisive majority, and it was supported by nearly a third of the white voters. On Oct. 24, 1964, the country became the independent Republic of Zambia, within the Commonwealth and with Kaunda serving as executive president.

ZAMBIA UNDER KAUNDA

During the early years of independence, Zambia was comparatively prosperous. Copper prices rose steadily from 1964 to 1970, boosted by the Vietnam War, and Zambia became the world's third largest producer of copper. Meanwhile, the leakage of copper profits abroad was greatly reduced. In 1964 the government acquired the mineral rights of the BSAC, and thereafter it also increased mining

taxation. The country embarked on long-overdue investment in communications and social services. In 1960 there had been only 2,500 Africans in secondary schools; by 1971 there were 54,000. At independence there were fewer than 100 Zambian university graduates; in 1965 the University of Zambia was founded, and by 1971 it had 2,000 students. Zambians finally began to predominate in the upper ranks of the civil service, the army, business, and the professions. The copper industry still relied heavily on white expertise, but the colour bar had vanished, and in 1966 black mine workers secured a large increase in pay, which soon affected wage levels generally.

On the other hand, Zambia incurred massive costs from the survival of white supremacy across the Zambezi. Following (Southern) Rhodesia's Unilateral Declaration of Independence (UDI) in 1965, the United Nations imposed sanctions intended to isolate that country, but these bore much more heavily on Zambia. Copper exports were expensively rerouted northward, and a tarmac road and oil pipeline were built to Dar es Salaam, Tanz. Trade with Rhodesia was steadily reduced, and the border was finally closed in 1973. A new coal mine and new hydroelectric schemes made Zambia largely independent of the Rhodesian-controlled power station at the Kariba Dam (built in 1959). In 1970–75 China built a railway from the Copperbelt to Dar es Salaam, which committed Zambia and Tanzania to extensive trade with China.

National integration had been a major task for Zambia's leaders at independence. White settlers presented no great difficulty, and those farmers who stayed on were valued for their major contribution to food production. African "tribalism" was a more serious problem. This had less to do with the survival of precolonial political loyalties than with regional differences aggravated under colonial rule and the absence of any African lingua franca. The Lozi and other peoples in the west and south had long depended on labour migration across the Zambezi; the Copperbelt was dominated by Bemba speakers from the northeast. Kaunda did not himself belong to any major ethnic group, but his continuation in power required constant reshuffling of colleagues in the party and the government to preclude the emergence of a rival. In the name of national unity, UNIP sometimes made exaggerated claims to allegiance; such claims had brought it into armed conflict in 1964 with the Lumpa church founded by Alice Lenshina and in the late 1960s with Jehovah's Witnesses. UNIP also challenged the independence of the judiciary, though from 1969 the authority of the bench was strengthened by the appointment of black Zambian judges.

In the early 1970s Zambia's economic fortunes took a turn for the worse. Copper continued to provide the great bulk of export earnings, but prices fluctuated erratically and suffered a prolonged fall in 1975. The price of oil shot up in 1973, and inflation, already serious, rapidly increased. The government,

committed to high spending, both public and private, reacted by borrowing heavily abroad and drawing on reserves. Investment declined, as did the efficiency of the transport network. State control of the mining industry, achieved in 1969–75, artificially prolonged its life but also increased the scope of corruption, as did parastatal corporations set up to promote industrial diversification.

The government became increasingly authoritarian. Kaunda felt threatened by critics at home and by the illegal Rhodesian regime, which harassed African guerrillas based in Zambia. UDI had already prompted Kaunda to impose emergency regulations, which thereafter were regularly renewed by the National Assembly and enabled the president to detain political opponents without trial. In 1973 the National Assembly approved a one-party constitution, and in 1975 UNIP took over Zambia's main newspaper. To some extent, fear of foreign attack diminished with the advent of independence in Portuguese Africa in 1975 and in Rhodesia (Zimbabwe) in 1980. But warfare in Angola and South African interference continued to provide pretexts to curb internal opposition.

Still more worrying, however, was the deepening economic crisis. Kaunda urged Zambians to look to agriculture rather than mining for a solution, but rural development policies, though consuming foreign aid, were mostly ill-conceived and failed to stem the historic drift to the towns. By 1980, out of a population of 5.7 million, more than 2 million lived in towns—many without jobs or housing—and inevitably, disease and crime flourished. Urban dwellers refused to pay the high prices that might have encouraged more farmers to produce for the market. Government subsidies sometimes bridged the gap, but their partial removal in 1986 and 1990 provoked major food riots in the towns. The restoration of subsidies in 1987 cost Zambia the support of the International Monetary Fund, though such support had been critical in coping with enormous foreign debts. Mounting discontent was reflected in recurrent closings of the University of Zambia, and in August 1991, in response to widespread pressure, the National Assembly abolished the one-party state. Multiparty elections were held in October, and Kaunda was decisively defeated by a trade union leader, Frederick Chiluba of the Movement for Multi-party Democracy (MMD). UNIP was left with fewer than one-sixth of the seats in the National Assembly.

CHILUBA PRESIDENCY

Although the 1991 election positioned Zambia to become one of Africa's leaders in the area of political stability, its fulfillment of that promise was hampered by a variety of domestic issues. Chiluba's administration worked to bring about economic reform, but ironically economic progress was limited due to the widespread corruption that became a problem under his rule. In addition, Chiluba's presidency was marked by unsuccessful attempts by opposing forces to topple the ruling party, termed "coup attempts," although they involved neither bloodshed nor widespread popular support.

On May 16, 1996, the National Assembly approved amendments to the constitution that declared that presidential candidates must be Zambian citizens born of parents who are Zambian by birth and that a candidate must not be a chief. These amendments were widely viewed in both domestic and international circles as a deliberate attempt to prevent Kaunda—whose parents were from Malawi—and his running mate, Senior Chief Inyambo Yeta, from running for office. Despite broad opposition, however, the National Assembly passed the amendments, thereby preventing Kaunda's candidacy. Later that year Chiluba was reelected to a second term. Some viewed his reelection as an empty victory, however, since Kaunda had been prevented from contesting and UNIP had boycotted the elections.

Chiluba faced another weak coup attempt on Oct. 28, 1997, when a group of Zambian army commandos seized control of the national radio station in Lusaka and proclaimed that they had toppled Chiluba's government; within hours, however, the group was overpowered by Zambian troops loyal to the president. Several people were later charged in connection with the event, including Kaunda, who was arrested on December 25. He was released six days later, but he was placed under house arrest until June 1998, when all charges were withdrawn.

The presidency of Frederick Chiluba was fraught with controversy and upheaval. Chiluba, who faced coup attempts and nationwide strikes, stepped down as Zambia's president in 2001. Paul Vicente/ AFP/Getty Images

Discontent with the state of the economy was evident in May 2001 when the country's public sector workers went on strike, demanding an increase in salaries and improved working conditions. The strike lasted several weeks and had a detrimental effect on the daily functioning of the country, closing schools and hospital wards and bringing the judicial system to a halt. The government resolved the strike in July, just days before Zambia was to host an international summit. Chiluba was also concerned with the growing refugee population in the country: beginning in 1999 and continuing for several years, Zambia received more than 200,000 refugees fleeing conflicts in the neighbouring Democratic Republic of the Congo and Angola.

Limited to two terms in office, Chiluba stepped down in 2001. His handpicked successor, Levy Mwanawasa of the MMD, was declared the winner of the hotly contested election and was sworn into office in January 2002.

MWANAWASA AND BANDA ADMINISTRATIONS

Despite being mired in election controversy, Mwanawasa moved quickly to assert his authority and launched a campaign against corruption. The initial targets of the campaign—the individuals alleged to be responsible for the corruption that damaged Zambia's economy in the 1990s—included former president Chiluba and many of his associates. Mwanawasa also initiated a review of the country's constitution in 2003 in an effort to bring about political reform, but some organizations invited to participate in the review declined, claiming that the review process itself was flawed.

Concerns over Mwanawasa's health emerged late in his first term, after he suffered a stroke in April 2006. He reassured the country that he was fit for office and stood for reelection later that year, garnering more than two-fifths of the vote. His nearest competitor, Michael Sata, made claims of voting irregularities and contested the election. Sporadic violence ensued in areas loyal to Sata, but the result of the election stood, and Mwanawasa was sworn in for his second term in October 2006. Mwanawasa again suffered a stroke in late June 2008. Rumours of his death circulated a few days later but were quickly refuted by Zambian government officials. He never fully recovered, however, and he died several weeks later.

Under the terms of the constitution, a special election to choose a new president was eventually scheduled for later that year. In the interim, Vice President Rupiah Banda served as acting president. The election, held on Oct. 30, 2008, was contested by four candidates, including Banda and Sata. Banda won, although by only a narrow margin, and Sata, who finished a close second, alleged that the vote had been flawed.

CHAPTER 13

ZIMBABWE

Zimbabwe is a landlocked country in Southern Africa. A former British colony, it gained independence in 1980. The capital is Harare.

EARLY HISTORY

The remains of Stone Age cultures dating to 500,000 years ago have been found in Zimbabwe, and it is thought that the San, who still survive mostly in the Kalahari desert of Botswana, are the last descendants of these original inhabitants of southern and central Africa. They were driven into the desert by Bantu-speaking groups during the long migrations from the north in the course of which the Bantu-speaking peoples populated much of Africa from Lake Chad to present-day South Africa. The first Bantu are thought to have reached Zimbabwe between the 5th and 10th centuries CE. Zimbabwe is home to many stone ruins, including those known as Great Zimbabwe (designated a UNESCO World Heritage site in 1986). Some ruins date from about the 9th century, although the most elaborate belong to a period after the 15th century and are of Bantu origin.

PORTUGUESE EXPLORATION

The Portuguese, who arrived on the east coast of Africa at the end of the 15th century, dreamed of opening up the interior and establishing a route to connect their eastern settlements with

GREAT ZIMBABWE

Aerial view of the ruins of Great Zimbabwe. *ZEFA*

The extensive stone ruin of an African Iron Age city, known as Great Zimbabwe, lies in southeastern Zimbabwe, about 19 miles (30 km) southeast of Masvingo (formerly Fort Victoria). The central area of ruins extends about 200 acres (80 hectares), making Great Zimbabwe the largest of more than 150 major stone ruins scattered across the countries of Zimbabwe and Mozambique.

It is estimated that the central ruins and surrounding valley supported a Shona population of 10,000 to 20,000. With an economy based on cattle husbandry, crop cultivation, and the trade of gold on the coast of the Indian Ocean, Great Zimbabwe was the heart of a thriving trading empire from the 11th to the 15th centuries. The word zimbabwe, the country's namesake, is a Shona word meaning "stone houses."

The site is generally divided into three main areas: the Hill Complex, the Great Enclosure, and the Valley Ruins. The Hill Complex, which was formerly called the Acropolis, is believed to have been the spiritual and religious centre of the city. South of the Hill Complex lies the Great Enclosure, the largest single ancient structure in sub-Saharan Africa. The Valley Ruins, located between the Hill Complex and the Great Enclosure, include a large number of mounds that are remnants of daga (earthen and mud-brick) buildings.

Great Zimbabwe was largely abandoned during the 15th century. With the city's decline, its stoneworking and pottery-making techniques seem to have transferred southward to Khami (now also in ruins). Portuguese explorers probably encountered the ruins in the 16th century, but it was not until the late 19th century that the existence of the ruins was confirmed, generating much archaeological research. European explorers who visited the site in the late 1800s believed it to be the legendary city of Ophir, the site of King Solomon's mines.

In the late 19th century numerous soapstone figurines in the form of a bird were found in the ruins; this Zimbabwe Bird later became a national symbol, incorporated into the Zimbabwe flag and shown in other places of high honour.

Angola in the west. The first European to enter Zimbabwe was probably António Fernandes, who tried to cross the continent and reached the neighbourhood of Que Que (now Kwekwe). Nearly 50 years later the Mwene Matapa ("emperor"), Negomo Chirisamhuru Mupunsagutu, was baptized by a Jesuit father, and in

1569 an abortive Portuguese military expedition entered the interior in search of gold.

A second great movement of the Bantu peoples began in 1830, this time from the south. To escape from the power of the great Zulu chief Shaka, three important groups fled northward. One of them, the Ndebele, carved out a kingdom. The Ndebele were warriors and pastoralists, in the Zulu tradition, and under their formidable chief Mzilikazi they mastered and dispossessed the weaker groups, known collectively as Shona (Mashona), who were sedentary, peaceful tillers of the land. For more than half a century, until the coming of European rule, the Ndebele continued to enslave and plunder the Shona. During this period, however, British and Afrikaner hunters, traders, and prospectors had begun to move up from the south, and with them came the missionaries. Robert Moffat visited Mzilikazi in 1857, and this meeting led to the establishment in 1861 of the first mission to the Ndebele by the London Missionary Society.

THE BRITISH SOUTH AFRICA COMPANY

In South Africa Cecil Rhodes formed the British South Africa Company, which received its charter in October 1889. Its objects were (1) to extend the railway from Kimberley northward to the Zambezi, (2) to encourage immigration and colonization, (3) to promote trade and commerce, and (4) to secure all mineral rights, in return for guarantees of protection and security of rights to the chiefs.

In 1890 a pioneer column set out from Bechuanaland and reached the site of the future capital of Rhodesia without incident on September 12. There the new arrivals settled and began to lay claim to prospecting rights. The Ndebele resented this European invasion, and in 1893 they took up arms, being defeated only after months of strenuous fighting. Lobengula, Mzilikazi's son and successor, fled, and the company assumed administrative control of the Ndebele region, known as Matabeleland. In 1895 many of the pioneers were persuaded to take part in the Jameson Raid into the Transvaal and were captured and sent to England for trial. In the same year, the company-administered territories, which had previously been loosely known as Zambesia, were formally named Rhodesia by proclamation. In 1896 the Ndebele rose again. Returning from London, Rhodes met with the Ndebele chiefs and persuaded them to make peace. The Shona had at first accepted the Europeans, but they too became rebellious, and the whole country was not pacified until 1897.

ECONOMIC AND POLITICAL DEVELOPMENT

By 1892 about 1,500 settlers from the south had arrived in Rhodesia. The railway reached Bulawayo in 1896 and Victoria Falls in 1904. By the following year there were 12,500 settlers in the country, and in 1909 gold exports were worth more than £2,500,000. Agricultural development, however, was slower, and it was not until 1907 that steps were taken to facilitate the acquisition of land. By 1911 nearly £35,000 worth of tobacco was being exported annually, and the European population had risen to 23,600.

From the earliest years, the settlers had demanded representation on the Legislative Council, which in 1903 comprised seven company officials and seven elected representatives of the settlers. In 1907 the settlers were given a majority of seats. In 1914, when the 25-year term of the company's charter was due to expire, the settlers, faced with the alternative of joining the Union of South Africa, asked for the continuation of the charter pending the grant of self-government. The British government therefore extended the charter for 10 years, with the proviso that self-government could be granted earlier if the settlers showed themselves capable of administering the country unaided.

Self-Government

Immediately after World War I the pressure for self-government was resumed, and a royal commission was appointed to consider the future of the territory. As a result of the commission's report, a referendum of the electors among the 34,000 Europeans in the country was held in 1922; the choice was between entry into the Union of South Africa as its fifth province and full internal self-government. In spite of the offer of generous terms by the Union's prime minister, Gen. Jan C. Smuts, a majority voted for self-government. On Sept. 12, 1923, Southern Rhodesia was annexed to the crown and became a self-governing colony. The British government retained control of external affairs and a final veto in respect to legislation directly affecting Africans.

The interwar period was one of material progress, with the development of a reasonably prosperous economy based on copper, gold, and other minerals, corn (maize), tobacco, and cattle. By 1953 Southern Rhodesia had a European population of 157,000 and an annual revenue of more than £28 million.

Sir Godfrey Huggins (later Lord Malvern) served as prime minister of Southern Rhodesia for 20 years. He believed that political power should not be given to the Africans until they were sufficiently experienced to know how to exercise it in cooperation with the Europeans and thus to maintain the economic development built up over the years. A second principle in which Lord Malvern and most other Europeans in Southern Rhodesia and Northern Rhodesia (later Zambia) profoundly believed was that the two countries should be joined together, both for their mutual economic benefit and to ensure the establishment of a powerful state based on British culture and traditions. Malvern failed to secure their amalgamation, but he supported the federation of Southern Rhodesia, Northern Rhodesia, and Nyasaland (later Malawi) when that solution was eventually accepted by the British in 1953.

GODFREY HUGGINS, 1ST VISCOUNT MALVERN

(b. July 6, 1883, Bexley, Kent, Eng.—d. May 8, 1971, Salisbury, Rhodesia [now Harare, Zimb.])

Godfrey Huggins was the prime minister of Southern Rhodesia (1933–53) and architect of the Federation of Rhodesia and Nyasaland, which he served as its first prime minister (1953–56).

After practicing medicine in London, Huggins migrated to Salisbury, Southern Rhodesia, in 1911 for reasons of health and soon established a reputation as a surgeon. When Southern Rhodesia became a self-governing colony in 1923, Huggins was elected to the Legislative Council. In 1933 his Reform Party won about half the Assembly seats, and he became prime minister and also secretary of native affairs (until 1949). He was knighted in 1941. In contrast to the British government's wish for a policy of "trusteeship," in which the interests of black Africans were paramount, Huggins supported the South African concepts of separate development, speaking of a "two pyramid" policy with black Africans at the top of one pyramid but barely equal to white settlers and their descendants at the bottom of the other.

His scheme to unite the two Rhodesias (Northern and Southern) and Nyasaland was finally realized in 1953, and a decisive victory at the polls by the Federal Party confirmed his premiership. Black Africans in all three territories opposed the Federation, however; although Huggins had gradually moved away from the "two pyramid" policy to one of "partnership," he revealed his vision of interracial partnership between white settlers and their descendants and black Africans to be that of "the rider and the horse," with the majority of political and economic power continuing to elude black Africans. He was created a viscount—Godfrey Martin Huggins, 1st Viscount Malvern of Rhodesia and of Bexley—in 1955.

FEDERATION

In 1957 a new electoral law was passed providing for a common roll of voters (the "A" roll, composed only of whites) with a special roll for those with lower qualifications (the "B" roll, a tiny minority of the blacks). At the same time, there was growing political consciousness among the African population, together with increasing hostility to the idea of federation. Joshua Nkomo was one of the fiercest opponents of federation as the local leader of the African National Congress, and, when that organization was banned, he became president of the National Democratic Party in 1960. It, too, was soon banned, and he formed the Zimbabwe African People's Union (ZAPU), which in turn was banned in 1962. In 1963 Robert Mugabe broke with ZAPU to join the Zimbabwe African National Union (ZANU) and thereby split African support along ethnic lines—Nkomo retained the Ndebele ethnic minority (mostly in the Matabeleland region), while Mugabe garnered the Shona ethnic majority.

In June 1962 the UN General Assembly called for a more liberal

ROBERT MUGABE

(b. Feb. 21, 1924, Kutama, Southern Rhodesia [now Zimbabwe])

Robert Mugabe was the first prime minister (1980–87) of the reconstituted state of Zimbabwe, formerly Rhodesia. A black nationalist of Marxist persuasion, he eventually established one-party rule in his country, becoming executive president of Zimbabwe in 1987.

As prime minister, Mugabe initially followed a pragmatic course designed to reassure Zimbabwe's white farmers and businessmen, whose skills were vital to the economy. He formed a coalition government between his party, ZANU-PF (which drew its support from the majority Shona people), and Joshua Nkomo's ZAPU (which drew its support from the minority Ndebele people), and he abided by the new constitution's guarantees of substantial parliamentary representation for whites. At the same time, Mugabe took steps to improve the lot of black Zimbabweans through increased wages, improved social services, and food subsidies. In 1982 Mugabe ousted Nkomo from the coalition cabinet, and ethnic strife between the Shona and the Ndebele subsequently troubled the country. Zimbabwe's economy steadily declined despite Mugabe's measures, and whites emigrated in substantial numbers.

Mugabe had always intended to convert Zimbabwe from a parliamentary democracy into a one-party socialist state. In 1984 ZANU-PF held a congress, made Mugabe its unchallenged leader, and set up a new party structure with a Central Committee and a Politburo that were designed to rule both the party and Zimbabwe. In 1987 Mugabe's and Nkomo's parties merged into one under the name of ZANU-PF, and as first secretary of the new party, Mugabe retained absolute control over it. On Dec. 31, 1987, he became Zimbabwe's first executive president, effectively establishing one-party rule. In 1990 he was reelected president in a multiparty election that was marked by intimidation and violence. His subsequent rule was also marked by intimidation and violence and by a decreasing tolerance of political opposition. Long-simmering political tensions between Mugabe and and an opposition party, headed by Morgan Tsvangirai, led to a hotly contested presidential election in 2008 and a protracted political crisis.

constitution for the territory. The election of December 1962, during which the 1961 constitution came into force, was boycotted by the African nationalists. The ruling United Federal Party was defeated by the more conservative Rhodesian Front (RF), and Winston Field became prime minister. At the end of 1963 the federation was dissolved, and Southern Rhodesia reverted to its former status as colony.

RHODESIA AND THE UDI

The goal of the RF was Rhodesian independence under guaranteed minority rule. Field was replaced as prime minister in April 1964 by his deputy, Ian Smith. The RF swept all A-roll seats in the 1965 election, and Smith used this parliamentary strength to tighten controls on the political opposition. After several attempts to persuade Britain to grant independence, Smith's government announced the Unilateral Declaration of Independence (UDI) on Nov. 11, 1965.

Britain declined to respond to the UDI with force, instead attempting economic tactics such as ending the link between sterling and the Rhodesian currency and seizing assets. Smith's government countered by defaulting on its (British-guaranteed) debts, leaving the British liable while at the same time balancing its budget. The United Nations Security Council imposed mandatory economic sanctions on Rhodesia in 1966, the first time that the UN had taken that action against a state. The sanctions were broadened in 1968 but still were only partly successful; some strategic minerals, especially chromium, were exported to willing buyers in Europe and North America, further strengthening the economy.

On June 20, 1969, a referendum was held in Rhodesia regarding adoption of a constitution that would enshrine political power in the hands of the white minority and establish Rhodesia as a republic; Rhodesia's predominantly white electorate overwhelmingly approved both measures. The constitution was approved by Parliament in November, and on March 2, 1970, Rhodesia declared itself a republic.

Unsuccessful negotiations with Britain continued. A 1971 proposal to lessen restrictions on the opposition led to the creation of a third nationalist movement, the United African National Council (UANC), led by the Methodist bishop Abel Muzorewa. Unlike ZAPU and ZANU—both banned and operating only from exile in Zambia and Mozambique, respectively—UANC was able to organize inside Rhodesia and held talks with the government during the 1970s. During the early 1970s ZAPU and ZANU had sporadically organized raids into Rhodesia, but in December 1972 the violence of the conflict intensified after a ZANU attack in the northeast. The Zambia-Rhodesia border was closed in 1973, but Mozambican independence in 1975 provided a valuable base of operations for ZANU, which had close links to the Frelimo government.

The white Rhodesian government was thus under diplomatic, military, and, increasingly, economic pressure for a settlement. The 1976 rapprochement between Nkomo and Mugabe led to the formation of the Patriotic Front (PF), which received frontline support from Rhodesia's majority-ruled neighbours. The fighting escalated in both area and intensity, and the emergency measures adopted by the government to counter it also served to increase antigovernment feeling. By 1979 the combination of pressures had forced Smith to accept the necessity of an "internal settlement."

INDEPENDENCE

A 1978 agreement with internal black leaders, including Muzorewa, had promised elections for a transitional government that would provide for both enfranchisement of blacks and protection of white political and economic interests. The UANC won a clear majority of the seats allotted to blacks in the April 1979 election, and the country adopted the name Zimbabwe. Without PF participation or support for Muzorewa's new government, however, Zimbabwe was unable to end the warfare. Diplomatic recognition of the new government was not forthcoming given the stalemate; after talks between Muzorewa, Mugabe, and Nkomo at the Lancaster House conference in London in late 1979, Britain briefly retook control of Southern Rhodesia as a colony until a new round of elections was held in February 1980. Of the 80 contested black seats, ZANU (now using the name ZANU-PF) won 57, ZAPU 20, and the UANC 3. Mugabe became the first prime minister as Zimbabwe achieved an internationally recognized independence on April 18, 1980.

A New Government

Mugabe's new government moved deliberately to redress inequalities of race and class, redistribute land held by the white minority, and promote economic development, with a one-party socialist state as its long-term goal. During the 1980s, drought and white emigration badly damaged the economy, which was already strained by the need for massive government spending in the long-neglected areas of education, health, and social services for the black majority. In 1982 Mugabe charged that Nkomo was plotting a coup and dismissed him from his cabinet, while arresting other leaders of ZAPU. Nkomo's supporters in the Matabeleland region retaliated, precipitating a civil war. Fighting did not cease until Mugabe and Nkomo reached an agreement in December 1987 whereby ZAPU was subsumed into ZANU-PF, Mugabe became the country's first executive president, and Nkomo became one of the nation's two vice presidents. Mugabe was reelected in 1990, 1996, and 2002.

The economy continued to lag throughout the 1990s as inflation soared, and a high level of unemployment led to significant unrest. In 1998 Mugabe's intervention in the civil war in the Democratic Republic of the Congo—purportedly to protect his personal investments—resulted in suspension of international economic aid for Zimbabwe. This suspension of aid and the millions of dollars spent to intervene in the war further weakened Zimbabwe's already troubled economy.

The Issue of Land Reform and the Rise of the Movement for Democratic Change

Throughout the 1980s and '90s the government continued to struggle with the issue of land reform. Some 4,000 white farmers collectively controlled about one-third of Zimbabwe's arable land, and hundreds of white-owned farms were either officially redistributed by the government or partially taken over by squatters responding to government promises and the lack of police deterrence. Nevertheless, public support for the farmers and opposition to Mugabe's increasingly autocratic rule were evidenced by the defeat of a referendum in February 2000 calling for a new constitution that would have extended Mugabe's rule for two more six-year terms and given him the power to confiscate white-owned farms without compensation, as well as by the June elections, in which the opposition party Movement for Democratic Change (MDC), led by Morgan Tsvangirai, won almost half of the parliamentary seats.

Despite the apparent reprieve for white owners, a law was passed in 2002 that allowed Mugabe to pursue an aggressive program of confiscating their farms, forcing more than half of the country's white farmers to relinquish their property and rendering tens of thousands of black farmworkers homeless and unemployed. As was the case in the 1990s, property was often claimed by politically connected individuals with little or no farming experience rather than by the landless peasant farmers or war veterans who were supposed to benefit from the redistribution program. The government's lack of forethought in forcing out the white farmers and not replacing them with experienced farmworkers contributed to a significant decline in agricultural productivity; this, as well as drought, led to severe food shortages.

INCREASING DISCORD

At the beginning of the 21st century, with Mugabe's popularity well in decline, his regime became increasingly brutal and repressive. Media freedom was curtailed by restrictive laws, and several newspapers were shut down by the government. The MDC and others critical of the government were dealt with harshly. Mugabe's reelection victory over Tsvangirai in 2002 was tainted by violence and criticized by observers, leading the Commonwealth to suspend Zimbabwe for one year. After the Commonwealth decided to extend the suspension indefinitely, Zimbabwe withdrew from the organization in December 2003. The 2005 parliamentary election was clouded by accusations of irregularities and was not deemed free or fair by the opposition and most observers, though the Southern African Development Community (SADC)—the only foreign observers officially accredited by the Zimbabwean government to observe proceedings—determined that the election met the will of the people. Shortly after the parliamentary election, the government launched "Operation Murambatsvina," a cleanup campaign that destroyed thousands of homes and stores in shantytowns on the outskirts of Harare and other urban centres. More than half a million people were displaced, and critics of the government claimed that this was a punitive measure aimed at the supporters of the opposition, who were mainly located in the shantytowns.

The MDC began to experience internal dissent in late 2005 as some members became disenchanted with Tsvangirai's leadership, especially his decision to boycott elections for the newly reinstated Senate, and a faction of the MDC,

Zimbabwean President Robert Mugabe, prior to addressing the United Nations General Assembly in 2009. Michael Nagle/Getty Images

led by Arthur Mutambara, a former student protest leader, professor, and consultant, broke away. Harassment of the opposition continued, and in March 2007 Tsvangirai and several other members of the MDC were viciously beaten; the Mugabe administration drew international criticism after images of the injured circulated throughout the world. Increasing pressure to resolve the conflict between the MDC and ZANU-PF led to mediation efforts by the SADC, facilitated by South African president Thabo Mbeki, but talks broke off in early 2008 without reaching a resolution.

ECONOMIC CRISIS

Meanwhile, economic troubles continued as sanctions were imposed on Zimbabwe and loans and economic aid from many donors, including the International Monetary Fund, were limited or completely withdrawn for various reasons, most notably in protest of the government's land-seizure program and because the country had fallen behind on repayments of previous loans. Inflation was rampant: the official government estimate reached nearly 8,000 percent in September 2007 (other, nongovernment estimates were up to several times that figure) before the government's Central Statistic Office stated that they were unable to continue calculating inflation rates, because of a lack of data; the basic consumer goods needed for the calculations could no longer be found in shops throughout the country. In early 2008, after government calculations had resumed, the official estimate had risen to more than 100,000 percent; by the end of the summer, it had surpassed 10 million percent. Economic problems also included an extremely high rate of unemployment, estimated at some four-fifths of the population and among the highest in the world. Employment did not guarantee financial security though, as the wages earned by those who were employed were unable to keep pace with inflation. Many Zimbabweans left the country—often going to South Africa—to find work; many of those who remained relied on relatives abroad to send remittances.

In the midst of the country's worsening economic situation was the debate on the root causes of it. Some—primarily supporters of the government—blamed what they deemed to be unfair economic sanctions, the failure of the British government to honour the terms of the 1979 Lancaster House agreement regarding the transfer of land to black ownership, and a Western plot to oust Mugabe from power. Others, especially critics of the government, blamed the land-seizure program and the economic mismanagement under the Mugabe administration. Both groups acknowledged that corruption also played a role. Regardless of the reasons for the economic troubles, many Zimbabweans were adversely affected, lacking basic commodities and suffering from food insecurity, fuel shortages, record-high rates of unemployment, and hyperinflation.

2008 Elections and Aftermath

Through all of Zimbabwe's political and economic troubles, Mugabe retained the support of many African heads of state and remained popular within ZANU-PF. In December 2007 the party endorsed Mugabe as its presidential candidate in the 2008 elections. However, as the country continued its downward spiral in the months leading up to the elections, support for Mugabe appeared to waver: former finance minister and ZANU-PF stalwart Simba Makoni announced that he was running against Mugabe for the presidency, and the MDC, with Tsvangirai as its presidential candidate once again, saw its popularity increase throughout the country, even in areas that were typically ZANU-PF strongholds. As the elections drew near, both opposition candidates and their followers were subject to harassment and attacks by the police and ZANU-PF loyalists.

Presidential, parliamentary, and local elections were held on March 29, 2008. Unofficial preliminary results indicated a favourable outcome for Tsvangirai and the MDC, but, as days passed with only a slow, partial release of parliamentary results (and the complete absence of presidential results), many feared that Mugabe and ZANU-PF were manipulating the outcome of the elections in their favour. The MDC released its own accounting of the presidential election results on April 2, which indicated that Tsvangirai

had captured slightly more than half the votes; the MDC's claims were dismissed by ZANU-PF, and the country continued to wait for official results. Later that day, results indicated that Tsvangirai's faction of the MDC had won the most seats in the House of Assembly. Senate results announced several days later revealed a split between the MDC and ZANU-PF, with the latter receiving an only slightly larger share of the votes. The final results for the presidential contest were not officially released until May 2, when it was announced that Tsvangirai had garnered more votes (47.9 percent) than Mugabe (43.2 percent), but, since Tsvangirai had not secured a majority of the votes, a runoff election would be necessary, which was later scheduled for June 27.

In the weeks leading up to the runoff election, MDC supporters were harassed and victimized by violent attacks, which the MDC asserted were sponsored by the ZANU-PF-led government; the government in turn claimed that the MDC was responsible for the violence. An increasingly tense climate was further heightened by several government actions, including the detention of Mutambara, Tsvangirai, and several other MDC officials and supporters, as well as several diplomats from the United Kingdom and the United States who were in the midst of investigating reports of preelection violence, the suspension of all humanitarian aid operations in the country, and statements from Mugabe implying that he would not cede power to the opposition if he lost the runoff election. As the politically motivated violence, intimidation, and rhetoric continued, on June 22 Tsvangirai announced that he was withdrawing from the election, citing the impossibility of it being free and fair in the country's current political climate. Nevertheless, the election was still held, and Mugabe was declared the winner despite assertions from independent observers that the election was neither free nor fair.

The fact that the election was even held—as well as the outcome—prompted widespread international condemnation, most notably from some of the governments of African countries that had previously supported Mugabe, and there were calls for the MDC and ZANU-PF to form a power-sharing government. To that end, SADC-led talks, again facilitated by Mbeki, were held with ZANU-PF and the two factions of the MDC. Although the parties were able to reach a consensus regarding the Memorandum of Understanding (MOU) to direct the terms and scope of the discussion, an agreement regarding a new power-sharing government did not progress as quickly. Meanwhile, Mugabe announced that he intended to convene Parliament on Aug. 26, 2008; this announcement was met with protest from the MDC and others who complained that doing so before a power-sharing agreement was reached contradicted the terms of the MOU. Nonetheless, Parliament was convened per Mugabe's directive. Notably, however, the House of Assembly speaker was elected from Tsvangirai's faction of the MDC—the first time since the

country's independence in 1980 that the speaker position was held by an opposition party member.

SADC-led negotiations for a power-sharing government continued, and on Sept. 15, 2008, Mugabe, Mutambara, and Tsvangirai signed a comprehensive power-sharing agreement—referred to as the Global Political Agreement. As part of the agreement, Mugabe would remain president but would cede some power to Tsvangirai, who would serve as prime minister; Mutambara would serve as a deputy prime minister. Initial jubilation quickly turned to disappointment in the following months when it became clear that Mugabe and Tsvangirai could not come to terms on how to implement the agreement, arguing over how to allocate the new government's key ministries between ZANU-PF and the MDC. Stalled talks and repeated attempts by the SADC to get discussions back on track continued against a backdrop of worsening economic and humanitarian conditions in the country. Rampant inflation continued, with official estimates at more than 200 million percent (unofficial estimates were much higher), and there were severe food shortages. The country's municipal and health services, lacking the funds and supplies to function adequately, rapidly deteriorated; this fueled a deadly cholera epidemic. Dozens of MDC supporters, human rights activists, and reporters had disappeared; the MDC alleged that they had been abducted by ZANU-PF- and government-allied forces. International support for continued negotiations for the power-sharing government began to wane, with some critics calling for Mugabe to step down from power; he adamantly refused to do so and later announced his intention to form a government on his own if Tsvangirai and the MDC would not participate. In late January 2009 Tsvangirai—under pressure from the SADC—agreed to join Mugabe in a new government, despite lingering misgivings. On Feb. 5, 2009, Zimbabwe's legislature passed the necessary constitutional amendment that altered the structure of the executive branch, allowing for the creation of the prime minister and deputy prime minister posts. On Feb. 11, 2009, Tsvangirai was sworn in as prime minister and Thokozani Khupe, of Tsvangirai's faction of the MDC, and Mutambara were sworn in as deputy prime ministers.

The unity government was a troubled one, however, as the MDC and ZANU-PF struggled to agree on various appointments, and Tsvangirai denounced ongoing human rights violations. On the one-year anniversary of the formation of the unity government, several issues of contention remained between the parties.

CONCLUSION

Given that Southern Africa has been inhabited for some 3 million years or more—nearly the entire known existence of human beings and their ancestors—it is no wonder that it has a rich and varied history. From the wandering of small bands of hominins through the savanna, through the inception of herding and farming as ways of life, to the construction of large urban centres, inhabitants of the region continued to adapt, change, and evolve. Through this diversity of human experience, several trends have been evident: the interplay between physical evolution and learned behaviour, or culture; technological and economic change; and shifting systems of belief. Some of these trends can also be seen in Southern Africa's present, and they will continue to shape the region's future.

Southern Africa has seen a vast and varied amount of interactions among its inhabitants, which also has shaped its history. The interactions between the region's first indigenous groups, between these indigenous groups and the Bantu-speaking groups that came from the north in waves over the course of more than a millennia, and between both of these African groups and "outsiders"—most notably, the Europeans who began entering the region in the 15th century and would later come to dominant the area—have all left their impact on the region. Sometimes groups were able to peacefully coexist, although such existence was, at times, tenuous at best. Some groups were eager to interact, such as those who found it advantageous to engage in trade. Many groups, however, found themselves engaged in conflict, whether it was to gain dominance over new territory or resources, or because they were being forced to defend themselves in an effort to survive.

The Southern African region today is a reflection of the complex experiences of all these groups as they interacted throughout the millennia. In particular, the region's countries and their borders today reflect the events of the colonial era, which lasted well into the 20th century. Some of the region's countries were able to peacefully shed their colonial status and embark upon their newly found independence with little strife, while others were embroiled in long, violent conflicts before ultimately winning their hard-fought independence. Likewise, some of the region's countries have experienced a relatively peaceful and prosperous existence since gaining independence, but many have seen some degree of conflict and economic struggle. Nonetheless, many of the countries in the region have demonstrated their ability to aptly meet challenges as they arise, and several are among the most politically and economically stable countries on the African continent today.

At the dawn of a new millennium, the story of Southern Africa continues to be written. The Southern African region of tomorrow will be a reflection of how its inhabitants continue to adapt to meet the challenges before them today.

GLOSSARY

Afrikaner Any South African of Dutch, German, or Huguenot descent whose native language is Afrikaans.

Apartheid A former policy of segregation and political and economic discrimination against non-European groups in the Republic of South Africa.

Australopithecines Upright-walking creatures who are the earliest human ancestors.

Caste Any of the ranked, hereditary, endogamous (exogamy and endogamy) occupational groups that constitute traditional societies in certain regions of the world.

Hegemony Leadership or predominant influence exercised by one group over another.

Indenture To contractually bind the service of one to another.

Indigenes A person who is indigenous, or native, to a particular area.

Kaffir An archaic term used to describe Bantu-speaking peoples in Southern Africa; modern use of the term is considered pejorative..

Laager An encampment protected by a circle of wagons or armored vehicles.

Pastoral Of or relating to the countryside and/or the raising of livestock.

Patrilineal One's family connections or heritage as traced through the father's line.

Pejorative Having a belittling effect or or negative overture.

Polygynous Having more than one wife at once.

Prazeros Primarily Portuguese settlers in Southern Africa who were able to procure land grants and judicial rights from local rulers.

Protectorate A less powerful state that is partially controlled by a stronger state but is still autonomous in internal affairs.

Rinderpest An acute infectious disease of ruminant mammals such as cattle.

Savanna A type of vegetation that grows under hot, seasonally dry climatic conditions and is characterized by an open tree canopy (i.e., scattered trees) above a continuous tall grass understory.

Serf A commoner who is required to perform work for a landowner in exchange for certain rights and privileges.

Trekboer A Dutch semi-nomadic farmer in Southern Africa.

Trekker A South African epithet used to describe a person who travels by ox cart; an early settler of South Africa who traveled inland.

Tribalism Tribal consciousness and loyalty; exhibiting exaltation of the tribe above other groups.

Veld Open country or grasslands in Southern Africa that is used for pasturage and farmland.

BIBLIOGRAPHY

General works on Southern Africa include Neil Parsons, *A New History of Southern Africa*, 2nd ed. (1993), an introductory text dealing with the region as a whole. A.J. Wills, *An Introduction to the History of Central Africa: Zambia, Malawi, and Zimbabwe*, 4th ed. (1985), is still a useful guide to British south-central Africa. Leroy Vail and Landeg White, *Power and the Praise Poem: Southern African Voices in History* (1991) signals a major turning point in the interpretation of Southern Africa's past by insisting on the centrality of African interpretations through poetry, performance, and other oral expressions.

SOUTHERN AFRICA TO 1800

David W. Phillipson, *African Archaeology*, 2nd ed. (1993), is an introductory text with coverage ranging from prehistoric times to European contact. Overviews of early societies are found in *The Kingdoms of Africa* (1978, reissued 1990), an excellent introduction to the Iron Age in Southern Africa. Graham Connah, *African Civilizations: An Archaeological Perspective*, 2nd ed. (2001), discusses the period of Great Zimbabwe's influence (c. 1250–1450) and Bantu occupation of east coast areas from the end of the 1st millennium CE. Martin Hall, *The Changing Past: Farmers, Kings, and Traders in Southern*

Africa, 200–1860 (1987; also published as *Farmers, Kings, and Traders*, 1990) offers an overview of Southern African history and archaeology, starting with the first settlement of the subcontinent. Portuguese ventures in west-central and east-central Africa are chronicled in Edward A. Alpers, *Ivory and Slaves* (also published as *Ivory & Slaves in East Central Africa*, 1975); and Jan Vansina, *Kingdoms of the Savanna* (1966). Slavery in the region is discussed in Joseph C. Miller, *Way of Death: Merchant Capitalism and the Angolan Slave Trade, 1730–1830* (1988); and John Thornton, *Africa and Africans in the Making of the Atlantic World, 1400–1800*, 2nd ed. (1998).

SOUTHERN AFRICA, 1800–c. 1900

Donald Denoon and Balam Nyeko, *Southern Africa Since 1800*, new ed. (1984), is a good overview. The era of mineral discoveries and the scramble for Southern Africa are the subject of Geoffrey Wheatcroft, *The Randlords* (1986); and Randall M. Packard, *White Plague, Black Labor: Tuberculosis and the Political Economy of Health and Disease in South Africa* (1989). The scramble for Africa and the establishment of colonial society are dealt with in Thomas Pakenham, *The Scramble for Africa: White Man's Conquest of* the Dark Continent from 1876 to 1912 (1991); and Bill Freund, *The Making of Contemporary Africa: The Development of African Society Since 1800*, 2nd ed. (1998). Events in Angola and Mozambique are outlined in Malyn Newitt, *Portugal in Africa: The Last Hundred Years* (1981), a lucid overview with a synopsis of the earlier period of Portuguese rule.

SOUTHERN AFRICA, C. 1900 TO THE PRESENT

Martin Chanock, *Britain, Rhodesia, and South Africa, 1900–45* (also published as *Unconsummated Union*, 1977), contains a masterly account of interregional politics. The struggle in the Portuguese colonies, South Africa, and Rhodesia following the Portuguese coup of 1974, covered from differing viewpoints, can be found in Basil Davidson, Joe Slovo, and Anthony R. Wilkinson, *Southern Africa: The New Politics of Revolution* (1976). Margaret Jean Hay and Sharon Stichter (eds.), *African Women South of the Sahara*, 2nd ed. (1995), discusses women and their roles in African society. Prosser Gifford and W. Roger Louis (eds.), *Decolonization and African Independence: The Transfers of Power, 1960–1980* (1988), considers the decolonization process.

INDEX